W9-ARQ-541

Pickles to Relish

Pickles to Relish

By
Beverly Ellen Schoonmaker Alfeld

Foreword by Ron Couch

Photography by Jim Smith

PELICAN PUBLISHING COMPANY
Gretna 2008

Library of Congress Cataloging-in-Publication Data

Alfeld, Beverly Ellen Schoonmaker, 1946-
Pickles to relish / by Beverly Ellen Schoonmaker Alfeld ; photography by Jim Smith.
p. cm.
Includes index.
ISBN 978-1-58980-489-0 (hardcover : alk. paper) 1. Canning and preserving.
2. Pickles. 3. Cookery (Relishes) I. Title.
TX603.A37 2008
641.4--dc22

2007041692

Photographic assistance by Justin Allen, Ryan Basten, and Jason Torres
Food styling by Beverly Alfeld
Research assistance by Kim Alfeld
Technical assistance by Tim Alfeld

Printed in Singapore

Published by Pelican Publishing Company, Inc.
1000 Burmaster Street, Gretna, Louisiana 70053

This cookbook is dedicated to my mother, Doris P. Schoonmaker,
who has always been supportive of my work and my adventures.

Contents

Foreword

Pickles and relish and, indeed, the cucumbers from which many such things are made often conjure memories of picnics and cookouts. But of course over the centuries pickled items of all kinds have been featured at the most formal tables of royalty, as well as being set out as fancy side dishes for the rich and famous. Fact is, folks around the world would enjoy far poorer diets were it not for the plethora of delightful things produced in the age-old pursuit of pickling and fermenting.

And Bev Alfeld certainly pursues the best in any culinary endeavor, not the least of which is perhaps her forte, pickling and preserving. In short, she is an expert. If readers of *Pickles to Relish* have enjoyed her earlier successful work, *The Jamlady Cookbook,* they will know that in her latest effort little of value or interest in the art of pickling has escaped the attention of Bev or the Jamlady. She thinks big; when she takes on anything, especially in the culinary field, she can be counted on to research it in depth.

As extensive as the information presented in *Pickles to Relish* is, you will find it fully accessible to both chef and home canner. This is because Jamlady and Bev Alfeld believe canning is more than food preservation, a tenet certainly evidenced by this book; it is useful to youngsters as well as adults because it teaches application of math and history and pride in self-sufficiency. Illustrating accessibility even to neophytes is the book's how-to for making small batches of pickles without canning—you can put them in the refrigerator or leave them out to develop at room temperature.

Of special note are the more technical aspects of *Pickles to Relish.* Although a bit complex for novice canners, the Alfeld Notation System still alerts them to the importance of processing times and altitude considerations. There is an excellent discussion of relative acidity and a pH chart in the back of the book.

Few cookbooks offer so many recipes for chutneys, or such a diversity of pickle and relish recipes, from mild to wild—like pickled green walnuts to top filet mignon, pickled kumquats in champagne or pickled dilly beans and asparagus in a Bloody Mary.

Ron Couch

Acknowledgments

Thank you market patrons; Mr. Ron Couch, editor of *Fruit Gardener* magazine; Mr. Bill Grimes, president of the California Rare Fruit Growers Inc; Mr. George Vicory; Mr. Bob Aicher; Mr. Joe Watson; Ms. Barbara Davies; the Crystal Lake Public Library staff; Mr. and Mrs. Bill Brooks of the International Pickle Festival; Ms. Susan Marquis; Dr. Kathleen Grambling; and Bonnie Will. Thanks to my publisher, Dr. Milburn Calhoun; my editors, Nina Kooij and Heather Green; my photographer, Mr. Jim Smith, and his three assistants, Ryan Basten, Justin Allen, and Jason Torres. A special thanks to my two children, Kim Alfeld and Tim Alfeld; to my mother, Doris Schoonmaker; and to my extended family and friends. Without all of you special people, Jamlady and Bev Alfeld could not thrive, teach, and influence.

Finally, thank you Jamlady for allowing me to write some of this book by myself. Not everyone appreciates you all the time, but I do. For those who don't believe in Tinker Bell, Jamlady is hard to explain. Jamlady, like Betty Crocker, is the ideal cook and canner, although Bev Alfeld influences Jamlady and visa versa. Bev Alfeld hears Jamlady's little voice above her shoulder when she cooks. Maybe you have a little voice that talks to you, but perhaps your Tinker Bell does not know how to cook and talk. Jamlady does.

Three jars of jardinière.

Introduction

***Pickles to Relish* provides information on food preservation for the homemaker, canner, gardener, professional chef, food scientist, doctor, artist, pickler, chemist, farmer, nurse, nutritionist, food historian, anthropologist, ethnobotanist, backyard-grill master, and anyone else who is interested in condiments, cooking, self-sufficiency, food history, education, art, new experiences, and healthful food. Various types of food-preservation techniques or methods, such as fermentation, curing, pickling, freezing, refrigeration, and canning, are discussed, along with related information from allied fields of knowledge. See how various techniques of food preservation have impacted, and continue to impact, human survival, security, and advancement. Learn how to get "pickle power." Learn about balancing your own potential and roots.**

Some of the multiple-subject, or cross-cat, information in *Pickles to Relish* isn't generally found in one book as our educational system, in general, tends to promote a single-subject mind-set. **School courses tend to divide information by fields, and many students don't think very deeply about food as it relates to nation building or feeding two billion hungry people via old-fashioned techniques such as fermentation.**

Pickling and canning! "Why do we need them? Can't we just buy food at the grocery store?" Artists, the creatively intelligent lot, are often seen as less learned or unqualified. What does an artist know about scientific, mathematical, or historical issues? **So many creative solutions are unrealized because the unique intelligence of one group or another is underrated, unrecognized, and underutilized.**

This title, *Pickles to Relish,* demonstrates the double meaning and intent of this book. While you read or use a recipe from this book, consider the historic, economic, artistic, and self-survival importance associated with something so basic as fermentation and food preservation. Has its impact and importance changed over time? How does a nation's collective philosophy of life affect its food choices and its food supply, and visa versa? **Are the pickling skills needed for pickling food being advanced or are they being slowly lost?** If they are being lost, what should we do about it? What values and knowledge are we losing, if any, as we attempt to relegate this homemaker's art to a position of "slow food" or relative obscurity? Should we rely on distant farms and factories to supply us with modified and cloned food? If properly applied, could pickling and fermentation knowledge be saving and enriching many lives? **Are we trying to use high-tech solutions to solve problems of the low-tech, third-world nations or of the low-tech home kitchen?** What might happen if we used more simplistic preservation methods in these places? How many lives might be saved or greatly improved at a relatively low cost per person? Do we educate people to eat for less cost while improving their nutrition or visa versa.

***Pickles to Relish* is more than a cookbook or recipe book. This book seeks to teach people to thrive by applying the various concepts of cooking, chemistry, art, horticulture, and historical knowledge to their everyday lives.** It seeks to teach people to modify and improve facets of their own lives. **Jamlady espouses a philosophy of balance.** It attempts to help people to be proud of their accomplishments. Jamlady and Bev Alfeld believe more local food sources should be developed, and more people need to pay attention to what they are eating. To this end, people need to slow down some and teach their children with hands-on activities so the allied knowledge children are learning in school is supported by meaningful, real-life, home experiences with nurturing adults. Educate yourself about food. Don't just purchase anything on the grocery store shelf, because it is there and, therefore, "must be okay to eat." Take control of your own life. Live a fuller, healthier, and happier life with self-acquired knowledge and increased self-sufficiency. Urge governments around the world to fund more programs that teach methods of fermentation, seed selection, and food preservation.

Support cooks, artists, scientists, and culinologists™ who seek to create more exciting foods, foods that are more interesting and healthful than ever. **This new field of culinology™, besides being the official magazine of the RCA (Research Chefs Association), is a new subject, field, and college major, which blends the fields of food science and culinary arts.** This blending and study of the blending of these two fields of knowledge are long overdue. Previously, simplistic and arbitrary lines of subject demarcation were beginning to restrict advances in both fields. Besides culinology™, the new field of ethnobotany has emerged. Ethnobotany studies the interrelatedness of cultures and their uses for plants. **One might see this information sharing as a swing of the pendulum back in time while also eyeing the future, as we grasp new theories like ECIWO and the fermentation of our vitamins and medicines into our foods.**

Within this cookbook are five chapters containing recipes and information on food history, process, chemistry, horticulture, spices, and philosophy. There are recipes for pickles, relishes, sauces, juices, and chutneys. Please refer to the table of contents and index for more information concerning the topics and recipes presented in this cookbook.

This publication hopes to spark your creative spirit and show you how much there is to learn and gain from just making a jar of pickles, relish, or chutney. I have not made every type of pickle in the world, but I have made many different pickles for farmers'markets, recipes easily duplicated by any dauntless reader. If you have fears about canning, read *Pickles to Relish* and overcome them. **If you have children, set the example of self-sufficiency and quell their fear. Can! Freeze! Make fresh, raw pickles! If you are a gardener, chef, scientist, doctor, nurse, or artist, make use of your special talents and bountiful garden by sharing the results of your applied philosophical and scientific knowledge as you hand out "jars of love."**

To pickle is to preserve a vegetable, fruit, or meat in an acid. Many dictionaries and other sources confuse people about pickling or fermentation. These sources imply vinegar or a brine solution must always be added to a vegetable to make a pickle. **Actually, a dry-salted vegetable, like a cucumber, will give up its own water via osmosis. This action triggers the fermentation process of lactic bacteria. The resulting acid preserves the vegetable and inhibits the growth of harmful bacteria.** This process is complex and has not been studied adequately for all types of pickles. **In some recipes an acid, like vinegar, is added to the vegetable, and it is then pasteurized to kill or make dormant the bacterial spores that may be harmful. The third method of preservation requires acidification of the vegetable or fruit combined with refrigeration.** The acid and the low temperature keep any harmful bacteria dormant. **Sometimes, lemons or limes are used instead of vinegar.** For example, *ceviche* (raw, pickled fish) may be made with lime juice instead of vinegar.

Water, wine, sugar, salt, or other spices might be part of a pickling solution, and it is possible to make a less-vinegary pickle by increasing the salt and water and decreasing the vinegar. When hermetically sealing a pickled product, the acidity, or pH, must always be considered. **It is also important to consider the quantity of salt and sugar in any product.** Do not alter pickling recipes unless you use a pH meter to check the ground-up product. **Make sure the pH of any rolling-water-bath-processed pickle is well under 4.6.**

This cookbook attempts to teach canning and pickling from a multi-sensory, philosophical, and multi-disciplinary point-of-view. Educational researchers and other psychologists tell us students learn better when the learning is meaningful and multi-sensory, yet instruction in many schools is still predominately by lecture or paper and pencil. **Present day students have sensory preferences: visual—46 percent, kinesthetic-tactile—35 percent, and auditory—19 percent** (Sousa 1997 and Swanson 1995). If one looks back, one sees "old-time" educators and individual family members teaching students with visual and kinesthetic-tactile methods. Such is the nature of everyone "pitching in." There was farm work to do, and everybody was working and talking with one another. There was more adult-child interaction and probably less isolated and unmonitored child-to-child interaction. Consider teaching a child how to milk a cow, curry a horse, or collect, clean, and count eggs. I don't think they often wrote out the instructions for the child to read or spoke all the instructions. Instead, it was, **"Watch me! Now, you do this."**

Consider home economics classes where the students had to measure, compute, prepare ingredients, and cook food. **Students would learn and then duplicate recipes for their own families.** Cooking opportunities were available at church, 4-H, and grandma's house. All the cooking skills were practiced—reading, measuring, temperature-setting, attending, and accountability. **Repetition of steps and putting information into short-term memory eventually allows information to be saved in long-term memory.** Learning was taking place. The same analysis could be applied to other self-sufficiency activities, such as building furniture or sewing a dress. **Information placed in long-term storage was then available for future examination and use.** The continued expansion of learning or higher-ordered learning could take place only when there was learned information available, which might be synthesized with the new information. **Over-learning was a good thing; revisiting learned information usually meant this information was being synthesized with new knowledge.**

In years past, there were fewer lines of demarcation for different subjects. Multi-disciplinary and multi-sensory learning was encouraged. Just look at an old dime book, and see all the allied areas of knowledge discussed within those little books. With all the new research about how we learn, it seems prudent to begin to use more hands-on instruction and instruction with meaningful and delicious results. **Making a pickle involves much more than just cooking. Pickling involves an understanding of horticulture, chemistry, cooking, cultural information, mathematics, art, and, sometimes, governmental regulations. But of course, if you insist, you can gleefully use this book as a "copy book." Just follow the recipes, and try to ignore the many encouragements for individual research and development. However, it probably won't work. That would be like eating only one chocolate-covered cherry from a box of twenty-four.**

Some will say pickling and canning take too much time and are slow. **The process of pickling can be either fast or slow, depending on the recipe. Keep in mind, the slowness of the art is not necessarily a negative, and making a pickle may not be the only objective. What some see as work, may be play to others. Learning is taking place as the process unfolds. Creative and analytic brain activity is spurred onward by the would-be inventor of a new flavor or kind of pickle. To create a new pickle, one draws on previous knowledge and manipulates the variables.** That is what learning is: the process of acquiring and retaining knowledge for future application.

So many cookbooks and recipe books are intended to be "copy books." Copy the recipe and don't think about it. It is easy and fast that way. Production is the main focus. Of course, first, one must do and copy to acquire and retain knowledge. Jamlady recommends you think a little bit more about your roots and how you can invent and apply these new ideas. Spend some downtime with yourself and your family. "Fast" should not always be the primary objective. **A "true cook" masters the techniques and underlying principals, so they have a toolbox of information to manipulate and synthesize with new information—sometimes from a most unexpected and inspirational source.** A learned, well-paced cook acquires knowledge, retains it, applies it in the future, and furthers family well-being, knowledge, and happiness in one fell swoop. Fast cooks produce food fast without necessarily meeting all of the objectives cited here. **The knowledge acquired is not just culinary in nature but is knowledge drawn from many allied fields of scholarship.**

Today's news is all about "fast food" and "slow food." The two philosophical schools discuss various food issues, back and forth. As with all things, a balance of both philosophies makes the most sense.

In the 1970s, there were classes in which professors required students to keep track of every minute they spent during the day and night, observing and maximizing their use of time. While time efficiency sounds good and aspiring, some professors failed to consider the consequences for a student who might actually carry out this experiment—to the max. The human body is not a machine and is not intended to run continually at full potential. The havoc such perfected self-discipline can create with the human nervous system can be gradual and harmful. Studies of assembly-line workers who work without adequate breaks, in dim light, and without changes from certain repetitive motions show that these actions can dramatically and negatively affect their bodies. Carpal tunnel is one possible problem. **The human body needs breaks, balance, and a variety of activities.** How similar is this scenario to some classrooms where the students sit at desks, writing all day long? The go-go person who has no balance to his daily routine often develops all sorts of health problems. So, one should consider the actual outcome of a lifestyle based on fast, faster, and fastest. Where are we headed? **Maybe we go faster and faster but, ultimately, are we sentenced with a shorter life span, lower test scores, and less happy families?** Look what is happening in Japan. Japanese seniors once could boast of the longest life span of any major peoples in the world, but their records may not stand the test of time if their pace of life continues to escalate as they grow fatter and fatter on Western food.

Change pace. Try to accomplish something new. Grow a garden. Watch what you eat. Can or refrigerate some raw pickles. Grow and eat unusual or heritage vegetables. **Be concerned about untested genetic engineering of seeds, especially "suicide seeds"** (genetically-engineered plants that produce seeds that cannot germinate). Understand the dangers and relevancies of these new technologies. Teach your children how to be frugal and self-sufficient. One day they may need or want to use these skills. Insist on schools teaching to an individual's needs as well as teaching to support the government's needs of its citizens. Support local farmers. **Teach your children by example; integrate their everyday learning with functional projects and fun cooking.** Don't miss an opportunity to count telephone poles on the way to grandma's cucumber patch.

There probably isn't a better place to teach yourself or your children about the world, plants, different cultures, math, and the basics of reading than through art and cooking. Yet, what are the first subjects cut in an austere school budget? Do school board members listen to the saying—"Art is Basic?" Art and cooking are basic. These subjects allow students to practice new information in an exciting way, permitting feedback to come from many sources and students to apply their newly acquired knowledge in all sorts of situations with less and less help from others. Indeed, the practice and learning strategies become self-regulated, more executive in nature, and allow students to more easily recall information; they have practiced this information thoroughly and in a multisensory fashion. For doing a good job while combining math, science, and culinary information

Dr. Paul Pechman's entries at the 2006 International Pickle Festival, Rosendale, New York. Left to right: *Dr. Paul Pechman's "Mango-Mango" (a quick pickle, a mangoed zucchini, or hollowed zucchini, which is stuffed [mangoed] with black-radish and tropical-mango pieces), canned dilly beans, and a quick pickle made with halved tindora cucumbers.*

the reward is intrinsic. **Further, if measurements or calculations are incorrect, the cook may end up creating a new, wonderful product or may experience utter failure.**

Since risk is inherent in the cooking, one is more apt to pay close attention and to focus on the steps towards the goal. If a student cook has spent time and money making a pickle or relish and fails because of a calculation error, you can be sure he will pay more attention the next time and recheck his math. Hopefully, he won't give up altogether. So, there are built-in rewards and consequences. Students are more likely to be on task, concentrating and seeking the best possible outcome if their calculations will actually be used in cooking than if they are just doing mathematical-word problems on paper. **There is more motivation. The end product is eaten and accolades are garnered from those who love the food. Additionally, the importance of positive self statements cannot be underestimated.** As a teacher or parent, it is a whole lot easier to convince children they can measure out or double a recipe than to convince them they can do math with paper and pencil. **The motivation to try harder, begins with little, fun-filled successes.**

Some critics say children are "too young to cook." "They are too young to count; they will be burned." Many pickles and flavored vinegars can be made with little danger to small children. Adults may have to do one or two steps, but children, with little fingers, can efficiently pack pickle jars with green beans or cucumbers. "How many green beans did you put in that pickle jar?" "Make the jar one-third pepper strips." "How beautifully you have packed those alternating layers of sweet red peppers slices and green bean pieces." Some people may not believe this, but most infants as young as one can learn to add and subtract. Babies can be taught to count with carrot sticks in a bucket, cookies in a bowl, or Cheerios® in a cup. **Given this fact, young children can learn to measure and cook.**

Other benefits of learning through recipes are: they come in increasing degrees of difficulty, have clear expectations, usually are expressed in short sentences and simple vocabulary, and provide feedback from hungry taste-testers. This is a formula for success, a formula that allows students of any age to increase their own self-esteem. Since I work as an advocate and educational consultant for special education students, as well as a chef, I take the opportunity to point out that ADHD students and hyperactive students learn much better with activities allowing them some range of movement, activities with a degree of relevancy. You won't hear students saying, "Why do we have to learn what two cups plus three cups equals?" They can see why it is necessary. There is also a good likelihood students will go home, get some friends together, and teach them what they have learned. How often does that happen with a paper and pencil assignment? There is even a greater likelihood students will complete the project and look forward to the next one. **While these types of projects may not be as "fast" as some assignments, it is very probable the information from this "slow" or "slower" activity will get logged into their long-term memory.**

So teach yourself to make a few jars of pickles, relishes, and chutneys, or make some "quickles." Start a family tradition if you don't already have an Aunt Tillie who makes hot dilly beans. But, most of all, teach your children the love of learning. Teach them to study about other cultures, religions, traditions, and beliefs that are so intertwined with cooking, pickling, and a meaningful life.

Chapter 1

The Processing Method

Most of my experience, with pickles, relishes, chutneys, sauces, condiments, and vinegars, has been with canned product, because Jamlady sells pickled products in warm, open-air markets, where refrigeration isn't often available or practical. Many marketers appreciate a shelf-stable product and often buy pickles and chutneys to give as gifts. **Some of the recipes in this book will not require sealing by heat processing and are quick, refrigerator, or freezer pickles. Others are hermetically sealed in jars. Various other pickles are uncooked and fermented. This chapter is about sealing product in a jar.**

There are several ways to hermetically seal a canning jar. The easiest method, and the method used in this cookbook is the rolling-water-bath method (RWB). Correctly sealing a canning jar, using the RWB method, will produce a safe, shelf-stable product. Please don't consider sealing any product with wax seals, dishwasher processing, steam environments, inversion, or other "short-cut" methods. These methods are not safe. The rolling-water-bath method is easy to use and requires just a little training or specialized equipment. You do not need to use a pressure-cooker to seal an acidified pickle, relish, or chutney. If you don't have a canner or bottom disc, construct a bottom disc out of canning rings with "twisties" (see photo on page 22). Let's keep it simple. **You need ten things, plus your wits. That's it!**

a canning jar
a canning lid with ring
a ladle
a pair of tongs
a kitchen towel
a knife or "bubbler"
a heat source
a properly acidified product to seal in the jar
a water-filled pot deep enough for processing the jar
a metal disc for the pot's bottom or an inner, perforated basket

The rolling-water-bath method will be explained and illustrated here, but it is always recommended a novice consult several sources when learning about a new topic. Remember what Jamlady says, "We often don't know what we don't know until we know it." There are many free, informative, agricultural websites on the Internet; consult some. Normally, the most reliable information originates from government- or university-sponsored websites, but this is not always the case. While many

Minimal canning equipment

experienced canners can spot potentially dangerous recipes, most novices cannot. So, beginners, please use only expert-tested recipes, and read this book from cover to cover.

A potentially dangerous recipe usually contains a low-acid vegetable or fruit that has insufficient acidification, salt, or sugar. The inexperienced canner should be wary of all low-acid vegetable or fruit recipes from unknown sources. **Refer to the pH of fruits and vegetables chart, in the back of this book, to see which fruits and vegetables qualify as low-acid. These are fruits and vegetables with pH numbers in excess of 4.6.**

Canners-in-training or experienced canners, armed with their trusty pH meters, will be able to test suspicious recipes and notify site webmasters or editors about dangerous canning recipes. Expert food scientists and very experienced canners should be able to spot these dangerous recipes by reading them over and analyzing their ratios of low-acid foods to acidifiers, salt, and sugar. Take the time to scrutinize each new recipe you encounter.

In order to safely seal a canning jar, an adequate vacuum needs to exist in the air-space between the contents and the lid. **That air-space needs to be about 6 percent and never less than 5 percent of the entire jar's volume. The contents or food product in the jar will then take up about 94 percent of the jar's space.** Some books speak in terms of inches, or inches from the top of the jar rim, but this measure is not always an accurate measure, because the shape of the jar, the circumference of the rim, and the height of the jar will all impact the headspace. A tall, slender, 8-ounce canning jar filled to 94-percent capacity would not have the same fill requirements in inches (from product top to jar top) as a short, squatty, 8-ounce canning jar filled to 94-percent capacity. So, the percentage of fill in a jar is a better indicator of how far to fill a canning jar than the number of inches, or fractional inches, from the top of the canning jar to the proposed product fill line.

If consistently using one type of canning jar, determine the correct level of the fill line, and fill all identical jars in the same way each time you use them. In general, a 16-ounce, standard, upright,

Filling a canning jar, add a little more to this jar so it has six-percent headspace or about a half-inch of headspace from the rim of the jar.

canning jar should be filled to about ½ inch from the top. An 8-ounce, upright canning jar should fill to about ⅜ inch from the top, and a 4-ounce canning jar should be filled to about ¼ inch from the top. A regular-mouthed, upright quart might have a headspace of ¾ inch to 1 inch, depending on the style of jar you have and if the contents are chunky and more likely to float up. A *jardinière* that is likely to expand might be filled with a slightly larger headspace than, say, applesauce. **Be careful not to overpack a jar of *jardinière*. It is better to under pack than to overpack.** A wide-mouth, tapered quart jar, filled to 94 percent full, might measure differently in inches from the top of the jar in comparison to the 94-percent-full, regular-mouthed quart jar, as the top surface areas are different. **Both jars should be filled to 94 percent full (with 6 percent of headspace) to assure a reliable closure or seal.**

Keep in mind, new and differently shaped canning jars and imported canning jars can be found. For a good, safe seal, make sure there is sufficient headspace and sufficient processing time and temperature. **Without enough headspace, there will be insufficient steam trapped in the headspace to create sufficient vacuum.** Additionally, and with heat processing, there will not be enough space for product expansion in the jar.

Air in the product is another factor to consider. There are slender tools, or "bubblers," that may be slid down the side of a canning jar—to dislodge trapped air bubbles. Prior to lid application, check the jars for trapped air bubbles. Scoot the trapped air bubbles up to the surface of the liquid. **The air in the product and the processing temperature both affect the resulting vacuum. Vacuum is less where air trapped in the product is greater.**

Time and temperature are both important to obtain a proper seal. **Normally, the higher the product temperature at the time of sealing, the higher the final package vacuum.** The capper vacuum efficiency for any specific canning jar can be measured by a vacuum gauge.

PROCESSING STEPS

1. Sterilize the canning jars in boiling water for 10 minutes or, alternatively, boil water in the jars by heating them in a microwave. This sterilization step is a more important step if, when you seal them, you will be processing the filled jars for less than 10 minutes. Some canners wash the canning jars in a dishwasher and boil the water-filled jars in the microwave. This is an acceptable method, especially if the final product will be in the RWB for more than 10 minutes. **Actually, jars that will be boiled for 10 minutes or more need not be sterilized, but you might run them through the dishwasher.** Just remember, it is always good to have squeaky-clean jars. **Scrubbing canning jars well with soapy bleach water before you boil them is an extra-prudent step for increased safety and sanitation. Wipe your counters with this soapy bleach water, and rinse well.**

2. Sterilize canning rings, funnels, and rubberized, metal tops by boiling them for 10 minutes in a pan of water. Do not attempt to microwave metal rings or lids. Rings that will be processed for more than 10 minutes do not need to be pre-sterilized.

3. Use a canning funnel to fill canning jars to the appropriate level. Caution: Do not RWB process any product with a pH in excess of 4.2 (pH must be comfortably under 4.6).

4. Wipe off the top of the jar lip. Check for chips or cracks. Attach the canning lid and ring. Screw the ring down until it meets with some resistance; then stop. Do not screw the ring on too tightly.

5. Place the jar in a canner or similar set-up. Cover the jars totally with water of the same temperature as the jars. There should be at least one to two inches of water over the top of the jars.

6. Heat the filled canner until the water boils. Time the processing time. Start timing from the first sight of an actual rolling boil. This RWB-process does not include the small bubbles rising from the bottom of the pan. The large bubbles of a rolling-water bath will break the surface of the water and roll, assuming your range has sufficient BTUs to bring the pot to a rolling boil.

7. When the processing time is up, use canning tongs to lift hot jars out of the canner and onto a folded kitchen towel, or take out the entire rack-full of jars and set them on a folded kitchen towel. Be careful not to burn yourself with rising steam. Wear a long-sleeved garment, so steam does not make contact with your arms. As far as possible, keep your head and body away from the steam. Keep hot jars separated by at least one inch. When jars are cooling, do not attempt to check the seal or tighten or unscrew the rings. Within a short period of time, a "click" should be heard, and the centers of the metal lids should depress (go down). Congratulations! You have now made a vacuum-sealed, shelf-stable product.

Commercially, jars and cans are sealed in big pressure-cookers called retorts. **Still retorts remain stationary as they process. Agitating retorts shake or agitate thicker product, so the heat is evenly dispersed throughout the jar.** This processing occurs at a temperature of around 250 degrees F (121 degrees C), with 15 lbs./sq.-inch pressure or about 10 tons of force. **A hydrostatic retort operates at a constant process temperature, and the product to be sealed is transported through the retort on a conveyor system.**

ROLLING-WATER BATH—RWB

Any canning recipe in this book may be sealed by a process called a rolling-water bath or RWB.

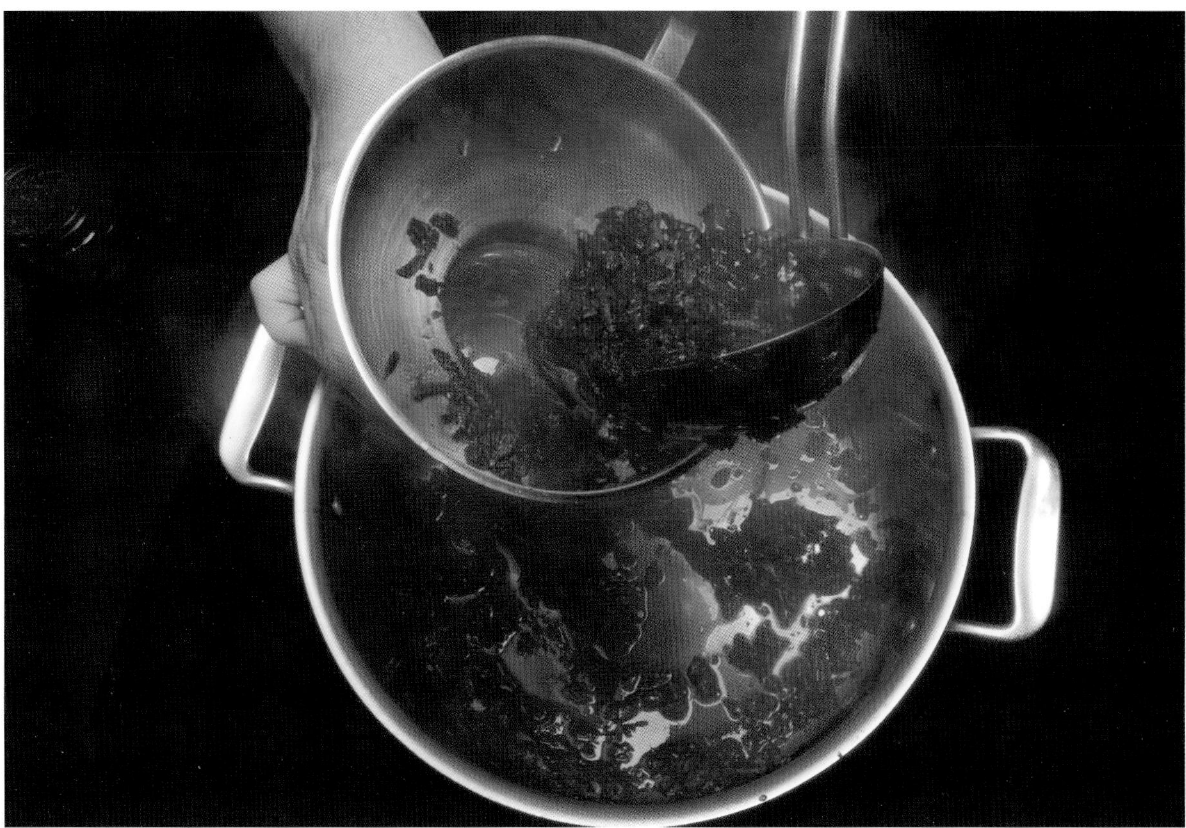

Filling the jar with a canning funnel and ladle.

A tall, cylindrical stockpot, like the All-Clad stockpot listed in the information guide, is preferable to a traditional canner with its shorter height and very-wide bottom. Jamlady wishes All-Clad would market a bottom disc for it. Outfit the taller stockpot with a round, perforated bottom disc or rack to create an elevation between the bottom of the pan and the bottom of the canning jar. Using a taller pot will reduce the amount of water that ends up all over the stovetop. Further, the filled pot will heat up faster, especially for cooks using a residential range with lower BTUs. **The pan's small-bottom circumference is important, because a lot of newer stoves don't have sufficient BTUs to take a large, wide-bottomed canner up to temperature. This is disastrous for pickles, because the pickles overcook before a rolling-water temperature is achieved.**

Taller canners are especially useful when sealing quart jars. Make sure your range has sufficient BTUs to boil water in a large pot. If the BTUs are insufficient, a different stove, one with sufficient BTU burners, may be needed. Look for a tabletop stock-pot range or some other type of range with higher BTUs at a local restaurant-supply store. Look for a minimum of 10,000 BTUs in a range burner; 12,000 or higher is better. If you try to use a 6,000- or 8,000-BTU burner, it might take too long to process the pickles, resulting in mushy pickles. Should a jar of pickles fail to seal during the first processing attempt, just refrigerate it. Remember, pickles cannot be successfully resealed by reprocessing, as they will be overcooked.

Caution: If a previously unsealed jar of product at room temperature seals in the refrigerator, do not assume it may be taken out of the refrigerator again and stored on a shelf. More than likely, this jar will unseal at room temperature and reseal again if cooled again. Neglecting to refrigerate this transitioning jar is potentially dangerous. Store all "low-vacuum" or unsealed jars of product in the refrigerator.

ALFELD NOMENCLATURE SYSTEM

The Alfeld Nomenclature System is an abbreviated notation system for canners to clearly label the times and process used to seal a canning jar. The following notation JSP/RWB10, or JSP/RWB10A, means jar, seal/close, and process in a rolling-water bath for 10 minutes, or 10 minutes plus the increase in time needed for the increased altitude. Adjusting processing time for altitudes over 1000 feet is normally assumed, but this **"A" notation may be used as a reminder.** The number of minutes to add to the processing time is indicated on the altitude chart shown on page 27. If the canning location is below 1,000 feet, no modifications are necessary, but, obviously, there is more leeway in the times at sea level than at 950 feet. One might also write JSP/RWB15(8OZ)A3100(20), which means the processing time for under 1,000 feet is 15 minutes, but the processing time for 3,100 feet is 20 minutes. An experienced canner might include the notation with the recipe when giving it away, especially to novice canners living at a higher altitude. **Instructing a cook to "seal" a jar is wholly inadequate information.** If you do not know the appropriate processing time for a recipe, just write—not available or NA(16OZ)R.

If no jar size is indicated at the end of the notation in parenthesis, the jar size is assumed to be 4 or 8 ounces. The notation JSP/RWB20(16OZ)A would mean jar, seal, and process a 16-ounce jar for 20 minutes in a rolling-water bath at an altitude of 1,000 feet or less; adjust the processing time for higher altitudes. The notation JSP/RWB15(16OZ)RA means jar, seal, and process a 16-ounce jar for 15 minutes, adjust for altitude (if necessary), and keep the product refrigerated. **It is further assumed a canner would properly label this product—"refrigeration required" or "Keep Refrigerated." JSR means jar, seal, refrigerate, and JSF means jar, seal, and freeze.** JSP/10SPI/75A means jar, seal, and process at 10 pounds per square inch for 75 minutes for a 4- or 8-ounce jar, and adjust for altitude. To change the jar size, add "16OZ", or whatever size you will be processing, to the end of the notation but before the "A." **The notation for low-temperature pasteurization is shown as JSP/180dF/30(16OZ)A. See low-temperature pasteurization.**

FILLING THE JAR

1. Inspect each jar for cracks or nicks, especially the jar lip. Discard damaged jars.
2. Make sure the jars are squeaky clean and sterilized. Boil canning jars, lids, and rings in water to sterilize them. Alternatively, run them through the dishwasher, and for extra sterility, you may microwave the water-filled jars. Lids and rings are easily boiled in a small pot on the stove. Do not microwave metal rings or lids. When hand-washing the jars, or washing them in the dishwasher, add a little capful of household bleach to the wash water; rinse well.
3. Do not overfill the jars. Fill the jars to 94 percent full, with 6-percent headspace (air-space). Check each lid's rubber seal for imperfections. Do not use rusty or bent lids or rings.
4. After filling the jar to the appropriate level, make sure the jar rim is clean. Place the rubber seal on the jar rim. Do not overfill the jars, or you will reduce the necessary vacuum.
5. Place the metal ring over the metal lid and tighten the ring. Do not screw it too tightly, but adjust it to the first bit of resistance. The jar is now ready for a rolling-water bath (RWB).

PROCESSING TIMES

Processing times vary according to the size of the jar and the thickness of the product. Today, the typical bread and butter pickle should be processed 15 minutes for a quart and 10 minutes for a pint. Historically, the times were less, 10 minutes for a quart and 5 minutes for a pint. Some people still choose to use historical processing times but then keep the pickles refrigerated, carefully labeling each jar with "Keep Refrigerated." **The USDA and others experts are now recommending longer processing times for some products.** Chutney may be processed 10 to 25 minutes, depending on the size of the jar. **Please make sure to read the section on the Alfeld Notation System, so you will understand the recipes. Jamlady recommends canners always consult more than one reliable source regarding processing times.** Canning jars, home and commercial, American and foreign, come in all sorts of shapes and sizes: 1-, 2-, 4-, 8-, 12-, 16-, 22-, 24-, 32-, and 64-ounce jars. **Normally, thicker product should be packed in smaller jars to assure good heat distribution during processing.** Home canners are usually told to avoid 64-ounce jars, because the heat cannot easily penetrate through the larger jars. However, it might be acceptable to use a 64-ounce jar for canning thin liquids like apple-water tea.

If the processing time is insufficient, a proper vacuum may not form to seal the jar. Then the product must be reprocessed or refrigerated. Some products like pickles shouldn't be reprocessed as they will be overcooked. **Caution: Even though a jar of product is sealed, be careful not to subject it to extreme temperature fluctuations, or anything that might disrupt the integrity of the seal. This especially includes freezing or placing the canned product in a car on a ninety-degree day.**

ALTITUDE CONVERSION

In recent years altitude-conversion charts have been updated, and processing times have been increased. For most sea-level canners, no altitude related changes are required. If you live in a place like Albuquerque, New Mexico, which is located at 5,000 feet, or in another high-altitude location (1,000 feet or higher), please pay attention.

Water-bath processing times need to be increased as altitude increases. The old, pre-1994 chart for RWB-processing suggested approximately one additional minute of processing time for every 1,000 feet in altitude. These recommended processing times have been increased to:

Altitude		**Increased Processing Time**
Feet	**Meters**	**Increase by**
1,001-3,000	306-915	5 minutes
3,001-6,000	916-1,830	10 minutes
6,001-8,000	1,831-2,440	15 minutes
8,001-10,000	2,441-3,050	20 minutes

Even these numbers are not totally accurate, because the boiling point of water varies according to the current barometric-pressure reading, and that value also fluctuates. For more information on high-altitude cooking and canning, please consult other sources such as Anderson and Hamilton's *The New High Altitude Cookbook.*

Processing times need to increase as altitudes

increase, because water boils at a lower temperature at higher altitudes. At sea level, water boils at 212.0 degrees Fahrenheit or 100.0 degrees Centigrade at sea level. **As altitude increases, the temperature at which water boils decreases. Lower temperatures are less effective for killing bacteria, so the processing times must be increased for the RWB method, and the canner pressure must be increased for pressure-cooker canning.**

Altitude		Boiling Temperature in Degrees	
Feet	**Meters**	**Fahrenheit**	**Centigrade**
2,000	609.6	208.2	97.9
4,000	1,219.2	204.4	95.8
6,000	1,828.8	200.7	93.7
8,000	2,438.4	196.9	91.6
10,000	3,048.0	194.0	90.0
14,000	4,267.2	187.3	86.3

* The above temperatures are approximate.

These different boiling points of water also change with variations in barometric pressure. To find the actual boiling point of water, take the standard barometric pressure (29.92 millibars) and subtract the local barometric pressure. Multiply the answer by 1.8518, add 212 to that, and you will have the current boiling point of water at that place and time.

High-altitude canners, bakers, and cooks should consult their local agricultural extension office for recommendations on extended cooking times for that specific area. **If you live at 940 feet, consider adjusting the processing times for over 1000 feet, depending on what you are processing (thickness of product, pH, size of pieces, etc.).**

REACTIVE METALS

Reactive metal should be avoided in canning. These metals include iron, aluminum, brass, copper, or zinc (galvanized). Select metals, pots, and utensils that do not react chemically with acids and salts. Use vessels or pots of enamelware, stainless steel, ceramic, or glass. Check with a reputable restaurant-supply store to purchase a tall, quality, stainless-steel pot—with a wire basket, built-in strainer, or bottom rack. The elevated rack from a regular pressure canner will usually fit in a tall, large, All-Clad stockpot and can work with the pot as a canner. Alternately, just look around, and buy a rack that fits your pan, or construct a make-shift rack by connecting canning rings with "twisties" or string. **Jamlady does not recommend the too-short, standard canner for canning quart jars, as water ends up all over the stove.** Besides that, many larger canners are too large in diameter for the BTUs on many home ranges. A taller and smaller-diameter pot is recommended.

Buy the best quality of cookware you can afford. Spend the extra money to get a thick-metal core in the bottom of the pot. Many would-be cooks have given up on cooking because "things always burn or stick." Perhaps the pan is at fault, not the cook. A quality stockpot and Dutch oven represent money well spent. Check discount stores like Marshalls and TJ Maxx. Sometimes there are real deals there on large, good-quality stockpots.

SPECIAL TECHNIQUES AND AVOIDING PROBLEMS

The best way to deal with any problem is to avoid it. Here are some suggestions for avoiding canning problems and some techniques to use.

1. **Do not use homemade vinegar for canning.** Use only 5- or 6-percent acidity vinegar.
2. **Do not use hard water, especially not for pickles.**
3. **Do not store canned goods in warm or light locations.** Store jars in a cool, dark place.
4. **Get your processing times right.** Cook on a range with adequate BTUs.
5. **Use fresh and chemical-free ingredients.** Don't use old or powdered spices. Use whole spices or fresh herbs for pickles. Don't use hollow cucumbers to make pickles. Discard any slimy pickles.
6. **Don't panic over pink, pickled cauliflower or green/blue garlic.** It isn't spoilage, but a non-harmful chemical change. Pickled cauliflower may be naturally colored with beets to eliminate the possibility of unwanted discoloration. **Immature and insufficiently dried garlic may turn blue or green in the presence of an acid because of the anthocyanin in the garlic. The green or blue color may also be due to sulfur compounds reacting with trace amounts of copper in the water.** If the enzymes in the garlic are not inactivated by heat, blue sulfate can form. Prior to use, some experts recommend temperature controlling the garlic to eliminate the problem. Don't use immature garlic heads. Prior to using, store garlic at room temperature for three weeks. Brown vegetables were either

Beets may be used to color cauliflower—the more beets, the darker the color. For photographic reasons, we made the beet color lighter than normal.

overcooked, overripe, or made with iodized salt. **Always use canning (pickling) salt for canning.**

7. **Don't overpack vegetables in a pickle jar, and don't pack a jar in such a way that vegetable pieces might migrate or block the neck of the jar.** A tightly packed jar cannot expand without forcing some of the juice out of the jar. If the water level in the pickle jar is greatly diminished, refrigerate it horizontally and use it first. Food trapped in a seal may ruin the seal; refrigerate it, and use it soon. Sometimes this problem is unavoidable.

8. **Discolored pickles are often traced to iron utensils, inappropriate cookware, metal-lid corrosion, iodized salt (use only pickling salt), too many or poor spices, and/or hard water.**

9. Shriveled and tough pickles are often traceable to overcooking, an excessively heavy syrup, an overly strong brine, old or diseased fruits, or to fruits that have been cooked too harshly in a brine or sugar syrup.

10. **Cloudy jelly may be caused by insufficiently strained juice, use of overly greenfruit, or because the jelly was allowed to sit for too long prior to being packed into jars.**

11. **Crystals in jelly or juice** may be from using too much sugar, cooking too little and too slowly, or because it was cooked too long. Crystals in grape jelly can be **tartrate crystals** and can be avoided by letting the extracted juice sit overnight in a cool place. Then strain the juice through two thicknesses of damp cheesecloth to remove the crystals.

12. **Don't touch the screw bands while the jars are still hot.** You might unseal an otherwise fine jar of pickles or relish.

13. **Do you can by the open-kettle method? If so, stop. With the open-kettle method, the food is not heated sufficiently to kill harmful bacteria and yeasts.**

14. **Do not use an oven, dishwasher, steam-canner, microwave, crockpot, or regular pressure-cooker to can foods.** Air does not conduct heat as well as water, so the foods processed with these methods can be under processed. Jars can also blow up when an oven door is opened. Steam-processing, according to some authoritative websites (for home canners), has not been sufficiently studied to be considered safe. Cold-water canning is also out, although you may read about this old technique in *The Jamlady Cookbook* (32).

15. **Do not use clamp-on style lids, old-fashioned rubber seals, wire bails and glass caps, or old zinc lids for canning in a RWB.** Use a metal, canning lid with a clean, metal ring. Old-fashioned jars may be used for refrigerator pickles or other fresh pickles. They look cute and charming, but don't expect them to be as reliable and safe as the two-piece lid and ring. Some one-trip, one-piece lids with attached "rubber seal" are also acceptable, but they are not often available to the home canner.

16. **Are you adding extra starch to recipes?** While starch usually does not change product pH that much, it can affect the rate of heat penetration into a product, and may necessitate longer processing times and/or rack agitation. If you are set on adding starch to a recipe, keep the product refrigerated after processing and use smaller jars. Consider adding starch to pie fillings when opening them, thereby, retaining the option to eat the fruit as canned fruit or pie filling.

17. **Don't add additional low-acid ingredients to a canning recipe or reduce the acidifiers. Don't reduce the sugar or salt. Certain harmful bacteria cannot grow in very salty, sweet, or acidic environments, but if the recipe is changed, the environment may become hospitable for these harmful bacteria.**

18. **Mold on jelly, or other products, indicates an improper seal.** Discard products with mold. Some toxins produced by molds may pose a health threat to some people.

19. **A faded pickle, relish, or jelly can be caused by improper storage or storage for too long.**

20. Bulging jars should not be opened in the kitchen or sink area because harmful bacteria might come into contact with uncooked foods. Reusing contaminated jars is not recommended. Seal these jars in double plastic bags, and dispose of responsibly as bio-hazardous material.

21. **Cracks in jars may occur when containers of product come into contact with something cooler or hotter.** Any filled jar of product needs to be placed in a water bath of the same temperature

as the jar. When removing a jar from a RWB, place it on a folded towel and not on a cold counter.

22. **Fermented product usually indicates a break or leak in the seal somewhere, even though it cannot easily be seen.**

23. Why don't my sauces, preserves, or fruit relishes thicken? Most fruits have some pectin. Apples, blackberries, crab apples, currants, gooseberries, and cranberries have a lot of natural pectin. Sauces, relishes, and preserves made with these fruits and sugars will usually thicken easily if they have or are combined with sufficient acid and sugar to allow the natural pectin to work. **Pectin is a fibrous carbohydrate containing entrapped water molecules.** When a fruit containing high pectin is cooked in the presence of an acid, the pectin changes its molecular structure and physical properties, so it is less possessive of its water and more attracted to the other pectin molecules. **Sufficient acid is essential for fruits to gel, or thicken.** When sugar is heated in the presence of an acid, it breaks down into simple sugars, glucose and fructose. These sugars accept the water molecules from the pectin chains. The pectin molecules then bind to one another, forming a web of pectin, and a jell is formed. **If there is insufficient pectin, sugar, or acid, the pectin chain does not form, and the thickening or jelling does not occur as expected.**

24. **Don't can bread in a jar.** The pH of any safely canned product has to be comfortably under 4.6, and the combined ingredients in most bread recipes aren't under 4.6 in pH.

25. If you are processing in a RWB, **respect the 4.6-pH line.** Make sure the product's pH is less than 4.3 or 4.2. **Always acidify plain tomatoes by adding 1 teaspoon of citric acid per quart.**

26. **Cut recipes in quarter or in half.** There is no problem with cutting most pickle, relish, and chutney recipes in half or in quarters. Just calculate the recipe correctly.

27. **Drain cucumbers and chopped vegetables well, usually squeezing out some of the excess water.** Avoid diluting the liquid portion of the recipe, as it may cause insufficient acidity. **Equate these instructions with "drain well" or "drain/squeeze."**

28. **Hot pack versus raw pack**—Pour hot brine into a jar of raw-packed vegetables to reduce the air in the vegetables. Raw-packed vegetables usually make crunchier pickles and keep their shape better than hot packed, but hot-packed vegetables float up less, have less air in the tissues, and tend to shrink more. Shrinkage allows for more vegetables to fit in a jar, but this might not be a good thing, especially if there is insufficient vinegar to acidify that quantity of low-acid vegetables. Hot-packed product may have a longer shelf life than cold-packed product, but all products should ideally be eaten in a year, as the nutritional value lessens with age.

29. **Low-Temperature Pasteurization Treatment** is a method used to reduce the incidence of soft pickles. Water baths are begun at 120 to 140 degrees F. Jars are inserted and covered with more warm to hot water. The temperature is raised to 180 to 185 degrees F and maintained there for 30 minutes. This method requires careful watching with a thermometer. Many canners opt to process for less time and keep the pickle refrigerated. A second refrigerator comes in handy for this purpose. Use small, fresh, and firm Kirby cucumbers for canned pickles, and this low-temperature pasteurization method may not be necessary. This method is often used for canning larger fermented pickles (crock pickles such as half-sours and sours), which normally can be refrigerated and eaten (without canning). **The Alfeld Nomenclature notation for this method would be JSP/180-185dF/30(16OZ) or JSP/83-85dC/30(16OZ). The 180dF stands for 180 degrees F. The 83dC stands for 83 degrees Centigrade.**

30. **Keep a process notebook.** Avoid problems and remember those you made before. Always write down a recipe or work from a photocopy of the cookbook page. Small, portable copiers are inexpensive and are a great way to save your cookbooks from damage. **Write or attach the recipe in a notebook, date the page, and check off each ingredient as you add it.** Make notations about any observations or problems. Label all jars with the contents, date, and recipe by keeping computerized files of these labels, or by cutting the recipe from a photocopied page of the cookbook. **Canning is not like regular cooking. Errors really must be avoided. Develop**

a system, and avoid distractions during critical measuring and timing operations.

31. If you love canning and wish to modify recipes, buy yourself a **pH meter.** Look for the new meters with all-metal probes. Talk to a technician at a good scientific-supply house. Tell him Jamlady sent you!

32. **Please don't confuse the use of apples/pears to mean only one-half of each.** The use of the forward slash in the ingredient listings for each recipe means either/or. In most cases, half of each ingredient could also be used.

33. **Refrigerate all RWB-sealed products after opening.**

34. **Peel the gingerroot for all recipes in this cookbook.**

35. **Not all recipes for canned pickles and relishes must be canned.** Many may be made in smaller batches of one-quarter or one-tenth the original batch and simply stored in the refrigerator. **A bread and butter pickle or a chow-chow relish, for example, may be cooked in a pan on the stove for the time equal to some or all of the processing time.** Then refrigerate the product. In many cases, pickles will be crunchier if you don't cook them as long as the regular recipe, as the length of the regular recipe's processing time was predicated by the need for sterility and vacuum. **In short, there's a whole book here you may easily and quickly convert from a canning recipe to a "quickle" or quick pickle or quick relish. The main reason for making large, canned batches is to preserve a glut of some vegetable or fruit. If you are purchasing small quantities of vegetables or fruits whenever you like, then just make your relishes and pickles and refrigerate them. Take a look at the recipe for red pepper relish, pepper hash, or beet and cabbage relish with horseradish. You should be able to make a couple of jars of either one of those in less than a half-hour. Label as "Refrigerate Only" and give some as gifts. Come on city, suburban, and country cooks, you can do this!**

35. **Seek instruction from cooks who have successfully made a product, and don't give out instructions for canned products you have never made and tested.**

CLOSTRIDIUM BOTULINUM

Around 1817, a German poet and medical officer, Justinus Kerner (1786-1862), first published an accurate description of the symptoms of botulism in food. Kerner did not identify the poison, but he called it "sausage poison" because of its association with sausages, not because of its rodlike shape. In 1895, Emile Pierre van Ermengem, a professor at the University of Ghent, discovered the actual pathogen. **After food-borne botulism was discovered, four other types were identified: wound, infant, hidden, and inadvertent botulism.** Because botulism is so deadly, some of our enemies have prepared to use this bacterium, and others like anthrax, in bombs and other weapons. As a response, scientists are now seeking to create vaccines to protect soldiers and others under biological attack.

The **symptoms of botulism** are: dizziness, double vision, blurred vision, dysphagia (difficulty swallowing), dry mouth, dysarthria (difficulty speaking), sore throat, dyspnea (difficulty breathing), constipation, nausea, vomiting, abdominal cramps, arm weakness, leg weakness, and paresthesia (sensations of the skin like burning, prickling, itching, or tingling). **The treatment for botulism is the administration of an antitoxin. To prevent botulinum spores from growing in canned product, make sure jars are sterile and products are acidified to well under 4.6 or keep the product refrigerated to 39 degrees F (4 degrees C) or below.**

Botulinum spores usually grow in conditions with less than 2-percent oxygen, in low-acid, moist food, and at temperatures between 40 and 120 degrees F. These spores, when conditions are right, produce vegetative cells that produce the deadly toxin. These spores can only be effectively killed at temperatures above boiling point (pressure canner required), but they can be controlled in high acid or high salt. If you have canned something low-acid and are unsure of its final acidity, do not eat it. Throw it out unless it is boiled for over 10 minutes to kill any possible toxins.

This botulism issue usually comes up when canners tell me they can non-acidified tomatoes and have been doing so for years. **Canning non-acidified tomatoes is not smart and could be deadly.** These canners probably boil their tomato products while making spaghetti sauce or soups, but the outcome could turn deadly if they were to use them for a cold Bloody Mary. The next question they usually ask me is, **"Would the drink taste different if there were active vegetative cells making botulinum toxin in the Bloody Mary?"** Probably not. **Caution: To avoid botulism, do not can low-acid food in a rolling-water bath.**

PH AND PH METERS

Acidity or pH refers to the potential of hydrogen. **The pH number is lowest for an acid (high-acid product) and highest for a base (low-acid product).** The pH chart may be confusing to some people, because they incorrectly assume a high number means there is more acid. This is not the case. **A low number means the product is acidic.** The pH of a lemon is usually between 2.2 and 2.8. The pH of a date is around 6.2 to 6.4. The lemon is acidic, and the date is barely in the acid range.

For the purposes of canning, and using the rolling-water-bath method (RWB) of sealing a jar, all products must measure well under 4.6 (4.3 or lower). **Products with a pH over 4.3 should be refrigerated or processed in a pressure canner (unless the product's water activity is less than 0.6). Please note: A pH of 2 (lemons) is actually the same thing as 0.01 (hydrogen ion concentration, gram mols per liter) or 10^{-2}, and 6.0 (dates) is actually the same thing as 0.000,001 or 10^{-6}.** Notice the exponent is used to show how many times the symbol or quantity is to be used as a factor. That number of times is equal to the single number used to express pH. **Numbers like 0.000,001 are just too unwieldy to use, so the single digit pH number is used to express the relatively small, fractional number. The pH chart runs from high acid at 0.0 to high alkaline at 13.0 with neutral at 7.0.**

To measure pH, obtain a pH meter that meets your needs. If you will test hot, thick, and viscous products, like hot jams, obtain an electrode and temperature probe that can handle that situation. Be sure to relate what you will test and under what conditions you will test to your scientific-instrument salesperson. Most scientific-instrument companies, such as Cole-Parmer Instrument Company, will personally assist customers regarding appropriate meter procurement and provide free consultation and trouble-shooting with a qualified meter technician. Be sure to ask about stainless-steel probes with ISFET (Ion Specific Field Effect Transistor) silicon chip pH sensors.

When testing any product with a pH meter, be sure to standardize the meter first. Purchase in-date buffer solutions, and don't use old and expired solutions. Prior to testing, pulverize and blend the product well. When testing, use a temperature probe, as temperature change greatly affects pH measurements. Don't eat product tested with a glass

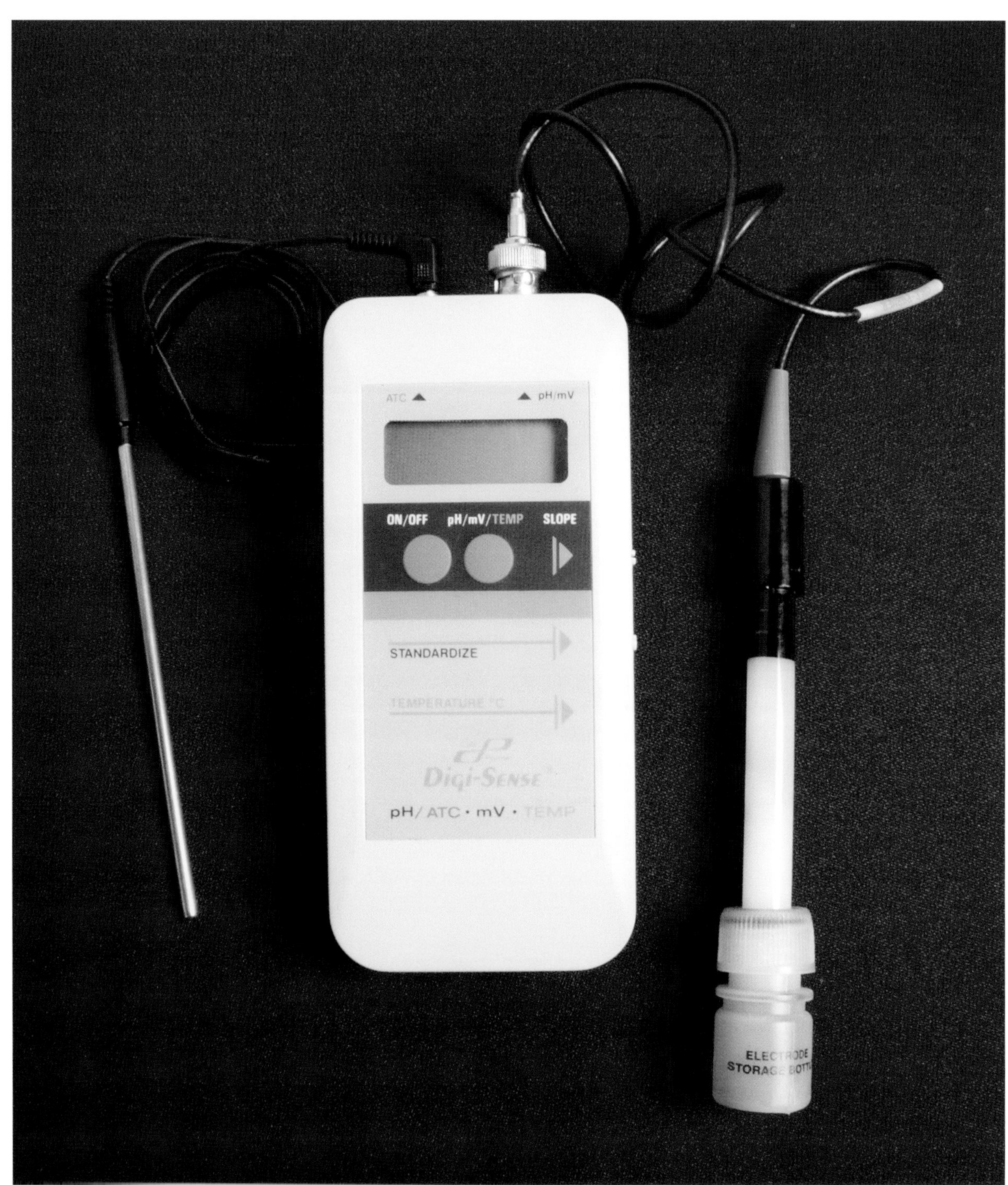

pH meter with temperature probe.

Relationship of pH, Hydrogen Ion Concentration, and Foods Commonly Used in Food Processing

	pH	Food or Other Substance (pH)	Hydrogen Ion Concentration, Gram Mols Per Liter	
Acid Range (0-6.9)	0 1	Hydrochloric N Acid (0.1) Sulfuric 0.1N] Acid (1.2)	1.0 0.1	10^{0} 10^{-1}
Process pH 4.6 or lower at 212 degrees F in boiling water bath	2	Lemons (2.2-2.8)	0.01	10^{-2}
	3	Grapefruit (3.0-3.7)	0.001	10^{-3}
Process pH 4.6 or higher at 240 degrees F in steam pressure canner	4	Bananas (4.5-5.0), Tomatoes (4.42-4.65)	0.000,1	10^{-4}
	5 6	Beans (5.60-6.50), Figs (5.0-6.0) Dates (6.2-6.4)	0.000,01 0.000,001	10^{-5} 10^{-6}
Neutral (7.0)	7 8 9	Fresh White Eggs (7.6-8.0) Hominy (Lye) (6.8-8.0) Borax (9.2)	0.000,000,1 0.000,000,01 0.000,000,001	10^{-7} 10^{-8} 10^{-9}
Alkaline Range (8.0-14.0)	10 11 12 13	Ammonia 0.01N (10.6) Ammonia N (11.6) Trisodium Phosphate, 0.1N (12.0) Sodium Hydroxide, 0.1N (13.0)	0.000,000,000,1 0.000,000,000,01 0.000,000,000,001 0.000,000,000,000,1	10^{-10} 10^{-11} 10^{-12} 10^{-13}

electrode as chemicals may have leached into the product from the electrode.

Not every recipe in this book is a canning recipe, but every canning recipe in this book is a "high-acid" recipe and may be canned in a rolling-water bath. If the overall pH of any canning recipe in this book was above 4.6, it has been acidified, so the resulting formulation is comfortably below 4.6. For this reason, no pressure canner is needed for recipes in this cookbook. Some recipes provide the average pH, as a guide for further understanding of pH and processing terminology. For "low-acid canning," please consult another source. **Ideally, beginners should start with rolling-water bath canning before advancing to pressure canning.**

ALTERNATIVE SWEETENERS

Natural sweeteners are: barley malt syrup, brown rice syrup, corn syrup, date sugar, dehydrated cane juice, fructooligosaccharides (FOS), fructose, fruit juice concentrates, glucose, high fructose corn syrup, honey, lactose, maltodextrin, maltose, maple syrup, molasses, moscovado sugar, sorghum molasses, stevia, and sucrose. **Artifical sweeteners** are: acesulfame K, aspartame, saccharin, and other sweeteners that are trying to get approved by the FDA. **Jamlady recommends readers digest the literature on each of these sweeteners before digesting them.** Reduced calorie sweeteners such as "sugar alcohols," maltitol, mannitol, sorbitol, and xylitol are also of interest.

Sugar alcohols are found widely in nature and don't promote cavities. While sugar alcohols are used in chewing gums and other foods, they may cause stomach upset and diarrhea if consumed in excess of 45 grams. Stevia and other sweeteners such as aspartame may chemically change with high heat or impart a "metallic taste." Some of these sweeteners may be incorporated into "quickles" or canned pickles, but issues such as undesirable tastes and high cost (xylitol is three times the cost of sugar) often leave formulators in a quandary. In Jamlady products, we have successfully used corn syrup, honey, fruit-juice concentrates, agave, molasses, maple syrup, sorghum, brown rice syrup, aspartame, saccharin, and date sugar. In recent years, I have refrained from using almost all artificial sweeteners and some natural alternatives because of health concerns or prohibitive cost.

Infusions of licorice tea have been used successfully, but the flavor imparted is that of licorice (see *The Jamlady Cookbook*—blueberry jam with licorice tea). Test the pH of products sweetened with any of these "new" sweeteners before you hermetically seal the jar, and research the possible and negative impact of high heat on that sweetener. For up-to-date articles on sweeteners by different researchers see **PubMed.com.**

CANNING SPICES AND HERBS

Allspice
Almond Extract
Bay Leaves
Brown Mustard
Capsicum
Cardamom
Chili Peppers (dried)
Chrysanthemum Flowers
Caraway Seed
Capers Bush Buds
Cassia Buds
Celery Seed
Chervil
Cinnamon
Cloves
Coriander
Cumin
Dill Seed
Dill Weed
Fennel
Fenugreek
Garlic Cloves
Geranium Leaves
Ginger
Horseradish Root,
Hyssop Leaves and Flowers
Juniper Berries
Lemon Verbena
Lovage Seeds
Mint Leaves
Mace
Mustard Seeds (Yellow)
Nutmeg
Oil of Cinnamon
Oil of Clove
Oil of Spearmint
Black Peppercorns
Parsley
Pickling Spice (a spice blend)
Pink Peppercorns
Rosemary
Saffron
Sage
Savory
Sweet Cicely Seeds
Tarragon
Thyme
Turmeric
White Peppercorns.

GINGER

Candied or Crystallized Ginger—May be made by boiling 1 pound sugar to 1 cup water with ½ teaspoon cream of tartar. When the sugar syrup is thick, drop in thin, dry, peeled, fresh ginger slices and cook. When candied, drop the ginger pieces on wax paper to cool, and then roll them in granulated sugar. Store candied ginger in a closed container. The pH of fresh ginger is 5.60 to 5.90.

Ginger or gingerroot may be (left) *fresh, dried/ground, or* (right) *candied.*

Common spices used for making dill pickles. Far back (left)*: dill weed; back row* (left to right): *dill seed, peppercorns, yellow mustard seeds, pickling spice, celery seed, and coriander. Front row* (left to right): *dried hot peppers and bay leaves.*

FURTHER COMMENT

If you have problems or question not answered by this chapter, please e-mail Jamlady@Jamlady.com to ask your question or to receive a free subscription to the ***Jamlady Newsletter.*** I recommend canners attend the various pickling festivals around the country; support local and state farmers by shopping at farmers' markets; question the inadequate labeling of genetically altered food and cloned meats; and, at the same time, resist excessive governmental regulations that unnecessarily impede the local production and sale of fruits, vegetables, herbs, honey, jams, pickles, baked goods, and maple syrup.

Okra and Chrysanthemum Pickle from Japan. First Place Winner, 2005 International Pickle Festival in Rosendale, New York.

The great diaspora of pickle makers and the cucumber.

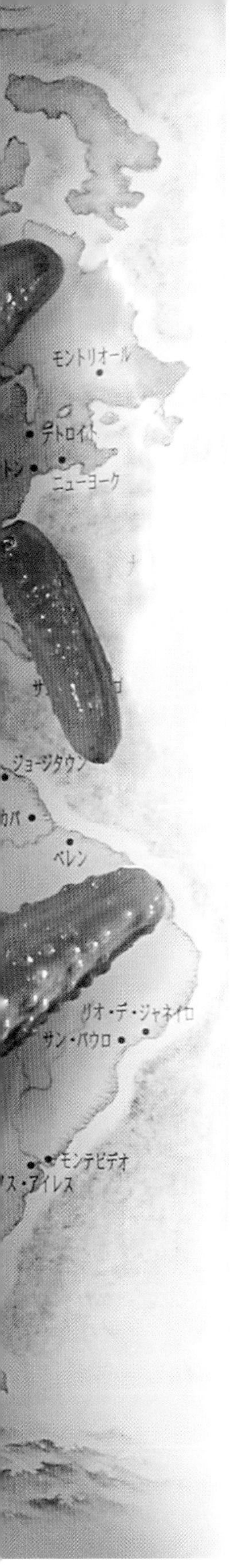

Chapter 2

Pickles, Power, and Agro-Processing

Pickling or fermenting fruits, vegetables, and other substances is an inexpensive and fairly efficient way to preserve food. It is a way to grow and then preserve food when other higher-tech methods like canning and freezing are not practical. This preserved food nourishes and provides food security for many peoples in the world and has done so for thousands of years.

It is very enlightening to study historic pickling and fermentation, because one can trace the great diaspora of cucumber seeds and pickle-makers through many centuries and countries. Starting around the year 2030 B.C., travelers from Northern India took cucumber seeds to the Tigris Valley, better known as Mesopotamia, and from there the cucumber enthusiasts trekked onward. In 850 B.C., Aristotle praised the medicinal value of cured cucumbers. Ancients, including Cleopatra, Pliny, Julius Caesar, and Tiberius, ate and loved pickles. From Mesopotamia, cucumber seeds made their way to Europe, and soon pickles were being relished by royalty. Queen Elizabeth I loved pickles. Napoleon valued pickles and other canned foods; they provided portable, preserved food for his army.

Early on, the Chinese and Koreans were picklers. A sixth-century agricultural text, *Qimin Yaoshu,* explains Chinese pickle-making methods step-by-step. These Chinese methods required high standards for detail and sanitation. Pickle-batch starters were made from scratch for each new batch. **This standardized, pickle-making methodology is noteworthy, because European methods were, by contrast, less clean and less precise.**

The Chinese created condiments such as fermented pastes, relishes, and sauces. These condiments or pastes are divided into two groups: ***chi,*** from soy beans, and ***jiang,*** from vegetables, meat, or fish. Other fermented Chinese products are: ***shih,*** a fermented black bean sauce (200 B.C.); ***tofu,*** a vegetable curd of beans and peas (tenth century and forward); and **miso (the name "miso" appeared circa 701 A.D. in Japan),** a thick, nutritious, fermented paste of grain and soybeans. To make miso, barley and rice are steamed, combined with the ***Aspergillus oryzae*** spores, and left to grow for two days. Washed, cooked, and crushed soybeans are added with salt and water. This mash is then fermented in cedar vats for two years.

Christopher Columbus grew cucumbers in Haiti. Amerigo Vespucci peddled pickles in Patagonia. **If you think about it, you'll see the tremendous impact salt and cucumbers have had on the world.** Nations were built, power changed hands, and knowledge spread. Peace-making and diplomacy skills were advanced in the pursuit of wealth, aided by friendly trade agreements and contracts. Maritime insurance was born, advancing the entire concept of insurance into other areas of life. All sorts of improvements in security for the individual, state, and world can be directly attributed to pickle power. **The manifestation of pickle power changed the world politically, culturally, and religiously.** In some countries, land owners and religious leaders lost power, as the shipping and trading companies got rich and powerful. It isn't hard to see why Mark Kurlansky entitled his book, *Salt: A World History.*

In 1535, Cartier found cucumbers growing in Canada. In 1609, pickling cucumbers were grown in Virginia. George Washington, John Adams, and Dolly Madison all relished their pickles! A famous quote by Thomas Jefferson expresses how Jefferson felt about pickles. **"On a hot day, I know nothing more comforting than a fine spiced pickle coming from a sparkling aromatic jar in Aunt Sally's cellar."** Early Americans made pickled mangoes, which are melons stuffed with chopped cabbage, onions, and a tad of horseradish. "Mangoes" were then submerged in vats of vinegar and stored for up to two years as insurance against a poor agricultural year. **In 1820, Nicholas Appert, the "Father of Canning," commercially packed pickles in jars.**

Sixteenth-century sea traders, especially the Dutch, considered cucumbers a necessary trade commodity for averting scurvy. The Bible and the Koran talk about cucumbers. Some written records of Europeans visiting Iran during the Safavi Era (1500-1736) state foods of the time included rice, stews, pickles, and jams.

Despite the early emergence and the relative ease of making pickles, the actual chemical processes that transforms a vegetable into a pickle are quite complex. The changes and the microbes responsible for the changes have not been adequately studied yet, except for a few pickles that are commercially produced. **Future scientists will need to learn more about pickling and fermentation and the techniques of less developed regions of the world.**

My investigation into pickling and fermentation opened doors. I learned more than I expected to learn and again observed how selectively we scrutinize ideas and practices. How many inventions or scientific discoveries are passed over by the hubris of the well-educated? Ethnic or class arrogance can be documented again and again. Take for example, an Indian named **Domagaia** who in the winter of 1535 led Jacques Cartier to a natural remedy for scurvy. This remedy was made from an indigenous tree. **It took two-hundred years for James Line, a British naval surgeon, to read about this historical event and then to prove the dietary basis of scurvy** (Vogel, Virgil. 1970. *American Indian Medicine.* Norman: University of Oklahoma Press.). Another four-hundred-and-fifty Indian remedies were finally published in 1925 by pharmaceutical historian Heber W. Youngken, in "The Drugs of the North American Indians" (*American Journal of Pharmacy* 97(3)).

Many natural herbs and drugs were initially ignored, possibly because upperclass people didn't discover them. Such appears to be the case with many pickling and fermentation methods of eco-specific areas. **Even contraceptive herbs were known to the Cherokees but were rejected by white man *a priori.*** Thomas Jefferson was informed about Virginia Indians using vegetables for contraception and abortions (Kock, Adrienne, and Peden, William. 1944. *The Life and Selected Writings of Thomas Jefferson.* New York: Random House. 211.).

There are many types of unique pickles in eco-specific regions of the world. Information on many of these traditional pickles has not been adequately documented. Some knowledge is being lost or delayed, but it now appears certain groups are studying these pickles.

At the 2005 International Pickle Festival in Rosendale, New York, I had a long conversation with Dr. Sei Tomio, chairman of the Sanjukei Corporation of Japan, and Ms. Eri Yamaguchi, author of *The Well-Flavored Vegetable,* about this very topic. Dr. Tomio gifted me with a box of *Meixing,* which proclaims the "beauty of health" from capsules of ginseng berries. For quite a few years, I have been reading about fermentation and other research being conducted in Japan. It appears the Japanese are very advanced in this area of fermentation.

A lot of interesting scientific research is also coming out of the People's Republic of China, specifically the **theory of ECIWO biology,** which has application in medicine, genetics, biochemistry, agriculture, and other sciences. **ECIWO means Embryo Containing the Information of the Whole Organism** (Zhang, Yingquin. 1987. *ECIWO Biology and Medicine.* Neimengga People's Press. [Other publications listed at www.the-tree.org.uk/TreeCultivation&Uses/Seedart/seed.htm]). **This theory says it matters from where you collect seed on a plant.** Collect from carrot tops and you've selected for large roots and tiny carrots. Therefore, by selecting from the proper place on a plant, worn-out varieties may be rejuvenated and yields increase. Zhang's theory includes a **bio-holographic law—"A sprout on a branch is a new little plant on the bigger plant"** (Coleman, Steven. 2004. *How to Rejuvenate Worn-out and Inbred Crops Using Localized Seed Selection.* [www.the-tree.org.uk/]). **If a leaf's bottom is wide and its top narrow, the plant will be similarly shaped.**

Want to increase cucumber yields? Select cucumber seeds harvested from the second or third fruit near the middle-lower section of the plant. Collecting pole beans seed? Select from the lower region. Want a sweeter sugar beet? Select from the side branches, but the plant will grow slower and its roots will be shorter. **What does this all mean?** It means a farmer can grow ten percent more cucumbers on the same field as last year. **It means using all the seeds from a plant will cause the variety to degenerate.** How about being able to grow seventeen-percent more rice in the same area? It can happen, and even that percentage can be improved upon by selectively cutting off parts of the plant to put all the plant's energy into the upper one-third of the plant that is forming seeds. **Coleman believes new crops can be developed from wild plants, using these principals.** Being able to grow more food in the same area and learning how to preserve it should greatly impact world hunger.

Today, as people in these eco-specific areas have become economically less dependent on their fermenting and pickle making, some of the recipes and knowledge to produce these unique and indigenous fermented pickles and pastes are being lost. **These eco-specific pickles, dismissed as "poor-people's food," are in danger of extinction. Yet, these very pickles might help stave off hunger in starving or marginal people.**

In areas where there is no money to import non-indigenous food, inedible plant materials, rendered edible through fermentation or "agro-processing," might be used to feed the hungry. Many of these fermented foods have superior nutritional value when compared to the highly processed foods of the Western world. Agro-processing exemplifies yet another new partnership to tackle the problem of world-wide hunger. Fermentation may be used to turn salvage plant and animal materials' "waste" into digestible food. Fish bones or tough abalone (fermented *paua* of the New Zealand Maoris) may be made soft or pastelike; vinegars may be made from fruit peels, and cassava may be made edible by removing its cyanide (**cyanogenic glucoside**) through fermentation (http://www.fao.org/).

The cassava is peeled, as sixty to seventy percent of the poison is in the peel. The cassava is then water-soaked or fermented in sacks for about three days. Sometimes, to speed up the process, the cassava is first grated. *Geotrichum candida* breaks down the cassava and makes an acidic product that kills off the unwanted microorganisms. Next, the acid-tolerant microorganism *Cornibacterium lactii* hydrolyzes the toxic chemical. **After three days, ninety-five percent of the dangerous chemical is neutralized, and the cassava takes on its distinctive flavor.** The cassava is then sieved and fired with some palm oil in an iron pan. **This last step removes most of the remaining toxins.** The liquor from a completed fermentation can be used as a starter. This practice reduces the fermentation time to about six to eight hours.

What exactly is fermentation? Fermentation is not putrefaction. **Fermentation does not degrade the protein but is a slow decomposition of organic substances, either anaerobically or partially anaerobically. Wikipedia, a free online encyclopedia, states, "fermentation (formerly called zymosis) is the anaerobic metabolic breakdown of a nutrient molecule, such as glucose, without net oxidation.** Fermentation does not release all available energy in a molecule; it merely allows glycolysis (a process that yields two ATP per glucose) to continue by replenishing reduced coenzymes.

Fermentation yields lactate, acetic acid, ethanol, or other reduced metabolites."

The term fermentation is usually used when the changes caused are advantageous and desirable—such is the case with the manufacturing of sauerkraut, pickles, vinegar, olives, *kimchi,* wine, beer, and some dairy products.

What makes some foods indigestible to humans? **What do these microorganisms have that we do not have? Microorganisms have cellulases.** Microbial cellulases hydrolyze cellulose into sugars, and humans can digest the sugars. **Further, *pectinases* change the texture of the food, mostly to a softer product.** So, the food is now soft and its sugars can be absorbed by humans as food. **Baby food can also be made by lactic-acid fermentation of starchy porridges so the starch is converted into sugars—*glucose* and *dextrose.*** This is done to reduce the food's bulk so a baby can consume enough to meet its nutritional requirements.

In many countries, fermented foods are used as medicine. Besides having a lower pH, which creates an inhospitable environment for pathogens, fermented foods also have increased digestibility and nutritional value (Lee, C.H. 2001. *Fermentation Technology in Korea.* Seoul: Korea University Press. 70-91.). **Increases in vitamin B12 and folic acid and the synthesis of some antibiotics have been observed, especially in fungal fermentations used to make "*natto*" or "*tempeh*"** (Van Veen, A.G., and K.H. Steinkraus, 1970. Nutritive Value and Wholesomeness of Fermented Foods. *Journal of Agricultural and Food Chemistry.* 18:576-578.).

In 2002, Dr. David Heber testified before the U.S. House of Representatives Government Reform Committee. Dr. Heber is a distinguished physician and professor of medicine and public health at the University of California, Los Angeles (UCLA). An expert on dietary supplements research, Heber testified about natural remedies, such as red yeast. His testimony can be found at http://www.cancercure coalition.org/articles/heber.htm. Dr. Heber states, **"At UCLA, I directed the first United States clinical trials showing that Chinese Red Yeast Rice can be as effective as prescription drugs for lowering cholesterol."**

In "Creative Fermentation Technology for the Future," Cherl-Ho Lee, Graduate School of Biotechnology, Korea University, dates Asiatic fermentation technology in Northern Asia as beginning in "the littoral foragers period of the Primitive Pottery Age (8000-3000 B.C.), which led the Neolithic culture of agriculture." Since then, fermentation technology has developed indigenously in different locations of the world, using natural products found in those areas. **Steinkraus divides the various methods of fermentation (the methods responsible for human survival over the ages) into six groups: alcoholic, lactic acid, leavened breads, meat substitutes, meat-flavored sauces, pastes, and protein/flavoring agents** (Steinkraus, K.H. 1993. Comparison of fermented food of the East and West. In *Fish Fermentation Technology*, edited by C.H. Lee, et al. Tokyo: United Nations University Press. 1-12.).

Lee characterizes the period before the twentieth century as the **"survival food age"** and the twenty-first century as the **"functional food age"** with great demand for convenience foods. He further states we have now moved into the **"era of tailor-made foods"** where the fermented foods will receive new attention as we move forward to combine both personal and health-benefit demands. **The job of food will now be to prevent disease and cure us, while at the same time meeting our personal demands.** From a Western perspective this goal or emphasis is probably accurate, but I keep thinking about those one- to two-billion people who are still hungry.

Lee predicts a new era in which we find useful microbes from indigenous fermented products and have these starter cultures available for study. Lee's article lists some of the biologically active compounds in *kimchi* and the **possible and beneficial effects of *kimchi:*** "antibiotic, anticarcinogenic, immune stimulant, reducing cholesterol, antioxidant, fibrinolytic, antagonistic, laxative, secretion of neuropeptides, and modulation of T-cell function."

If properly utilized, fermented foods can feed starving populations. Some foods can be fermented and then dried. ***Gundruk,* from Nepal, is a dried vegetable product that is first**

fermented and then dried. It is made from shredded leaves of mustard, radish, and cauliflower, which are pot fermented for approximately a week and then sun dried. This tasty, mineral-laden food is eaten with starchy foods. A recipe for making ***Gundruk Sadheko*** can be found at http://www.recipezaar.com/87974. **Even insects, seeds, hides, and bones may be fermented into nutritious foods.** Peanut and coconut by-products are converted into a "cake or cheeselike" product, via fermentation. In the Sudan, ***"kawal"*** is produced from fermented wild-legume leaves, ***"furundu"*** from fermented red sorrel seeds, and ***"sigda"*** from fermented sesame press-cake (http://www.fao.org/). In some countries, hibiscus seeds are fermented and used as food.

The usual organisms responsible for food fermentations are bacteria, yeasts, and molds. *Lactobacillaceae* are "good-guy bacteria." ***Lactobacillaceae* produce lactic acid from carbohydrates.** The ***Acetobacter* species produce acetic acid.** Acids act as preservatives and often improve the taste. Molds require oxygen to grow, so they don't thrive in the pasteurized canning jar, but molds may be found on open jams, as they can tolerate high salt and sugar concentrations. Some molds are useful, like the ones found in blue cheese. Other molds are "bad guys" or spoilers. The biochemical changes in fermenting foods are caused by the work of enzymes. **These complex proteins or enzymes are catalysts.**

Catalysts start chemical reactions and are affected by changes in their environment, changes in temperature, acidity, moisture, oxygen availability, nutrients, and inhibitors (Mountney and Gould 1988; http://www.fao.org/docrep/x0560e/x0560e07.htm). Food manufacturers and canners manipulate and control these environments to produce optimal results in the processing of fermented or pickled foods. Several microorganisms usually work in sync to create the desired food product. **For example, bacteria may grow first. Then yeast colonies take over, and finally molds finish the product. The growth of certain microorganisms often suppresses wannabe spoilers. Such is the case with "dry-salted" cucumbers.** Water and sugar are osmotically drawn from the cucumber using salt. The cucumber's sugar is converted into acid. This acid preserves the fruit and inhibits the growth of harmful microorganisms.

Water is necessary for cellular growth. When water interacts with a solute (a solid, gas, or liquid that is dissolved in a liquid to make a solution) or a surface, it is not available for other interactions. **If water is restricted, cellular activity is diminished.** Such is the case with dried foods. Freezing does the same thing because cells can't use water in a frozen state. **Adding a good quantity of salt causes water to interact with the salt, and the water is no longer available for hydration. In a canned product, there is water within the food (bound water) and water surrounding the food (free water). If the free water can be reduced, microorganisms cannot grow. The available free water for microorganisms is expressed as a_w and can be measured with an electric hygrometer (with a sensor to measure equilibrium relative humidity [ERH]).** Bacteria, yeasts, and molds all require water to grow (respectively, in descending order).

The water activity of plain water is around 1.0. Plain water is 100 percent water. The amount of water in a substance is its water activity if it is available for organisms to use. For example, frozen water in meat is water, but it isn't available, so the food is preserved. Pickles, on the other hand, have a lot of water in them, so they need either high salt, high sugar, high pH, or high vinegar to be preserved. Otherwise, organisms will use the water to multiply and cause food spoilage. **Most foods have a water activity above 0.95.** Most bacteria, yeast, and molds will grow above this point. **As a rule of thumb, almost all microorganisms can be controlled with a water activity (a_w) below 0.6—fungi below 0.7, yeasts below 0.8, and bacteria below 0.9. The spores of *Clostridium botulinum* are usually controlled or inhibited at an a_w of .93 or less.** If, within a product like cheese spreads a_w = 0.947), thick fudge sauce (a_w = 0.832), or peanut butter (15% moisture, a_w = 0.70), there is insufficient water for *C. botulinum* spores to grow, and mild heat is used to destroy the vegetative cells, we have a method of preservation that does not require high heat.

A food canned with a water activity greater than 0.85 and a pH greater than 4.6 is considered a low-acid food. The thermal process for a low-acid food needs to be appropriate; usually it is processed under pressure for a specific and recommended time. By contrast, if the water activity is adjusted to 0.85 or less, it needs no thermal process, regardless of the pH. **If the pH is 4.6 or less, and the a_w is greater than 0.85, the food is considered an acidified food and must be processed, usually in a rolling-water bath for recommended times.** If you need more explanation about this topic, please refer to FDA Regulation 21 CFR Part 113 and Part 114. Manipulation of salt and sugar concentrations, oxygen availability, water activity, and acidity can all be used by the food manufacturer or canner to control the process and inhibit the growth of spoilers. **Molds (e.g. *Aspergillus*) are common spoilers and must have at least an a_w of 0.75 in order to grow.**

Salt and sugar affect water activity. Dry-salted fish or salt-cured meats and fish are preserved because the salt inhibits the growth of spoiler microorganisms. **This is why you should never reduce the salt in any canning or preserving recipe.** *C. botulinum* can grow in a 7-percent salt solution but not in a 10-percent salt solution (or its equivalent, which is an aw of 0.93). Even though *C. botulinum* has grown in a 7-percent salt solution, thus far no toxin growth has been noted at this concentration. ***Clostridium botulinum* grows best at temperatures between 86 degrees F (30 degrees C) and 98 degrees F (37 degrees C). So, if in doubt about the water activity, salt concentration, processing time, and/or acidity, just don't take any chances and keep the product refrigerated.**

Caution: Non-spore forming bacteria, which cause some forms of food poisoning, are easily destroyed by heat. While non-spore forming bacteria can make you sick, they don't usually cause death. Such is not the case with spore-forming *C. botulinum*. When in doubt about a product's processing times or formulation, refrigerate! *C. botulinum* grows well in temperatures of 80 degrees F and above but can grow at temperatures between 40 degrees F (4 degrees C) and 100 degrees F (37.77 degrees C).

Some critics who are not supportive of home canners or third-world food processors will argue small-scale operations are not sanitary enough to make food, especially in areas that are impoverished. It should be noted that many fermented foods are normally safe because of their high acidity and low moisture content. Further, if some of these techniques were truly understood by a majority of the scientific community, perhaps improvements could be made in the method. The fact that many scientists don't understand a lot about some of these techniques also speaks to the power and intelligence of those indigenous peoples who created the processes in the first place. That power is resourcefulness, self-sufficiency, and outside-the-box thinking. It is power fueled by scarcity and necessity. It only takes one person to create a new method, one inventor, and it need not be a food scientist. It is the food scientist who should then perfect the methodology, test its usefulness, and partner with industry to deliver training or products where needed.

If we discourage homemaker experimentation and relegate new-pickle formulation exclusively to degreed food scientists, I feel quite sure we will greatly diminish the speed with which this art/science advances, and we may lose a lot of knowledge in the process. For sure, what we lose is our own spirit, self-reliance, and the belief in our ability to take care of ourselves. **We don't need to educate less; we need to educate more.** Those of you with knowledge about fermentation and pickling should pick up pen and paper, or computer mouse, and record this knowledge somewhere, so it can be read, processed, used, and improved. **Make computer files and labels for your products and attach the recipe to your products when you gift them away.**

Consult with experts when necessary. Stay current by reading abstracts from Pub Med (now easily accessible on the Internet). No one is suggesting you process food (can) or make pickles without knowledge; educate yourself about basic pickling concepts and safety. Those of you with culinary or medical interests, who travel to remote or primitive areas, record what you find and ask questions when you see traditional culinary methods in action. You may be the only person recording this experience or knowledge. **Remember, school learning is but one kind of learning. Self-motivated, intrinsically rewarding, life-long learning is the true laudable goal for a productive individual or society.**

Fermented foods like bread, cheese, wine, and fish sauces have been consumed for thousands of years. We aren't sure when man ate the first fermented fruits, but they probably consumed them directly from fruit bushes or the ground. Not long ago a fellow author wrote to me and asked what to do with a "surfeit of plums" as she "daren't leave them to rot," because she "didn't want a garden full of drunken blackbirds." This struck me as particularly funny, and I wasn't sure if blackbirds would actually consume so many fermented fruits as to affect their airworthiness. However, the very next week I ran across an article in the February 11, 2005, issue of *USA Today,* whereby dozens of cedar waxwings, pickled on fermenting holly berries, killed themselves by flying into window glass. So, it makes perfect sense that somewhere along the line humans consumed fermenting fruit and started to purposefully make wine or something akin to it.

Scientists believe fermented drinks were made in Babylon and Egypt 5,000 to 7,000 years ago. The Chinese also had fermented grains (*"Shu-Ching,"* Chou dynasty, 1121-256 B.C.). **Korean *kimchee* has been produced for over 3,000 years.** *The Roman Cookery Book,* a critical translation of *The Art of Cooking,* by Apicius, discusses fermented fish sauce (***liquamen*** or ***garum.***) (Flower and Rosenbaum 1958). Fish sauce was made from small, salted fish or fish entrails that couldn't be used for much else. Often wine was added during the fermentation process, and bones were softened by the combination of ingredients and time.

Bacteria responsible for beginning the fermentation or pickling process are uni- or multicellular organisms. They quickly reproduce by simple fission. Some, like *C. botulinum,* are almost ubiquitous and produce dormant spores, which are spores highly resistant to chemical or thermal damage. **Lactic-acid bacteria are a group of gram-positive, non-spore-forming bacteria in rod form (*cocci*). They convert carbohydrates to lactic acid, carbon dioxide, and other acids anaerobically (without oxygen).**

Yeasts (uni-cellular fungi) reproduce asexually by budding. Yeasts are larger than bacteria. *Saccharomyces cerevisiae* is a common yeast associated with food products; it ferments *glucose, sucrose, maltose,* and/or *raffinose.* **Yeasts need oxygen for growth but anaerobically can turn sugars into ethyl alcohol and carbon dioxide. In an oxygen environment, with an acetobacter, the alcohol is turned into acetic acid—a fruit vinegar.** For example, when an air lock on a winemaker's jug comes dislodged, wine becomes vinegar. Yeast are acid-tolerant; they are active in temperatures from 0 to 50 degrees C and thrive in neutral environments (pH = 7.0) but can grow in pH ranges around 4.3. **Yeasts require less water to grow than bacteria but require more water than molds. Some yeast can grow in high sugar, but most like product with less than half sugar.**

There are several types of bacterial fermentations. **Lactic-acid fermentations** occur when the glucose is converted into lactic acid, or the glucose is converted into lactic acid, ethanol, and carbon dioxide. In **acetic-acid fermentation,** the acetobacter changes alcohol to acetic acid in the presence of too much oxygen (wine turns to vinegar). The alcohol is converted to acetic acid and water. In **alkaline fermentations,** the *Bacillus* species bacteria (usually *Bacillus subtilis*) breaks down the protein into amino acids and peptides and also releases ammonia, which increases the alkalinity. **This alkalinity inhibits spoilage by creating an environment unsuitable for the growth of spoilers.** There are few foods produced by this fermentation method, but one so made is protein-rich Sudanese *kawal.* ***Kawal*** is made by fermenting pounded, wild-legume leaves of the Sickle-Pod Plant, *Cassia obtusifolia.* These leaves are covered with sorghum leaves and ferment in a buried, mud-sealed jug for fourteen days. The contents are stirred every three days, and the resulting smelly, black paste is rolled into balls and sun dried (Harper, D.B., and Collins, M.A. 1992. Leaf and Seed Fermentations of Western Sudan. In *Applications of Biotechnology to Traditional Fermented Foods.* Office of International

Affairs National Research Council. Washington, D.C.: National Acadamy Press.). ***Ombolo wa koba*** is made in Zaire from cassava leaves, using an alkaline-fermentation recipe. Wang lists the following alkaline-fermented foods in an article in *Critical Reviews in Microbiology* (1996, 22(2):101-38), "Japanese ***natto,*** Thai ***thua-nao,*** and ***kinema*** from cooked soybeans; ***dawadawa*** from African locust beans; ***ogiri*** from melon seeds; ***ugba*** from African oil beans; ***kawal*** from fresh legale leaves; ***owoh*** from cotton seeds; and ***pidan*** from fresh poultry eggs."

In America, self-reliant types use yeast fermentation to make wine. I've made some very good wine from wild grapes, often using a Campden tablet (from a wine supply store) to kill off the wild yeast and then inoculating the crushed grapes with yeast known to produce excellent wine or champagne. I usually use less Campden than is recommended, as the taste of the final product is better. If doing so, the equipment must be fastidiously sterilized. **Air locks are positioned to keep the oxygen out of the process; sterile equipment is used to keep unwanted microorganisms at bay.** It's helpful to take a Brix reading (to evaluate the existing sugar in the fruit mash) before adding the sugar syrup, which ameliorates the juice. **The measure of sugar added will determine the wine's sweetness or dryness. Temperature also affects the readings and the fermentation.**

To make homemade wine, first destem the grapes. Then crush the grapes, preferment them in a vat, remove the seeds and skins from the juice (by straining), add a Campden tablet (sulfur dioxide) to inhibit wild yeast, ferment the wine in a jug (with a water-filled air lock, which allows gas out but no air in), rack off the wine by siphoning, and mature the wine until it is bottled and corked.

African banana beer is made with bananas and sorghum flour. This prebeer mixture ferments into an orange alcoholic beer, which last for just days. I have actually made sweet banana wine. It was difficult to determine when it was done fermenting, and several bottles of the wine almost exploded in my refrigerator. Luckily, I had wired on the tops, because it appeared I had made banana champagne!

A good-tasting wine, similar to Dry Sack® sherry, may be made from mountain-ash berries, *Sorbus aucuparia.* Andrew Chevallier's *Encyclopedia of Medicinal Plants* (1996) recommends prepitting rowanberries because of cyanide in their seeds but doing so is very labor-intensive. Years ago, I made rowanberry wine from whole berries. We drank it and, belatedly, read an article about the dangers of cyanide from the rowanberry seeds. Since drinking this wine, I have spoken to many chemists who stated they weren't afraid to drink my wine. The EPA standard for "safe drinking water" is 0.2 parts cyanide per 1 million parts of water (0.2 ppm), but I have no comparable measures, unless I make it again. Further discussion about cyanide and copper sulfate can be found at http://homedistiller.org. This site states there is no danger from low amounts of cyanide. Plants for A Future's (http://www.pfaf.org/) database states small amounts of cyanide "stimulate respiration and improve digestion." Of course, rowanberry jelly or jam is safe because the cyanide is eliminated with high heat, but if a wine mash is never heated, there will be some cyanide. After hearing Louis Pasteur pasteurized wine, one might theorize a 189-degree water bath capable of destroying the cyanide without wrecking the wine? I have not tried, but let me know if you do it successfully. It is also possible the fermentation actually reduces the cyanide, as it does in cassava fermentation, but I have been unable to find any scientist who can confirm this for me.

Wine may be made from many plants. Local elderberries make wonderful wine, as do tomatoes, but raw elderberries also contain some cyanide. In Latin America and Asia, cashew wine is made from *Anacardium occidentale.* Fermented plant saps can be made into wine. A palm wine, such as ***nsafufuo,*** from Ghana, is made in several African countries, and **toddy,** a very short shelf-life drink, is made in Sri Lanka from coconut palm sap. Fermented ***pulque*** is the national drink in Mexico. When pulque is distilled, it's called "mezcal" or tequila, depending on who manufactured it.

All of this brings us to **dry-salting,** or dry-salted, fermented vegetables. German sauerkraut is an example of an **acid fermentation of vegetables,** and it is one type of pickling that has been thoroughly studied. **Primarily, three groups of organisms contribute to a successful batch of sauerkraut:** 1) *Leuconostoc mesenteroides,* 2) *Lactobacillus plantarum* and *Lactobacillus cucumeris,* and 3) *Lactobacillus pentoacetius* (*L. brevis*). Basically, these organisms produce acid and gas, and hopefully, the acid is sufficient to control the spoilers. **Bacteria in the first group are activated when the salt is put on the cabbage** (weighted down and temperature maintained at around 69.8 degrees F, or 21 degrees C, or maybe 68 degrees F, or 20 degrees C). Warmer temperatures of 22 degrees C or above will encourage the premature growth of the second group of organisms. **When the acidity or lactic acid reaches about .3 percent, the number two bacteria take over until the acid level reaches 1.5 to 2.0 percent.** Finally, group three bacteria complete the job. A successful batch of sauerkraut has lactic acid, some acetic acid and propionic acid, some aromatic esters, some alcohol, and gases like carbon dioxide. **The acid controls the spoilers (largely acetic acid at the end) because these spoilers aren't bothered much by the resultant salt content of 2.0 to 2.5 percent.**

If you make sauerkraut, remember to use pure pickling salt. Starter cultures can also help your batches along. *Streptococcus lactis* may be used, but *Leuconostoc mesenteroides* is recommended. **Soft kraut can result from poor salting, varying temperatures, too much air, or out-of-sequence bacterial growth (usually too much growth of the *Lactobacillus* group).** If normal fermentation does not get started, spoilers can break down the protein and ruin the texture and/or taste. Dark kraut is caused by spoiler action during fermentation, which might be due to uneven application of salt, wrong temperatures, and/or insufficient liquid coverage.

Brines can be used to ferment low-moisture vegetables. The amount of salt in brine is written as degrees "Salometer," or a percent saturation of sodium chloride by weight. **A salometer is a hydrometer calibrated to measure the density of sodium chloride in brine.** As with pH and sugar measures, these measurements are affected by temperature. According to my grandmother, a fresh egg floats in a 10-percent brine solution, but who sells "fresh" eggs in the burbs? The older an egg gets, the lighter it becomes as gas builds up inside and its water evaporates. So, find an egg that sinks in plain water (fresh), and then add the salt until it floats (10-percent brine). This little, salty exercise makes a good **"eggsperiment"** for the kids, especially if you toss in the 1,000-year-old egg story (alkaline-fermented *pidan*) and recent mitochondrial DNA evidence that the first chicken is related to the red jungle fowl's ancestor, which probably originated more than 8,000 years ago in Thailand. How do they know this? Ancient chicken bones found in Thailand had the same DNA markers. Go to http://www.google.com/ for more information, including how to make your own hydrometer.

Brine solutions can be made from 15- to 20-percent salt, but a brine solution below 15 percent will stop the fermentation. Most pickle makers add additional salt as the fermentation progresses. Different types of vegetables can be brine-salted for fermentation. **Fresh-picked, unwaxed, and washed pickling cucumbers may be pickled in a 15- to 20-percent brine solution. Weigh down the crock to avoid spoilage.** During the process, the water and sugars are drawn out of the cucumbers, lowering the salinity of the solution. More salt is usually added over time.

The fermentation begins in a few days, and the brine will "boil." **As acids are produced, the pickle should begin to turn a darker shade of green, and the inside of the pickle should become more translucent.** The pickles should start to sink in the vat. These stages of bacterial growth should be fairly similar to those described for sauerkraut and should continue for 1½ to 4 weeks or longer, depending on the ambient temperature. The optimal temperature for *Lactobacillus cucumeris* is around 84 degrees F, or 29 degrees C, or a few degrees warmer. **Sometimes sugar is added to keep the fermentation going. Then the pickles are rinsed or soaked in hot water to remove the excess salt and packed in a jar with an acetic acid (vinegar) solution.** Brines of final and completed pickles are usually around 15-percent salt. Keep in mind, these are generalizations about the process. Some pickle producers put liquid paraffin on the top of the brine to stop yeast scum from destroying the lactic acid, and then leave the pickles to be consumed from the vat. If **shriveled pickles** are made, this unfavorable defect might be due to too much acid, too much air (from stirring), or to too much activity by the *Lactobacillus mesenteroides* bacteria.

Some vegetables can be fermented without the addition of salt. ***Gundruk,*** from wild mustard leaves, is one example. Oxygen is usually restricted so the yeast cells don't grow, and the lactic-acid bacteria produce acid quickly, which lowers the pH and preserves the vegetables.

Pit fermentations, as practiced in the South Pacific Islands, are sometimes fermentations of starchy vegetables without the addition of salt. It is probable early man utilized some sort of fermentation pits, as animals use similar preservation methods and bury foods. According to Soomro in *Pakistan Journal of Nutrition* (2002, 1(1): 20-24), **there is "evidence of food preservation from post-glacial era, from 15,000 to 10,000 B.C.** The first use of biological methods was from 6000 to 1000 B.C. when fermentation was used to produce beer, bread, wine, vinegar, yogurt, cheese, and butter."

Fermentation pits are still used today. Zhang says in his article on Chinese Zuzhou-flavored Liqueur, in the *Journal of the Institute of Brewing* (2005, 111(2)), **"A pit is used as the container for the fermentation of Zuzhou-flavored liqueur."** ***Zaopei,*** a mixture of fermented grains such as sorghum, corn, wheat, and rice, is distilled. The distilled *Zaopei* and some newly steamed grains, plus Chinese Qu, are then transferred to a mud-lined pit and sealed. The fermentation mechanism for the production of this liquor was studied, and **"one bacterium phylotype was dominant . . . bacteria closely related to *Lactobacillus acetotolerans* appear to play a key role"** in the production of this liqueur.

These early pits may have produced fermented drinks, as well as fermented foods. Over the years, anthropologists Robert Braid (University of Chicago) and Johnathan D. Sauer (botanist from the University of Wisconsin) have debated, **"Which came first, beer or bread?"** For quite a few years, it was assumed that bread came first, as who would take the time to plant crops just to drink? Other anthropologists argued the opposite—that beer was the inspiration to grow crops and settle down in one place. Now, anthropologists believe barley was domesticated about 10,000 years ago in the area of southern Levant; it is likely that wild grains were collected long before then. **Barley can naturally ferment; when it sprouts, it produces sugar, which can ferment into alcohol.** Grain in a wet container might sprout and produce an alcoholic beverage. Bioanthropologist Solomon H. Katz and Fritz Maytag, president of Anchor Brewing Company, addressed the debate in the article "Brewing an Ancient Beer," appearing in the journal *Archaeology* (1991, 44(4): 24-33). **A Sumerian beer recipe, which was found on clay tablets, was used to manufacture beer.** Translation of the "Hymn to Ninkasi" sang the praises of the Sumerian goddess of brewing. Researchers found Sumerian beer parlors existed, and beer-related offenses were dealt with harshly by the **Code of Hammurabi.** The punishment for overcharging for beer was death by drowning. An eye for an eye, and a soak for a soak, I guess. Artifacts and straws, found by Sir Leonard Woolley in the tomb of Lady Puabi at Ur, ca. 2650 to 2550 B.C., showed beer was drunk from straws of gold and lapis lazuli.

Further investigation showed **the Hymn was "a linear description of brewing**—the preparation and heating of a mash in which enzymes convert the cereal starch into sugar, the boiling of the processed mash or wort, the addition of flavoring, and the fermenting of nutritional contents of the beer. By following the stanza-by-stanza instructions, we could duplicate the process used by the Sumerians." The researchers use a honey and barley flour mixture to make their **bappir, which was a storage, twice-baked, biscottilike barley bread.** The Sumerians probably used dates as a sweetener. The flour used to make the bread was from unmalted, malted, and roasted barley. This twice-baked bread is similar to bread still made in Crete today. Researchers mixed one-third bappir with two-thirds malt in the mash or wort tank to insure all starch would convert to sugar. The beer turned out well.

If I may speculate, it seems logical to me that if early man buried food to hide or store it, some of the stored

The history of bappir, salt, beer, and pickles.

grain would have eventually gotten wet and fermented. Likewise, if some of the bappir bread got wet in a container, the container contents might have fermented into an alcoholic drink. Since pottery only appears to be in evidence starting around 25,000 B.C. (and I am not an anthropologist—but this appears to be the date I see in literature), what large containers would they have had except containers of wood, hides, or pits in the ground? In any event, ancients fermented in pits and mixed items in pits because "The Hymn to Ninkasi," as translated by Miguel Civil, states:

> You are the one who handles the dough, [and] with a big shovel,
> Mixing in the pit, the bappir with sweet aromatic

The later stanzas discuss the filtering vat and collecting vat for the beer.

The researcher's beer had an alcohol concentration of 3.5 percent by weight, which is similar to modern-day beer.

Given all this information, what do you think about the impact of fermentation and pickling on world events? To pickle or to be pickled, that is the summary of all things. It appears we've come full circle. Salt, bread, beer, cucumbers, and the pickle—a long, historic story about feeding resourceful ancients, providing nautical provisions for oceans of sailors, delighting kings and queens, and enriching traders and nation builders. Magical, life-sustaining fermentations, bread, beer and pickles! And now it's time to resurrect the pickle's power. Today's scientists can harness pickle power to help third world nations ferment their own foods from indigenous resources and to help eradicate world hunger.

When scientists study these indigenous pickling and fermentation techniques and selectively choose seeds from specific parts of plants, they might hope to feed the world's one- to two-billion people who are malnourished and starving. High-tech scientists need to get very practical and study older, low-tech solutions and start working with what we have, rather than trying to put expensive Band-Aids on real, long-term problems.

Clockwise from right: *Speckled Horse Relish, Garden Corn Relish, Chow-Chow, India Relish*. Center: *Sweet Pickle Relish*.

Chapter 3

Relishes

Relishes are chopped pickles, peppers, and other pickled vegetables or fruits. Relishes can be used on sandwiches, in salads, as side condiments, or wrapped in meats. Relishes and pickles are acidic. To make them, vinegar or some other acid (such as lemon juice or naturally produced lactic acid), salt, water, and sometimes sugar are used. **For this reason, the pots and pans used to make relish should be non-reactive to vinegar and other acids. The salt and vinegar (or created acid) used in the pickling process serve as preservatives, as do other ingredients like sugar, honey, or maple syrup.** Fermented relishes or fermented pickles may be made. Fermented relishes may also be made from chopped fermented pickles.

For the best relishes, use only fresh produce. Do not use overly ripe, shriveled, hollow, or very large fruits. Use vinegar with at least 5- to 6-percent acetic acid. **Use only pickling salt—plain, food-pure, and free from additives. Follow the recipes carefully. Never reduce the vinegar or salt without testing the pH of the completed relish.** To decrease tartness, add more sugar, but never decrease the vinegar or salt without testing the acidity. Do not change ingredients in acidified recipes without the knowledge of how to adapt recipes. **Do not assume you have acidification knowledge if you have never studied the topic.**

Use stainless steel, glass, or enamelware to eliminate the possibility of a reaction between the pan's metal and the vinegar or salt. Use non-hard water or rainwater to avoid discoloration of any pickles. Carefully evalvate old-time recipes.

One of the more historic relishes is pepper hash. **Since the peppers are not brined, pepper hash is unique. Instead of brining, hot water is poured over the peppers to remove the spoiler enzymes.** For this reason, pepper hash is lower in salt than most other relish recipes and contains adequate vinegar to compensate for the reduced salt.

There are many variations of pepper hash, some with only 2 cups onions per 24 peppers. Classically, **"Pepper Hash is 12, 12, and 12,"** which means equal numbers of red peppers, green peppers, and onions. If you like, vary the number of red to green peppers, but use only medium-sized peppers. **Be careful not to use overly large peppers in any old-time recipe, as their peppers were generally smaller than today's peppers.**

Old-Fashioned Pepper Hash (c. 1864)

Large Batch

12 red sweet peppers (7 cups)
12 green sweet peppers (7 cups)
12 peeled onions (4¼ cups)
Boiling water
3 cups vinegar
2 cups sugar
2½ tablespoons pickling salt

Small Batch

1 red sweet pepper
1 green sweet pepper
1 peeled onion
Boiling water
¼ cup vinegar
2⅔ tablespoons sugar
½ teaspoon pickling salt

Use large or small batch proportions only. Use 5-percent acidity vinegar. Seed the medium-sized peppers. Finely grind or chop the onions and peppers. Pour enough boiling water over the vegetables to cover; wait 5 minutes. Drain/squeeze; discard the liquid. Add the remaining ingredients to the drained vegetables. Cook for 10 minutes. JSP/RWB10(8OZ)10(16OZ)A. For one-twelfth recipe (small batch), cook the relish for an extra 5 minutes and JSR. pH = 4.1 to 4.24.

Variation: Spicy Pepper Hash—Add a hot pepper pod to each jar and 1 to 2 tablespoons ground or whole mustard seed to the whole recipe, or substitute some hot peppers for non-hot peppers (1-1 exchange), or spice the entire recipe with a teaspoon or two of dried hot peppers.

Variation: Multi-Colored Pepper Hash—Use several colors of sweet peppers.

Variation: Pepper Hash with Dill Seeds—Use red wine vinegar instead of white vinegar and add 1 tablespoon dill seed to the larger batch size.

Variation: Classic Onion Relish—Reverse the ratio of peppers to onions (i.e. use 14 cups onions and 4¼ cups peppers). Spice with dill seed and/or mustard seed.

Variation: Hot Onion Relish—Use some hot peppers instead of sweet. For extra heat, reduce the sweet peppers in the regular recipe by ½ cup, and insert ½ cup hot peppers on the jar sides.

Variation: Classic Red Pepper Relish—2 dozen red peppers, 7 medium onions, 2 tablespoons yellow mustard seed, 2 tablespoons salt, 3½ cups red wine vinegar, and 3 cups sugar. This sweet relish is low in salt and high in vitamin C.

Variation: Sunshine Relish—Use half red and half orange peppers.

Often the classification of a canned product is in question. Is it a relish, chutney, or jam? Since this next product is very sweet, my mother says it is jam, and she puts it on top of her omelet. I say, "Mother, if it's on top of your omelet, it's chutney!" She says, "Where's the kicker? And, on top of cold cuts, surely it's used as chutney, or relish, unless, of course, it's used like a mint jelly. Then it's jam. With Brie cheese and crackers, it's jam or chutney, but not relish . . . and on a hot dog?" Notice the following recipe has just about the same amount of vinegar as pepper hash, allowing for some vinegar to mix with the extra sugar. There is more than two times the sugar in this recipe as in pepper hash for about the same amount of peppers.

There's no "kicker." See the definition of chutney! I think this recipe is too sweet to be a relish, too sweet to be chutney, and will concede to my mother who says it is a sweet-and-sour jam that's sometimes used like a chutney or relish.

Classic Red Pepper Relish in endive boats with lobster meat and basil leaf. Squeeze the hors d'oeuvre with a lemon wedge and enjoy.

Sweet and Tart Pepper Jam

25 medium bell peppers*	2½ pounds sugar (4½ cups)
About 4 tablespoons pickling salt	3¾ cups red wine or cider vinegar

Wash, seed, and chop the medium-sized peppers. Spread the peppers out on a cold, large-rimmed, stainless-steel tray** and sprinkle with pickling salt. The exact amount of salt need not be measured as the peppers are rinsed off later. Weep the peppers for 3 to 4 hours. Rinse the peppers well with cold-running water. Heat the peppers, sugar, and vinegar to a boil. Simmer until thick and translucent. Cook down (on-off method). JSP/RWB10(8OZ)15(16OZ)A. pH = 4.0.

There are many variations of Southern or Dixie Relish, with varying ratios between the cabbage, peppers, and onions (*Brassica oleracea, Capsicum annuum var. annuum,* and *Allium cepa,* respectively). The pepper to onion to cabbage ratio may be altered if using an equivalent number of cups or pounds of low-acid vegetables, but do not increase the cabbage to more than 3 pounds, and measure the final pH. Cabbage has the highest pH and is already the predominate vegetable, so it isn't likely one would want to increase its quantity. Lowering its quantity is more likely. The current ratio of cabbage to pepper to onion is approximately 9:6:5. These ratios might be 8:7:5 or 7:8:5 or 6:8:6, respectively. **To increase the cabbage beyond 3 pounds, increase the vinegar, and check the pH carefully to make sure it is well under 4.6 (4.2 or lower).**

Dixie Relish

3 pounds green cabbage*
12 sweet red/green bell peppers
6 medium onions
5/8 cup salt
4 teaspoons whole clove
1 tablespoon whole allspice
2 cinnamon sticks
4 tablespoons mustard seed
3 tablespoons celery seed
1 quart red or white wine vinegar**
3 cups sugar

Don't use Savoy cabbage. Chop and mix all the vegetables with the salt; wait 4 hours. Squeeze out the liquid. In a pan, add the spice bag (clove, allspice, and cinnamon sticks), mustard and celery seeds, vinegar, and sugar. Cook for 2 to 3 minutes. Add the drained vegetables. Cook for 5 to 10 minutes. JSP/RWB15(16OZ)A. pH = 3.86.
* May substitute red cabbage
** May substitute cider vinegar or white vinegar

This next relish probably evolved when cooks began substituting vegetables. The **Rummage, Garbage, Chow-Chow, Kitchen Sink** and **End of the Garden** relishes are all exemplary of this type of mixed or multi-vegetable formulation. This rummage relish appeared in the September 1931 issue of *Comfort Magazine.* I thank Ms. Barbara Davies for bringing a copy of her old *Comfort Magazine* to the Wilmette Farmers' Market. The original recipe calls for celery root, but celery may be used instead. It is interesting to see **celery root** or **celeriac** (turnip-rooted celery), *Apium graveolens* L. var. *rapaceum* (Mill.), in a canning recipe. The original recipe called for 8 cups green tomatoes to 4 cups ripe tomatoes. On October 18, 1999, I was almost out of ripe tomatoes and, of necessity, substituted some green for red.

Rummage Pickle (Relish)

10 cups chopped green tomatoes
2 cups diced ripe tomatoes
4 cups chopped cabbage
2 cups chopped onions
2 cups chopped celery*
1 1/2 cups red or green peppers
6 cups cider vinegar**
2 cups brown sugar
1 teaspoon mustard

Cover the vegetables with 1/2 cup salt; ice the pan. Wait 8 hours then drain well. Simmer all ingredients together for 1 hour. JSP/RWB10A.
* May substitute celery root
** May substitute red wine vinegar

He-Man Relish was especially formulated for construction workers who frequented Jamlady's stand, demanding more "hot stuff." **He-Man Relish is a hot rummage relish.** Like Dixie Relish, make it with red or white cabbage.

He-Man Relish

8 cups diced cucumbers
2 cups chopped zucchini
1 cup diced red bell peppers
8 tablespoons salt (for dry-salting)
10 cups chopped red cabbage
7 cups diced jalapeño peppers
2 cups chopped onions
8 cups red wine vinegar*
1 cup minced fresh gingerroot
7 cups sugar
6 tablespoons dried fenugreek leaves**
6 tablespoons dry mustard
2 tablespoons mustard seed
2 tablespoons salt (cook in recipe)
1 ½ tablespoons turmeric
1 tablespoon ground cinnamon
1 teaspoon ground mace

Dry-salt the cucumbers, zucchini, and red peppers with 8 tablespoons salt for 1 hour. Squeeze/drain; combine all ingredients. Cook for 5 to 10 minutes. JSP/RWB10A.

* Marconi-brand recommended

** Can be found in Indian food stores

Some recipes may be changed without disrupting the pH readings substantially.

Note the changes between this recipe and the previous one.

Mild He-Man Relish

5 cups diced cucumbers
2 cups chopped zucchini
1 cup diced red bell peppers
8 tablespoons salt (for dry-salting)
16 cups chopped red cabbage
3 cups diced jalapeño peppers
2 cups chopped red onion
8 cups vinegar
1 cup minced fresh gingerroot
7 cups sugar
6 tablespoons dried fenugreek leaves
6 tablespoons dry mustard
2 tablespoons mustard seed
2 tablespoons salt
1 ½ tablespoons turmeric
1 tablespoon ground cinnamon
1 teaspoon ground mace

Dry-salt the cucumbers, zucchini and red peppers with 8 tablespoons salt for 1 hour. Squeeze/drain; combine all ingredients. Cook for 5 to 10 minutes. JSP/RWB10A. pH = 4.03.

One of the problems a small-plot gardener has is finding enough of any one vegetable to make a batch of relish. Here's the remedy.

This and That Relish

5 cups chopped cucumbers
4 cups chopped green tomatoes
4 cups chopped red tomatoes
4 cups chopped green cabbage
3 cups chopped onions
2 cups chopped celery
2 chopped green peppers
2 chopped red peppers
½ cup salt
4 cups brown sugar
8 cups distilled or wine vinegar
2 tablespoons celery seed
1 tablespoon chopped garlic
1 tablespoon mustard seed
1 tablespoon ground cinnamon
1 teaspoon ginger
½ teaspoon ground clove

Salt the vegetables for 6 hours; keep cool. Drain/squeeze the vegetables and combine with all the other ingredients. Cook for 30 minutes. JSP/RWB10(8OZ)10(16OZ)A.

Kitchen Sink Relish

3 cups zucchini squash
3 cups onions
2 cups baby pan-pan squash
2 cups green peppers or hot peppers
1 cup cucumbers
1 cup green tomatoes
½ cup pickling salt
3 trays of ice cubes
8 cups red wine vinegar*
4 cups brown sugar
2 minced garlic cloves
1 tablespoon celery seed
1 tablespoon ground cinnamon
1 tablespoon mustard seed
1 teaspoon ground ginger
½ teaspoon ground clove

Chop all the vegetables and measure. In a cool place, let the first 8 ingredients sit for 12 to 18 hours. Drain/squeeze the vegetables; add the last 8 ingredients. Cook for 5 minutes. JSP/RWB10(8OZ)10(16OZ)A.
* May substitute cider vinegar

Chow-chow and India relishes are classics. Some chow-chows have lima beans or string beans in them; other formulations contain cabbage, green tomatoes, peppers, cauliflower, and onions. Some formulations have only green tomatoes, peppers, and onions. **The common element is the use of dry mustard powder. For this reason, chow-chows and India relishes are known as "mustard pickles."**

India Relish, chow-chow's cousin, is delicious with any sandwich, hot dog, or burger. The ginger provides the zip to this flavor-filled relish. Serve India relish, made with high-Scoville-unit peppers (substituted for some of the regular green peppers), and watch the rhetorical gesticulations fly or tame it down by mixing it with mayonnaise!

Hot India Relish

18 cups chopped cucumbers
16 cups chopped green tomatoes
12 cups diced red/green bell peppers*
2 cups chopped onions
¾ cup salt
6 cups red wine vinegar
5 cups sugar
4 cups chopped cabbage
20 chopped Serrano peppers**
6 tablespoons mustard seed
2 tablespoons minced gingerroot
2 teaspoons turmeric
2 teaspoons cinnamon
6-10 crushed bay leaves

Mix the first 5 ingredients; keep cool for 8 hours. Squeeze/drain and add the remaining ingredients. Cook 3 minutes. JSP/RWB10(8OZ)10(16OZ)A.

* May substitute some hot peppers for sweet

** May substitute other hot peppers of equal measure

Chow-chow, a mustard-pickle relish, may be made hot or mild. Use hot chow-chow on sandwiches, burgers, brats, or with beans. Make this relish with small chunks of vegetables or with relish-size pieces.

Hot Chow-Chow

8 cups chopped cabbage
6 cups diced red/green bell peppers
4 cups chopped onions
4 cups chopped green tomatoes
4 tablespoons pickling salt
2 cups sugar
6 cups red wine vinegar
7 cups chopped jalapeño peppers
1 tablespoon ground dry mustard
1 teaspoon ground ginger
1 teaspoon turmeric*

Salt the cabbage, sweet peppers, onions, and green tomatoes; leave refrigerated for 8 hours. Drain/squeeze. Boil the sugar, red wine vinegar, jalapeño peppers, mustard, ginger, and turmeric. Then add the drained vegetables. Simmer 10 minutes. JSP/RWB10(8OZ)10(16OZ)A.

* Optional, a natural colorant like annatto

Variation: Jamlady's Hot Burger Chow— Follow the same directions with 8 cups cabbage, 2 cups sweet green peppers, 1 cup red sweet peppers, 6 cups green tomatoes, 4 cups onions, 1¼ cups hot jalapeno peppers, ¼ cup Serrano peppers, 6 cups vinegar, 2 cups sugar, 4 tablespoons pickling salt, 1 tablespoon dry mustard, 1 teaspoon ground ginger, and 1 teaspoon turmeric.

Chow-Chow Relish

4 cups chopped cabbage
2 cups coarsely chopped cauliflower
2 cups onions
2½ cups chopped green tomatoes
2½ cups chopped red/green peppers
3 tablespoons salt
3 ½ cups vinegar
1½ cups sugar
2 teaspoons dry mustard
2 teaspoons celery seed
½ teaspoon ground ginger
1 teaspoon mustard seed
1 teaspoon ground turmeric

Mix the first 6 ingredients. Keep cool; wait 4 hours. Drain/squeeze. Boil the spices, sugar, and vinegar for 10 minutes; then add the drained vegetables. Cook 10 minutes. JSP/RWB10(8OZ)10(16OZ)A. Makes about 4 pints.

Mrs. Humiston's chow-chow recipe is taken from *Light of the Kitchen* (the Willing Workers Society of the Methodist Episcopal Church n.d.). This cookbook belonged to my paternal grandmother, Elizabeth F. Decker Schoonmaker of Accord, New York, who married Gross B. Schoonmaker on July 26, 1913, in Greenfield, New York. As a child, I would make floral deliveries with my father, Donald L. Schoonmaker, to Humiston's Funeral Home in Kerhonkson. **Almost all the women I knew in the Rondout Valley cooked, baked, and canned something, for they were all bonafide "church-ladies" or "synagogue-ladies."**

Mrs. Humiston's Chow-Chow—
"½ bu. green tomatoes, 6 green peppers, 12 onions. Chop fine and sprinkle 1 pt. of salt over it. Let it stand overnight and drain. In the morning, put some vinegar on it and let it simmer for an hour on the stove then pour it off. Have ready in a pan, 1 teaspoon pepper, 2 teaspoons clove, ½ cup mustard, 2 lbs. (scant) sugar, 1 pt. grated horseradish, a little vinegar. Let it boil and pour over the chow-chow while hot." Refrigerate Mrs. Humiston's Chow-Chow or check the pH before canning as exact measurements are not given. Many times chow-chow is just made and refrigerated or taken to a picnic or pot-luck supper.

At the end of the season, green tomatoes are usually left in most gardens. It's a shame to let them freeze. Bring in green tomatoes, wash them in cool water, dry them, grade them by degrees of ripeness, and layer them between layers of brown paper in a box. Keep them cool, or they will ripen quickly. Make green tomatoes into relish, pickles, mincemeat, frozen green-tomato pies, or fried green tomatoes and leave some to ripen.

Chow-Chow Relish is a "mustard pickle" that has been made with smaller pieces of vegetables.

Green Tomato and Apple Relish

8 cups peeled apple chunks
16 cups green tomatoes
8 cups onions
5 cups sugar
5 cups red wine vinegar
2 teaspoons salt
2 teaspoons celery seed
2 teaspoons mustard seed
1½ teaspoons ginger
1 teaspoon ground clove
1 teaspoon turmeric
1 teaspoon ground cinnamon
1 teaspoon allspice
½ teaspoon nutmeg

Separately, in a food processor, chop the apples, tomatoes, and onions. Add the remaining ingredients. Simmer for 1½ hours. Stir well. JSP/RWB10(8OZ)15(16OZ)A.

Green tomatoes are versatile and so are apples. Together in relishes their flavors complement one another. These two fruits may be used together in pies (see *The Jamlady Cookbook*). A similar apple and green tomato recipe appeared in an old church cookbook in Kerhonkson, New York. **Take special note of the ingredient "mangoes."**

The following recipe has apples and green tomatoes, like the recipe above, but it also has **"mangoes"** and raisins.

Mrs. Grant's Apple and Tomato Relish—Taken from *The Light of the Kitchen* (58): "12 apples, 6 mangoes* [see definition], 6 green tomatoes, 1 pound of raisins, 1 tablespoon salt, 2 cups brown sugar, 1 tablespoon celery seed, 1 quart vinegar, grind everything and cook 1 hour. Put in glass jars and seal. Will make 3 qts." **Note: This recipe should be no problem to can, as there is a quart of vinegar to compensate for the only ingredient that is substantially over 4.6 (see the pH chart).**

* **Mango (definition)—"any of various types of pickle, especially a pickled stuffed sweet pepper."** (*American Heritage Dictionary of the English Language: Fourth Edition*).

Webster's Revised Unabridged Dictionary (1913 ed.) defines a mango as, **"A green muskmelon stuffed and pickled."**

John F. Mariani's *Encyclopedia of American Food & Drink* (1999) states, **"In the Midwest (especially the Ohio Valley) a sweet pepper is called a 'mango.'"**

In *Craig Claiborne's The New York Times Food Encyclopedia* (1985), Claiborne writes, **"I have been familiar with this preparation since childhood, but I did not know why the filled peppers or tomatoes were referred to as mangoes until I heard from many people, mostly in the Middle West, who said that the word mango commonly refers simply to the sweet green pepper known as a bell pepper."**

The *Oxford English Dictionary:* Second Edition states, **"To pickle as green mangoes are pickled."**

Moreover, John Ayto's *The Glutton's Glossary: A Dictionary of Food and Drink Terms* (1990) mentions that **"in the eighteenth century mango was even used as a verb: To mango Cucumber."** There's also a mango bird, *Oriolus kundoo;* mango fish, *Polynemus risua;* and a mango tree, *Mangifera indica,* which produces the tropical mango fruit. Jamlady suggested to me: an inebriated person might well be referred to as "mangoed." See discussion below.

Stone Ridge Public Library's copy of *Tried and True: Cookbook of Domestic Receipts* (Ladies Air Society of the Methodist Episcopal Church n.d., 88) gives a recipe for **Mangoes** and **Pepper Hash made from Mangoes.** In the first mango recipe below, I am assuming the stuffed mangoes are placed back into a brine solution or are covered with hot, scalding vinegar, weighted down, and kept cold. The recipe is not specific.

"Mangoes—Take large green peppers, remove the top, leaving the stem on, take out the seeds and put in salt and water overnight; take out and drain well; fill with two quarts of chopped cabbage, one-half cupful of mustard seed, three tablespoons of celery seed, two tablespoons of salt, two small tablespoons of sugar;

mix well together and put into the pepper with some small cucumber and a few nasturtum (sic) seed; put on the covers and tie them on; keep in a cool place."

"Pepper Hash—Two dozen mangoes, fifteen onions, remove seeds from peppers, chop all fine, cover with boiling water and let stand five minutes, pour off and put on more and let stand ten minutes; one and a half pints of vinegar, one and a half cups sugar, three tablespoons of salt; boil together fifteen minutes."

Clearly, the Pepper Hash is an old recipe, known to be made with only peppers and onions, and classically made with the hot water being poured over the top, drained, and a sugar/vinegar solution added. **Given this information, it must mean the word mango was used to denote a sweet green pepper, perhaps the size of one that might be stuffed. It seems reasonable to assume Mrs. Grant's Apple and Tomato Relish was made with large peppers or peppers prepared in brine, so they could be stuffed, but were instead used in relish. Try brine-storing some garden peppers in the refrigerator. Weight them down.**

Mrs. Elliott's Housewife (1870), by Mrs. Sarah A. Elliott, gives recipes for melon, cucumber, and peach mangoes. **Anyone researching everyday cookbooks from 1700 to 1800 will see recipes for mangoed pickles of melons, green tomatoes, peppers, cucumbers, and peaches.**

John Evelyn's *Acetaria* (1699):

> Take the biggest Cucumbers (and most of the Mango size) that look green: open them on the Top or Side; and Scooping out the Seeds, Supply their Place with Small Clove of Garlick, or Some Roccombo Seeds. Then put them into an Earthen Glazed Jarr, or wide mouth'd Glass, with as much White-Wine Vinegar with Pepper, Cloves, Mace Ec. and when off the Fire, as much Salt as will make a gentle Brine; and So pour all boyling-hot on the Cucumbers, covering them close till the next Day. Then put them with a little Dill, and Pickle into a large Skillet; and giving them a Boyl or two, return them into the Vessel again: And when all is cold, add a good Spoonful of the best Muftard, keeping it from the Air, and So have you an excellent Mango. When you have occasion to take any out, make use of a Spoon, and not your Fingers. [Rocambole (rok'-am-bohl) is a common name for *Allium scorodoprasum,* the Giant Garlic.]

Recipes for stuffed peppers or mangoes were often seen in small advertising cookbooks, given away, or sold for a dime, hence the name "dime cookbooks." *Mrs. Winslow's Domestic Receipt Book for 1871* (1870, 90), gives this recipe for **Mangoes of Melons:**

> Mangoes of Melon—Take green melons and make a brine strong enough to bear up an egg; then pour it boiling hot on the melons, keeping them under the brine; let them stand five or six days, slit them down on side, take out all the seeds, scrape them well in the inside, and wash them clean; then take cloves, garlic, ginger, nutmeg and pepper; put all these proportionately into the melons, filling them up with mustard seed; then lay them into an earthen pot, and take one part of mustard seed and two parts of vinegar, enough to cover them, pouring it on scalding hot. Keep them closely covered.

Mrs. S. Dally's recipe for **Pickled Mangoes** appears in *The Earnest Workers' Cook Book* (Trinity Church, Chicago 1886, 44):

> **Pickled Mangoes**—Young musk or nutmeg melons, one handful English mustard seed mixed with scraped horse-radish, one teaspoonful mace and nutmeg, pounded, two teaspoonful chopped garlic, a little ginger, twelve whole peppercorns, one-half tablespoonful ground mustard to a pint of the mixture, one teaspoonful sugar, one teaspoonful salad oil and one teaspoonful celery seed, to the same quantity. Cut a slit in the side of the melon, insert your finger and extract all the seeds. If you cannot get them out in this way, cut a slender piece, saving it to replace. Lay

A mangoed green pepper!

the mangoes in strong brine for three days. Drain off the brine and freshen in pure water twenty-four hours. Lay in cold water, until firm, fill with the stuffing, sew up the slit or tie with pack thread, pack in a deep stone jar and cover with scalding vinegar. Repeat this process three times, at intervals of two days, then tie up and set away in a cool dry place. They will not be "ripe" under four months, but are then very fine. They will keep for several years.

From E. Smith's *The Compleat Houfewife Or Accomplish'd Gentlewoman's Companion, Fifteenth Edition* (1753):

To mango Cucumbers. Cut a little flip out of the side of the cucumber, and take out the seeds, but as little of the meat as you can; then fill in inside with mustard-seed bruifed, a clove of garlick, some slices of ginger, and some bits of horse-radish; tie the piece in again, and make a pickle of vinegar, salt, whole pepper, cloves, mace, and boil it, and pour it on the mangoes, and do so for nine days together; when cold, cover them with leather. **To make Melon Mangoes.** Take small melons not quite ripe, cut a slip down the side, and take out the insides very clean; beat mustard-seed, and shred garlick, which mix with the seeds, and put in your mangoes; put the pieces you cut out into their places again, tie them up, and put them into your pot; then boil some vinegar (as much as you think will cover them) with whole pepper, some salt , and *Jamaica* pepper, which pour in scalding hot over your mangoes, and cover them close to keep in the steam; repeat this nine days, and when they are cold cover them with leather."

Gillette and Ziemann's *The White House Cookbook* (1976, 229) directs green-pepper mangoes be filled with chopped cabbage, green tomatoes, salt, mustard seed, and ground clove, and then be sewn closed. **The mangoes should have hot boiling vinegar with brown sugar poured over them for three mornings.**

Dr. D. Jayne's Family Medicine's 1917 booklet, *How to Do Pickling,* suggests toothpick closures and chopped cabbage with a tablespoon of salt, celery seed, red pepper, and a little ground cinnamon as a filling for mangoed peppers, and further says "small green tomatoes may be used in the same way."

The Woman's Exchange Cook Book, by Minnie Palmer, (1894, 49) gives a recipe for

> **Cucumber Preserves**—Gather young cucumbers, about four inches long. Lay in strong brine one week. Wash. Soak twenty-four hours in clear water, changing this four times. Line a bell metal kettle with grapevine leaves. Lay in the cucumbers with a little alum scattered among them. Cover with vine leaves. Fill the kettle with clear water. Cover closely. Let them simmer. As soon as they are well greened take out the cucumbers and drop in ice water. When perfectly cold, wipe, and with a small knife slit down one side. Dig out the seeds. Stuff with a mixture of chopped raisins and citron. Sew up the slit with a fine thread and weigh them. Make a syrup, allowing 1 pound of sugar to 1 pound of cucumber and 1 pint of water. Heat to boiling point. Skim. Drop in the fruit. Simmer half an hour. Take out. Spread on a dish in the sun and boil down the syrup with a few slices of ginger root added. When thick, put in the cucumbers again. Simmer five minutes and put in glass jars, tying up when cool.

Palmer's book cites a recipe for **Spiced Nutmeg Melon,** a sweet-sour pickle, spiced with cinnamon, cloves, and allspice.

> Select melons not quite ripe, open, scrape out the pulp, peel, and slice; put the fruit in a stone jar, and for 5 pounds fruit, take a quart vinegar, and two and a half pounds sugar; scald vinegar and sugar together, and pour over the fruit; scald the syrup and pour over the fruit each day for eight successive days. On the ninth, add 1 ounce stick cinnamon, 1 of whole cloves, and 1 of allspice. Scald fruit, vinegar, and spices together, and seal up in jars. This pickle should stand two or three months before using.

Professor H. Blit's Methods of Canning Fruits and Vegetables by Hot Air and Steam, and Berries by the Compounding of Syrups, and the Crystallizing and Candying of Fruits, Etc., Etc. (1890, 34) states,

> **To Make Mangos or Green Peppers,** Let them lie in salt and water for about a week (brine the same strength as for string beans). Then remove the seeds and fill them with shaved cabbage and a little mustard seed. Pour oven (sic = over) them scalding vinegar, then seal in jars or crocks.

Does anyone still question a mango was a pepper? This next quote on mangoes is from an 1870 cookbook.

Melon Mangoes

> Take young cantelopes (sic), large as a good sized orange, put them in a strong brine of salt and water, and let them remain twenty-four hours; then take them out and cut down one of the slices (only one cut; it will readily open after being in the brine, and is far better than cutting out the slice or plug); slip your finger in and clean the seeds out nicely, then put them in cold water to rinse them. After all are cleaned, return them to the brine, and scald them several mornings, by pouring the brine off in a brass kettle and giving it a boil up (small bit of alum in the jar improves them). When green as you wish, scald them in part vinegar and water and let them remain in it three days; then prepare a stuffing of cabbage cut fine, mustard seed, few celery seed, pickled cucumber cut fine, onion if you like it, horse-radish scraped, allspice, cloves, pieces of cinnamon, teaspoonful of sugar to each melon and a few grains of pepper. Fill them with this mixture, putting in one at a time, and put

them in a stone jar, and cover well with strong cider vinegar. Some persons like one teaspoonful of salad oil in every mango. Have strips of bleached cottons half an inch wide to tie around the melon and secure the stuffing. These are good two years old. (Elliott 1870, 218).

To understand what is happening inside a mangoed cantaloupe, please review chapter two: Dry-salting, the three stages of microbe growth in sauerkraut and anerobic fermentation.

Cucumber Mangoes

"Prepare your cucumbers as for plain pickle; have large, full-grown ones for mangoes; make an incision length way of the cucumber; don't take anything out, but gently fill it with the same stuffing given for melons. You will be surprised to see how much you can put in it; secure it with strips wound around it, put in a jar, and fill with cold vinegar, with pieces of horse-radish, ginger root, and allspice over them." (Elliot 219)

Peach Mangoes

"Use the same stuffing and open them carefully to extract the seed, after being in salt and water two days. Boil the vinegar with a teacup of sugar and pour on them."(Elliott 219)

Pickled peaches may be stuffed with chopped walnuts. Try this recipe for mangoes or stuffed peppers.

Mangoes or Stuffed Peppers

12 medium peppers, assorted
1 cup salt
7 cups shredded green cabbage
1 tablespoon salt
1 cup chopped onions
4 minced garlic cloves
2 tablespoons mustard seed
3-4 tablespoons celery seed
½ cup sugar
Vinegar or spiced vinegar
Cauliflower (optional)
Baby cucumbers (optional)
Celery (optional)
Baby pan pan squash (optional)

Seed the peppers; leave their shells intact. Weight down the peppers in a gallon crock of water with 1 cup salt for 12 hours. Rinse the peppers. Weep the shredded green cabbage with a tablespoon salt for 1 hour. Drain the cabbage. Stuff the rinsed peppers with filling (1 cup chopped onions, 4 minced garlic cloves, 2 tablespoons mustard seed, 3 to 4 tablespoons celery seed, ½ cup sugar, and the drained cabbage). Cover with boiling spiced vinegar or white wine vinegar and JS**R** or JSP/RWB15(8OZ)20(16OZ)**R**A. Note: The **R** means refrigerate. Matures in 6 weeks. **Keep refrigerated or test to confirm a pH of 4.2 or under.**

Variation: Use pieces of cauliflower, baby cucumbers, or pan pans with less shredded cabbage.

Some cooks dilute the vinegar by using 1 quart vinegar, 2 cups water, and ¼ cup sugar. Since *jardinières* of peppers (pH = 4.65-5.45), onions (pH = 5.37-5.85), and cabbage (pH = 5.20-6.80) usually call for a little more vinegar than water, it seems reasonable to make mangoes with less than full-strength vinegar, but be careful of adding too much cabbage. **For a canned recipe, I am inclined to reduce the cabbage and add in more lower-pH vegetables. For a new hermetically sealed formulation, always test the pH before eating or keep the product refrigerated.**

Spiced cabbage-relish recipes are usually made with full strength vinegar. Full strength vinegar with shredded cabbage nets a pH of 3.97 to 4.01. A ratio of 5 cups vinegar to 4 cups water is an acceptable mix for peppers and onions, but for cabbage, more acidity is needed to safely can it. One quart vinegar to 1 cup water is probably okay for mangoed peppers, if the peppers (and jars) are loosely packed, and the filling is of cabbage with other lower pH vegetables. If you have a pH meter, make the pickle, grind it up with the surrounding liquid, and test the over-all pH. **To safely can mangoes filled with cabbage, measure with a pH meter and temperature probe. Then look for a pH of 4.0 or less. Remember to create a recipe that will work with the greatest amount of possible variance anyone could possibly expect or just keep the mangoes refrigerated.**

A handwritten recipe "for making mangoes" in an unidentified recipe book #4, dated 1849 to 1877, at the Huguenot Historical Society Library and Archives, New Paltz, New York, simply states, **"put them in salt and water, and let them remain in for 2 days—fill them, add 1 pint of molaf?acs (sic = molasses?) to 1 gallon of vinegar & boil them in it till you can run a straw through them."** Clearly the molasses would help to take the edge off the full-strength vinegar, but it also has a higher pH than sugar. **Because of the 1849 to 1877 date and molasses' impact on pH, we can assume this is a "refrigerate only" recipe.**

For this cookbook, I made mangoed peppers that were not stuffed with cabbage, but stuffed with green and red tomatoes and onions (see previous photo by mango definitions and elsewhere). I did not use hot peppers, but they could be used. The peppers were not pre-salted or brined. It might help to do so, as it was difficult to put a hole in the peppers and sew them together without sewing down further on the pepper than one would think necessary. Nevertheless, this method worked.

Small Mangoed Peppers

Cut the tops off the peppers about ½ inch down from the stem and seed. Mix and wait: 1½ cups chopped green tomatoes, 1 small onion (diced), 1 3-inch red tomato (diced), and 1½ tablespoons salt. After 15 minutes, drain/squeeze. Stuff the peppers with the relish, sew them shut, and put them in sterile jars. Heat the vinegar solution: 3 ½ cups cider vinegar, 2 cups sugar, 1 teaspoon celery seed, ½ teaspoon allspice, and 2 teaspoons mustard seed, and pour over, SP/RWB10(4OZ)15(8OZ)15-20(16OZ)A. The pH = 3.41.

Peppers, tomatoes, and onions are used in regular jardinières, which may use 5 parts vinegar to 3 parts water. So try this 5:3 solution (with no sugar) to make mangoed peppers with no cabbage and no added sugar. Test the final pH, or JSR.

Use spiced cabbage in *roulades*. Spread spiced cabbage on thin pieces of raw beef or pork cutlets, roll, and tie up. Let the refrigerated rolls marinate for 6 to 12 hours. Then bake, broil, or grill the *roulades*. Try spiced cabbage inside rolls of deli meat or on grilled burgers and brats.

Spiced Cabbage

1½ tablespoons grated horseradish root
16 cups shredded red/white cabbage
½ cup pickling salt
4 cups cider vinegar
1½ cups sugar
1 tablespoon mustard seed
1 teaspoon whole clove
5 cinnamon sticks

Peel and grate the horseradish root. Chop or shred the cabbage (no Savoy); add the salt and weep for 8 hours in a cool place. Mix the vinegar, sugar, spice bag (spices and horseradish), and boil for 15 minutes. Rinse the cabbage with water; drain/squeeze. Mix the vinegar solution with the cabbage. JSP/RWB20-25(16OZ)25-30(32OZ)A(0-1000FT). Fill the jars to 6 percent full or ½-inch from the top of a standard 16-ounce jar. pH = 3.97 to 4.01.

The **tomato, *Lycopersicon lycopersicum,*** native to the Andes, bears edible fruits of red, orange, yellow, black, green, white, purple, and bi-color. Some tomatoes are striped, spherical, pear-, torpedo-, or plum-shaped. **The tomatillo, *Physalis ixoxarpa***

Brot., is commonly known as the husk tomato or Mexican Green Tomato and is related to the ground cherry. The perennial husk tomato, often grown as an annual, was used by the Aztecs. **The tomatillo fruit is very distinctive, with its paper-like husk (extended calyx) that completely envelopes the green, yellow-green, or purple fruit.**

The tomatillo is underutilized in the United States, but it is a major crop in Central America where it is used for chili sauces, tacos, and enchiladas. Relishes may be made from tomatillos anytime; they are usually in most Mexican markets year-round. **Tomatillos may be substituted for green tomatoes in most recipes.**

Tomatillo Relish

16 cups chopped tomatillos
3 large chopped Texas onions
6 chopped red peppers*
6 cups sugar
4 cups white wine vinegar**
4 teaspoons celery seed
2 teaspoons whole allspice
4 teaspoons mustard seed

Add the tomatillos, onions, and peppers to the salt gradually (as you chop them). The whole process takes about 30 minutes. Wait 10 minutes more; drain/squeeze. Simmer the sugar, vinegar, and spice bag (celery seed, allspice, and mustard seed) for 10 minutes. Add the drained vegetables; heat to boiling. JSP/RWB10(8OZ)15(16OZ)A or cook 5 minutes and JS**R.**
Makes 8 pints, or half the recipe for 4.
** May substitute white vinegar

Variation: Maisy's Green Tomato Relish—Substitute green tomatoes for tomatillos. For the mustard seed, use 3 teaspoons in the spice bag and 1 teaspoon in the relish itself.

Variation: Hot Tomatillo Relish—*Substitute hot peppers for some of the sweet peppers. Do not brine the hot peppers; cook them in the vinegar instead.

Variation: Green-Boy Relish or **Hot Green-Boy Relish***—Dry-salt 16 cups chopped, green Big Boy Tomatoes, 1 large Texas onion (or equivalent shallots), 2 large red onions, and 6 assorted red/orange peppers with 8 tablespoons salt for 15 minutes; drain/squeeze. Cook a spice bag of 5 teaspoons celery seed, 2 teaspoons allspice, and 2 tablespoons mustard seed in 4 cups cider vinegar (or red wine vinegar) with 6 cups sugar for 10 minutes. Add the drained vegetables and boil 5 minutes. JSP/RWB10(8OZ)15(16OZ)A.

Tomatillo Piccalli

8 cups chopped tomatillos
1 cup salt
8 cups weeped ripe tomato meats
4 cups sliced scallions/onions
2½ cups diced sweet yellow peppers
2½ cups sweet bell peppers
3½ cups white vinegar*
2 cups sugar

Dry-salt the husked, chopped tomatillos; keep cool for 12 hours. On hour eleven, plunge the whole ripe tomatoes in boiling-hot water, remove their skins and seeds, strainer-drain the tomatoes for 1 hour and measure out 2 quarts tomato meats. Drain the tomatillos and mix in all other ingredients; cook for ½-hour. JSP/RWB10(8OZ)15(16OZ)A. pH = 3.89.
* May substitute white wine vinegar

Variation: Green Tomato Piccalilli—Substitute green tomatoes for tomatillos.

Daisy's Hot Green Tomato Relish

12 red bell peppers
5 hot peppers*
5 cups chopped green tomatoes
3 cups chopped onions
2 cups chopped cabbage
2 cups sliced celery
½ cup salt
tray of ice cubes
5 cups white or brown sugar
4 cups vinegar
1½ cups non-hard water
2 tablespoons mustard seed
1 tablespoon celery seed

Seed and chop the peppers. Mix the first 8 ingredients together for 2 to 3 hours; drain. Add the rest of the ingredients; boil 5 minutes. JSP/RWB15(16OZ)A

* Hot peppers need not go with the salt. For hotter results, chop and boil the hot peppers with the vinegar.

Bowl of tomatillos or husk tomatoes.

Ploughman's Piccalilli

8 cups green tomatoes
6 sweet peppers, assorted hues
4-5 chopped onions (2½-inch thickness)
3 cups red or white wine vinegar*
1¾ cups white or brown sugar
4 tablespoons mustard seed
5 tablespoons celery seed
2 tablespoons pickling salt
2 cinnamon sticks
2 teaspoons allspice
¼-½ teaspoon turmeric (optional)**

Use 5- or 6-percent vinegar. Wash and chop the tomatoes, pepper, and onions. Add 1½ cups vinegar to the vegetables; boil for ½-hour. Drain the vegetables; discard the liquid. Add the remaining 1½ cups vinegar, sugar, spices, salt, spice bag (cinnamon sticks and allspice), and the drained vegetables. Simmer for 2 to 3 minutes. JSP/RWB10(8OZ)10-15(16OZ)A. Makes 12 8-ounce jars.

* May substitute sherry vinegar
** Used as colorant

Note: Clock the exact time a full rolling-boil is boiling. The small, rising bubbles seen prior to a full rolling-boil do not constitute a full rolling-boil or RWB.

In the Willing Worker's Society Cookbook of the Methodist Episcopal Church, *The Light of the Kitchen* (n.d.), I noticed two proximate recipes for **Bordeau Sauce.** Amusingly, they are almost identical, so I've morphed Mrs. J. J. Churchill's and Mrs. Moule's recipes together.

Bordeau Sauce

"4 qts. cabbage, 2 qts. green tomatoes, 6 large onions sliced, 3 large red peppers, ½ oz. turmeric, 11 whole allspice (or ½ oz.), 11 clove (or ½ oz.), 2 oz. white mustard seed, ½ oz. celery seed, 2 cups sugar, 2 qts. vinegar, 1 cup salt (or ½ cup). Mix all together. Boil 20 minutes. Can hot."

Moroccans make a fresh relish with similar ingredients to Jamlady's Hot Moroccan Relish. Half or quarter this recipe as you like. **This relish is quite unusual with the taste of lemons, hot peppers, capers, tomato, and celery.**

Hot Moroccan Relish

½ cup lemon juice
3-4 outer lemon rinds
15 cups sliced celery
1½ cups diced bell peppers
2½ cups diced Serrano peppers
2 cups canned capers
1 cup chopped fresh parsley
7 cups vinegar
24 cups tomato meats*
7 cups sugar
1 cup olive oil**
4 tablespoons salt
2 teaspoons black pepper

Blenderize the lemon juice and outer rinds (no pith). Mix together the celery, green peppers, Serrano peppers, capers, parsley, lemon juice, lemon rind, and vinegar. Bring to a boil; refrigerate for 24 hours. *Plunge the tomatoes in hot water, then in cold. Peel and seed the tomatoes, reserving only the meats. Reheat the mixture; add the tomatoes and sugar. Stir well. Add the olive oil; boil for 1 minute or can (**without adding the oil). JSP/RWB15(16OZ)**R**A. pH = 3.94. **Refrigerate the canned jars of this relish containing oil. To make a shelf-stable product without the oil and the overnight refrigeration step, just can the product. JSPRWB10(8OZ)15(16OZ)A. Add the oil to the relish after opening the jar. **Serve with grilled shrimp, fish, or chicken and *couscous.***

Caution: Regarding oil, the worry is that the oil might trap botulinus inside low-acid vegetables where it might grow at room temperature. Keeping the canned product refrigerated prevents any botulinus from growing. All peppers and similar vegetables that are canned with oil should first be cooked and soaked in vinegar for 24 hours. Keep products canned with oil in the refrigerator or can them without the oil, adding the oil after opening. Oil/lid-compound compatibility was investigated. A major lid company representative stated, "Home canning with oil is strictly a safety issue, and is not a lid/oil-compatibility issue."

The **cucumber,** *Cucumis sativus,* is a vining annual native to Asia bearing elongated green, white, or yellow fruits. The lemon cucumber is more globular than long. Beautiful golden relishes and pickles may be made from lemon cucumbers, but lemon cucumbers aren't easily grown in Illinois. When fresh, its outer skin is often unattractive, but in the jar, it is beautiful.

Dwarf varieties of cucumbers may be grown in patio containers. **Try to pick small or medium-sized cucumbers as overly mature or yellowing fruit cause plants to stop producing fruit.** Select garden varieties according to their intended use. Small Kirby's make great relish or bread-and-butter pickles. **If collecting seed, see ECIWO.**

Sweet Pickle Relish

5 cups chopped pickling cucumbers
2 cups chopped onions
¼ cup salt
1 tray of ice cubes
3½ cups sugar
2 cups red wine vinegar
1 tablespoon celery seed
1 tablespoon mustard seed

Use 4- to 6-inch pickling cucumbers. Cover the cucumbers, onions, salt, and ice with water; wait 2 hours. Drain/squeeze well. Mix cucumbers with the rest of the ingredients; cook for 10 minutes. JSP/RWB10(8OZ)10-15(16OZ)A.

A very popular hot cucumber-and-honey relish is Jamlady's Hot Beekeeper's Relish. Use a good beekeeper's raw clover-ginseng* (bees visit clover and ginseng blooms), light clover, or orange-blossom honey to make this relish. **The 5-star quality of this relish is directly related to the quality of the raw honey used.** Some people say, "Honey is honey!," but the proof is in the taste of the relish. Contact a state or local beekeeper's association to find raw honey for sale. A good raw honey from a qualified beekeeper will make an incredible, lip-smacking relish and may help some individuals with allergies.

Use raw honey as a topical dressing for wounds. (Moore, O.A. 2001. Systematic review of the use of honey as a wound dressing. BMC Complementary and Alternative Medicine 1:2). Quoting this study, **"Treatment with honey produced significantly more healing at seven days. At seven days, 58% (97/167) of patients were healed with honey, and 19% (29/151) with other treatments."** Sugar paste is successful in healing wounds. Moore says there is **"a**

lack of high-quality, comparative evidence for both conventional and unconventional treatments. It is difficult to see how the 21st century can be upon us without such evidence being available." Please see the index: contraception, scurvy, Chinese Red Yeast, agro-processing, and inedible-plant material.

Hot Beekeeper's Relish

8½ cups chopped Kirby cucumbers
6 cups chopped onions
1 large seeded, chopped bell pepper
½ cup salt
1 tray ice cubes
2 teaspoons mustard seed
2 teaspoons celery seed
4 cups clover-ginseng honey*
5 cups cider vinegar**
20 unseeded, chopped jalapeño peppers
5 hot finger peppers or Serrano peppers

Pick 4- to 6-inch Kirbys for this original Jamlady relish. Layer the chopped cucumbers, onions, bell peppers with salt and ice for 6 hours; drain/squeeze. Cook the spices, honey, and vinegar for 15 minutes. Add the hot peppers and cook for 10 minutes. Add the drained vegetables and cook 5 to 10 minutes. JSP/RWB10(8OZ)10-15(16OZ)A. pH = 3.5.

* See previous discussion on honey

** May substitute red wine vinegar

Left, *Hot Beekeeper's Relish;* right, *Maisy's Green Tomato Relish;* back, *Corn Relish.*

Classic Cucumber Relish

7 to 8 medium pickling cucumbers
4 cups chopped onions
2 chopped bell peppers
1 tablespoon salt
1 tray ice cubes
4½ cups red-wine vinegar*
2 cups sugar
1 teaspoon turmeric
⅛ teaspoon black pepper
2 teaspoons mustard seed

Wash the vegetables well. Processor-chop the cucumbers, onions, and peppers but don't over chop. Mix the salt, chopped vegetables, and ice cubes; wait 1-2 hours. Drain; squeeze out the excess liquid. Combine the vinegar, sugar, turmeric, pepper, mustard seed, and vegetables and cook for 5 minutes. JSP/RWB10(8OZ)10-15(16OZ)A.

* May substitue cider vinegar

Note: Please see the Linus Pauling Institute's Web site, Oregon State University, on the medicinal value of turmeric/curcumin, *Curcuma longa,* member of the ginger family.

Jamlady's Hot Honey Relish

7 cups diced baby zucchini*
3¾ cups chopped onions
2¼ cups white vinegar
1⅓ cups grated carrots
1 cup raw clover honey
¾ cup chopped Serrano peppers
¼ cup salt
1 tablespoon mustard seed
1 teaspoon celery seed
1 teaspoon turmeric

Cook all ingredients together for 15 to 20 minutes until tender-crisp. JSP/RWB10(8OZ)10-15(16OZ)A. pH = 3.91. DOB = 7/21/97.

* May substitute yellow squash (for beautiful results)

Jamlady Tip: Don't use huge, tough-skinned zucchini for relishes or pickles.

This zucchini relish may be made with various squash. Doris Schoonmaker's Zucchini Relish uses very little sugar, resulting in a healthful and "veggie-tasting" relish.

Doris Schoonmaker's Zucchini Relish

5 pounds chopped small zucchini*
6 large diced onions
½ cup salt
Cold water
2 cups white vinegar**
1 cup sugar
1 teaspoon dry mustard
2 teaspoons celery seed
½ teaspoon ground cinnamon
½ teaspoon ground nutmeg
½ teaspoon black pepper.
2-4 ounce jars chopped pimentos***

Salt the zucchini, raw peppers (if using***), and onions; cover with water. Refrigerate 4 to 8 hours. Drain, rinse, and drain/squeeze. Cook the squash with the vinegar, sugar, mustard, spices, and pimentos; stir well. Simmer; reduce to 3 quarts (20 minutes). JSP/RWB10(8OZ)12-15(16OZ)A. pH = 3.86.

* May substitute yellow or green zucchini or pan-pans

** May substitute cider vinegar or wine vinegar

*** May substitute 2 red sweet peppers

Golden Zucchini Relish

10 cups chopped golden zucchini*
3 chopped medium onions
4 chopped red sweet peppers
4-5 tablespoons pickling salt
1-2 trays ice cubes
2½ cups white vinegar**
6 cups sugar
1 tablespoon turmeric
2 tablespoons corn starch
2 tablespoons celery seed

Mix the zucchini, onions, peppers, salt, and ice cubes; wait 6 to 8 hours. Drain, rinse, drain again, and squeeze. Mix all ingredients together; simmer ½-hour. JSP/RWB10(8OZ)12-15(16OZ)A. **Good on brats, egg salad, or atop deviled eggs.**

* May substitute green zucchini
** May substitute white wine vinegar

The **carrot,** *Daucus carota var. sativus,* has been widely cultivated. Under cultivation, many new forms have emerged. **The carrot is actually a biennial, but it is usually grown as an annual.** Growing good carrots is an art and requires loose soil. One Kentucky family won "best of show" for their carrots grown in potting soil in 24-inch-deep deck containers (courier-journal.com 2001). Sow seeds in the early spring or late summer.

Speckled Horse Relish

24 cucumbers
4 red sweet peppers
4 yellow sweet peppers
4 small hot peppers
14 carrots
12 chopped onions
1 cup pickling salt
1-2 trays ice cubes
8 cups cider vinegar
4 cups sugar
1 tablespoon turmeric
1 tablespoon ground mustard
2 tablespoons celery seed
4 minced garlic cloves
1 cup grated horseradish root

For a smaller batch, see cup measurements below. Use peeled or unpeeled cucumbers; chop. Seed and chop the sweet peppers. Chop the hot peppers. Peel and grate the carrots. Mix the first 8 ingredients. Wait 12 hours and drain/squeeze. Cook the vinegar, sugar, spices, garlic, and horseradish for 3 minutes. Add the drained vegetables; cook 15 minutes. JSP/RWB10(8OZ)15(16OZ)A or cook 5 minutes longer and JS**R.** pH = 3.52 to 3.72. Add extra vinegar and sugar for batches 3.9 or higher.

For one-sixth the recipe, 2⅓ carrots (1 cup), 2 medium onions (1 to1¼ cups), 4 medium Kirby cucumbers (3 cups), ⅔ yellow pepper (⅔ cup), ⅔ red pepper (⅔ cup), ⅔ hot Serrano (⅔ cup), 3⅓ tablespoons salt, 1⅓ cup cider vinegar, 3½ tablespoons horseradish, and ½ teaspoon turmeric.

Putting Speckled Horse Relish into a canning jar.

Jamlady's Bunny Relish

5½ cups chopped zucchini
3 cups grated carrots
3 cups chopped onions
½ cup chopped green peppers
½ cup diced yellow banana peppers
½ cup chopped red peppers
⅕ cup salt
2¼ cups champagne vinegar*
¾ cup sugar
1 tablespoon celery seed

Seed the peppers. Cook all ingredients for 20 minutes. JSP/RWB10(8OZ)15(16OZ)A.
* May substitute 6-percent acidity vinegar or use ¼ cup more of 5-percent acidity vinegar

Corn, *Zea may* var. *rugosa,* is an annual plant growing 5 to 7 feet tall, with a central stalk surrounded by grasslike leaves and an edible grain found on its ears. These ears of corn contain white, yellow, or bi-colored kernels. **No recipe collection is complete without a good corn-relish recipe.**

Corn relish may be made from old corn, but age diminishes its quality. **The best corn relish is made from tender, mid-sized kernels.** Market patrons tend to gravitate to bi-colored corn relish because of the two-toned, visual effect, but any good-quality sweet corn can produce excellent corn relish.

Beekeeper's Corn and Pepper Relish

2 cups chopped bell peppers
8 cups steamed corn kernels
2 cups sliced celery
2 cups chopped onions
4 cups white vinegar*
1 cup light clover honey
2 tablespoons celery seed
1 tablespoon salt
1 tablespoon dry mustard
1 tablespoon mustard seed
¼ cup flour
Tomato meats** (optional)

Seed and chop the peppers. Mix all ingredients together, except the flour. Cook for 5 minutes. Mix some flour with a little vinegar, add, and cook 5 minutes. Side (slide the tomato meat into the jar so the meat is against the side of the glass and is visible) the filled jar with 1 to 2 drained, skinless/seedless tomato-meat accents. SP/RWB20(8OZ)20(16OZ)A.
* May substitute white wine vinegar
** See Hot Moroccan Relish for how to obtain tomato meats.

Variation: Hot Beekeeper's Corn Relish— Substitute some hot peppers for bell peppers, or slide two split Serrano peppers down the inside of each jar, adding 1 teaspoon vinegar and ½ teaspoon sugar per pint jar.

Ini Corn Relish*

6 cups steamed corn kernels
2 cups red or green bell peppers
2 cups vinegar
1 cup sugar
1 cup chopped baby zucchini
1 cup chopped celery
1 cup cauliflower flowerets
½ cup chopped onions
3-4 tablespoons flour
2 teaspoons salt
2 teaspoons dry mustard
2 teaspoons celery seed
¾ teaspoon turmeric

Heat all ingredients together (to a boil); cook 3 minutes. JSP/RWB20(8OZ)20(16OZ)A.

* **Note: The "ini" is inspired by the movie *Breaking Away!* "Ini food!"**

Variation: Hot Ini Corn Relish—Reduce the red or green bell peppers by the amount of hot pepper added.

Any corn relish recipe may be made with hot or sweet peppers, seeded or unseeded, and substituted in equal measure. For families requiring jars of mild, medium, and hot product, see Hot Beekeeper's Corn Relish above. Small, dried red piquins (find in Mexican food stores) may be used for heat. Different varieties of corn may be used for corn relish, but, for me, the variegated scarlet and yellow-orange varieties have produced good-looking but inferior-tasting corn relish.

Jamlady Tip: If you don't need corn cobs for the jake, use them to make **Corn Cob Jelly.** Boil 12 cobs in water for 20 minutes, strain off 3 cups corn cob juice, and boil it for 1 minute with 1¾ ounces powdered pectin. Add 4 cups sugar; boil 1 minute. Check the "set" on a frozen plate. JSP/RWB5-10A. Optional: Add 1 to 2 drops red or yellow food coloring. **Corn cob juice may be used in soups, and cobs may be tossed into myrtle ground coverings for increased mulch and for the squirrels.**

Jamlady and I have included three "Scoville-heat-adjusted" recipes, so **novice canners** can see the differences in the formulations. We know many new canners are afraid, and rightfully so, to make changes with low-acid vegetable recipes. For this reason, Jamlady has printed all five versions: extra hot, hot, medium hot, mildly hot, and not hot.

CUSTOMIZED OR SCOVILLIAN CORN RELISH

Jamlady's corn relish replaces the traditional ingredient of cabbage with cauliflower, which enhances product flavor and clarity. These recipes may be cut ½, ¼, or ⅛, but just don't make any math mistakes! In these corn relish recipes, do not increase the vegetables or decrease the sugar, salt, or vinegar. If pepper accents will be added or a lower pH is desired, add ½ cup extra vinegar and ¼ cup sugar to compensate for the added side-pepper accents (1-2 per pepper on the inside side glass wall of each jar). Steam the corn for about 4 to 5 minutes and cut it from the cob. Mix all ingredients together, except the accents (tomato meats and side peppers), and cook for 5 minutes. JSP/RWB20(8OZ)(16OZ)A. pH = 4.20

Ingredients	Extra Hot	Hot	Medium Hot	Mildly Hot	Not Hot
Corn kernels	32 cups	16 cups	15 cups	15 cups	15 cups
5-percent vinegar	11 cups	6 cups	5½ cups	5½ cups	5½ cups
Chopped green bell peppers	5 cups	2½ cups	4½ cups multi-colored	4½ cups	4½ cups
Sliced celery	6½ cups	3¼ cups	2 cups	2 cups	2 cups
Chopped cauliflower	6 cups	3 cups	3 cups	3 cups	2¾ cups
Sugar	5 cups	2¾ cups	2½ cups	2½ cups	2½ cups
Chopped onion	4 cups	2 cups	2 cups	2 cups	2¼ cups
Chopped jalapeño or Serrano peppers	3 cups	½ cup	1 cup	½ cup	—
Red hot finger peppers or Thai peppers	1 cup	1 cup	—	—	—
Flour mixed with enough vinegar to make a paste (add at the end)	¾ cup	⅜ cup	⅜ cup	⅜ cup	⅜ cup
Red pepper accents (sweet or hot) in each jar	sweet or hot	sweet or hot	sweet	sweet	sweet
Dry mustard	3½ tbsp	2 tbsp	1¾ tbsp	1¾ tbsp	1¾ tbsp
Pickling salt	3 tbsp	1½ tbsp	1½ tbsp	1½ tbsp	1½ tbsp
Celery seed	3 tbsp	1¾ tbsp	1¾ tbsp	1¾ tbsp	1¾ tbsp
Turmeric	1⅓ tbsp	2 tsp	2 tsp	2 tsp	2 tsp

Caution: Measure exactly and increase the sugar, vinegar, and salt, proportionately if you want a larger margin of error and are not using a pH meter. Do not alter these recipes in anyway unless you fully understand the chemistry and consequences of inadequate acidification of low-acid vegetables. Use a check-off sheet for ingredients added to the recipe. Double check any math computations made.

The following recipe may be canned without the sugar, but please keep the canned product in the refrigerator and label it **"Keep Refrigerated."** If you do not can the product, electing to refrigerate the corn relish instead, cook the corn relish for 15 minutes or so and allow it to cool some. Then stir in the sweetener (aspartame or agave) and refrigerate. Some of the many objections to aspartame have to do with aspartame and high heat. I do not recommend artificial sweeteners, but I recognize some people wish to use them. For the canned no-sugar corn relish, the corn relish should be canned without the aspartame or agave, adding the chosen sweetener at serving time (in liquid form).

Fresh corn's pH is between 5.90 and 7.30. **Jamlady and I recommend this next "no-sugar-added" corn relish be refrigerated, even if canned. Label the relish on the top and side—"Keep Refrigerated." The pH for this completed corn relish measures under 4.0.**

Jamlady Tip: All canned foods will keep better if refrigerated or kept in a cool and dark environment. Many smart canners keep their canned goods in second and third refrigerators or in a cool root cellar.

"No-Sugar-Added" Corn Relish

18 cups cooked corn kernels
6 cups sweet green peppers
6½ cups vinegar
5 cups sliced celery
2 cups cauliflower flowerets
1½ cups chopped onions
¾ cup flour
2 tablespoons salt
2 tablespoons dry mustard
2 tablespoons celery seed
2 tablespoons turmeric
45 packets aspartame (or liquid aspartame) or agave syrup to taste.

Cook all ingredients, except the sweetener. Add the packet or liquid aspartame when the product is almost cool. **JSR** or can without the sweetener, adding it later. The completed pH must be 4.0 or under if the canned jars are to be shelf-stable (stored above 40 degrees F). **The approximate pH of this recipe, as given, is around 3.97. Those wishing to change corn relish recipes should purchase a pH meter and use it.**

Consider what a few cooks with pH meters can do for the field of home canning. Stop wondering if a substitution is safe. If you tested it, you know it is safe. Experiment with a pH meter. Experiment with different sweeteners, and measure their impact on overall product pH. Maple syrup, for example, will elevate product pH. Test recipes made with agave (please see agave elsewhere). Refrigerate all products over 4.0 or increase the vinegar to decrease the pH prior to canning.

Medium-Hot Garden Corn Relish

6 cups chopped red or green bell peppers
20 cups steamed corn kernels
7½ cups red or white wine vinegar
5 cups sliced celery
3¾ cups sugar
2½ cups diced onions
2 cups grated carrots
1 cup sliced summer squash
1 cup chopped jalapeño peppers
¾ cup white flour
2½ tablespoons dry mustard
2 tablespoons turmeric
2 tablespoons celery seed
1½ tablespoons salt
5 minced garlic cloves

Make a full or quarter batch from dinner's left over sweet corn. Seed the red or green bell peppers. Mix with the other ingredients. Cook until hot. JSP/RWB20(8OZ)(16OZ)A, or cook 10 to 15 minutes and JS**R.**

FRUIT RELISHES

There is a very fine line between fruit relish and chutney. By Jamlady's definition, a sweet-sour with a kicker is chutney, and fruit relish would fall into that same category unless there were no spices at all. Relish, to Jamlady's standard, implies a coarse-ground product, and chutney usually has larger pieces but not always. There are recipes for apple relish using larger pieces of apple or quartered and peeled apples, which are usually pickled with spiced sweet-sour syrup. **Conclusion: The definitive line between fruit relish and chutney often is gray.**

Tart Apple Relish

1 quart tart apples
3 quarts water
1 teaspoon ascorbic-acid crystals
1 1/4 cups vinegar
1 cup sugar
1/2 cup corn syrup
5/8 cup water
1 1/2 teaspoons whole clove
1 1/2 teaspoons whole allspice
2 cinnamon sticks or one drop oil of cinnamon

Peel and dice, slice or quarter* tart apples. Measure approximately 1 quart apples; soak them in 3 quarts water plus 1 teaspoon ascorbic-acid crystals. Boil 1 1/4 cups vinegar, 1 cup sugar, 1/2 cup corn syrup, 5/8 cup water, 1 1/2 teaspoons whole clove, 1 1/2 teaspoons whole allspice, and 2 cinnamon sticks or drop of oil of cinnamon (add the oil of cinnamon drop (very potent) to part of the syrup and add back in gradually, to taste). Drain the apples and add to the mixture; cook for 2 minutes. JSP/RWB10(4OZ)15(16OZ)A.
* 20 to 25(16OZ) apple quarters (by size)

A recipe for peach and pepper relish is shown in a well-known pickling book. It is made much like pepper hash with hot water poured over 6 sweet and 6 hot peppers, and then drained. Six peaches or nectarines, 3 lemons (juice, plus cook it with rind, and then remove the rind), 6 cups sugar, and 2 cups cider vinegar are added. If you look at Jamlady's peach chutney recipe and other chutney recipes, you will see very little difference in the formulation of many of these fruit relishes and fruit chutneys.

Is this next recipe relish or chutney? The answer probably depends on the size of the pieces and the ratio of peppers to fruits! Comparing this recipe to Spicy Pear Chutney, there are many peppers in this relish and, classically, fewer peppers in pear chutney. There are no raisins either. **This recipe could just as well be named a pepper and pear chutney!** There is a kicker, the hot peppers! What do you think? Jamlady says the answer is not as important as the analysis! Sagacious canners always analyze recipes! Look at the Fall Chutney recipe; see what you think then?

Spicy Winter-Pear Relish

4 cups sugar
2 tablespoons turmeric
4 tablespoons pickling salt
1/3 cup dry mustard
6 cups white wine vinegar
15 cups peeled/chopped winter pears
5 pounds peeled/chopped onions
7 seeded/chopped sweet green peppers
8 seeded/chopped sweet red peppers
8 seeded/unseeded small hot peppers

Cook the sugar, turmeric, salt, mustard, and vinegar together for 2 minutes. Add the pears and vegetables; cook 25 to 30 minutes until thick. JSP/RWB12(4OZ)15(8OZ)15(16OZ)A.

Variation: Spicy Apple Relish or Spicy Pome Relish—Make with apples or ½ apples and ½ pears.

Italian Mostardi di Cremona is a fruit chili sauce for meats, fish, cottage cheese, sharp cheeses, curries, and fried vegetables. Try some on meatloaf or in deli-meat rolls.

Italian Mostardi di Cremona

8 to 10 medium tomatoes
6-7 large peaches
6 large Bartlett or d'Anjou pears
2 red or green sweet peppers
1½ large sweet Texas onions
1½ cups sugar
3 cups white wine vinegar
1-1½ tablespoons salt
½ teaspoon ground true cinnamon
1 true cinnamon stick, per jar (optional)
½ teaspoon clove
¼ teaspoon ground cayenne*
A pinch ascorbic acid**

Plunge the tomatoes in boiling-hot water for 1 minute; then cold. Discard the skins, juice, and seeds; retain the tomato meats. Peel, core, and fine or coarse chop the other fruits and vegetables. Add the rest of the ingredients; cook until thick. JSP/RWB10(8OZ)15(16OZ)A.

* May substitute minced hot pepper

** For "working the fruit," to prevent oxidation

Banana Relish

2 cups cider vinegar
½ cup white sugar, brown sugar, or honey
1 tablespoon whole clove
4 cinnamon sticks
1 teaspoon whole allspice
1-2 pieces broken nutmeg
4 pounds bananas

Heat 2 cups cider vinegar; ½ cup white sugar, brown sugar, or honey; and a spice bag (1 tablespoon whole clove, 4 cinnamon sticks, 1 teaspoon whole allspice, and 1 to 2 pieces broken nutmeg) for syrup. Peel, slice, and cook 4 pounds bananas in the syrup for 1 minute. Jar the banana pieces and pour the syrup over. Optional: add ¼ cup raisins, using ⅗ cup sugar and 2½ cups vinegar instead of ½ cup sugar and 2 cups cider vinegar. JSP/RWB12(8OZ)15(16OZ)A.

Unpeeled Apple Relish

5 small onions (3-3½ cups)
2-3 hot peppers
1 tablespoon salt
2 cups boiling water
5½ to 6 pounds organic apples
4 cups cider vinegar
1 cup sugar
1 tablespoon cloves
1 cinnamon stick

Peel 5 small onions. Processor chop the onions and 2 to 3 hot peppers. Add 1 tablespoon salt; wait 10 minutes. Pour 2 cups boiling-hot water over the mixture. Wait 2 minutes; drain. Add 5½ to 6 pounds organic apples (not waxed, not-peeled but cored and chopped). Cook the apples, drained onions and peppers, 4 cups cider vinegar, 1 cup sugar, and the spice bag (1 tablespoon cloves and 1 cinnamon stick) for 10 minutes. Wait 5 minutes; discard the spice bag. JSP/RWB10(8OZ)15(16OZ)A.

Sweet Crab Apple Relish

- 7 pounds prepared crab apples*
- 1 cup diced Clementine fruit
- 4 cups light brown sugar
- 2 cups cider vinegar or wine vinegar
- 1 pound golden raisins
- 1 pound dried currants
- 1 tablespoon whole clove
- 1 tablespoon ground nutmeg
- 2 cinnamon sticks

Peel and core the apples. Use only Clementine fruit, minus the pips, rind, and partitions. Cook all ingredients for 10 minutes. Break a piece of cinnamon stick for each jar. JSP/RWB10(8OZ)15(16OZ)A. Good with pork chops and Indian food.

* **May substitute prepared apples**

Brussels Sprouts, *Brassica oleracea,* are native to Belgium and require a long growing season. Brussels sprouts may be pickled alone or with other vegetables, but Jamlady has never seen Brussels sprouts used in a relish before. This is a recipe I made just to do it, but surprisingly, many market patrons and friends liked it and asked for it again. **Red radish relish** and **celery relish** were two other recipes Jamlady and I tried, but nobody thought much of them. Processed radishes lose their red color and taste. Celery does not do well alone.

Hot Brussels Sprout Relish

- 3 pounds chopped Brussels sprouts
- 6 chopped medium onions
- 3 cups seeded/chopped bell peppers
- ½ cup salt
- 1 tablespoon clove
- 1 tablespoon allspice
- 1 cinnamon stick
- 4 cups red wine vinegar (Marconi)
- 4 tablespoons mustard seed
- 3 tablespoons celery seed
- 3 cups light, raw clover honey
- 2 cups chopped jalapeño peppers

Mix the chopped Brussels sprouts, onions, and bell peppers with salt. Wait 3 hours; drain/squeeze. Boil the spice bag (clove, allspice, and cinnamon stick) in the vinegar with the mustard and celery seed for 10 minutes; add the honey. Add the jalapeños to the hot vinegar; cook for 5 minutes. Add the drained/squeezed vegetables and cook for 15 to 20 minutes. JSP/RWB15(8OZ)20(16OZ)A. (A = Adjust processing time for high altitudes). Use on brats and with Indian curries!

Beet and Cabbage Relish

4 cups coarsely grated raw beets
2-3 tablespoons grated horseradish root
6 cups coarsely chopped cabbage
2 cups coarsely chopped, peeled onions
2 cups sugar
2 cups red wine vinegar*
1 tablespoon salt

Peel the raw beets and horseradish root; grate them in a food processor. Chop the cabbage and peeled onions. Cook all ingredients for 20 minutes or until thick. JSP/RWB20(8OZ)(16OZ)A. Serve with cold cuts, fish, poultry, or fried vegetables.

* Marconi brand is recommended.

Step 1: *Vegetables for making Beet and Cabbage Relish.*

Step 2: *Prepared ingredients for the Beet and Cabbage Relish.*

Step 3: *Prepared beets, cabbage, onions, and horseradish in a stainless steel pan.*

Step 4: *Adding the sugar and vinegar to the prepared vegetables.*

Step 5: *Cook the relish until thick.*

Step 6: *Fill the 8-ounce jar, using a canning funnel and ladle.*

Step 7: *Leave ½ inch from the top. Wipe the rim clean, place the sterile lid, and screw down the ring.*

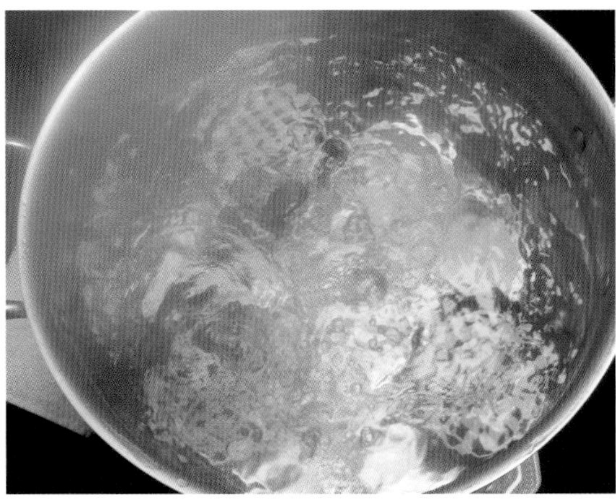

Step 8: *Place the jars in a canner. Cover the jars with water equal to the temperature of the jars. Heat to a rolling boil. Time the RWB for 20 minutes.*

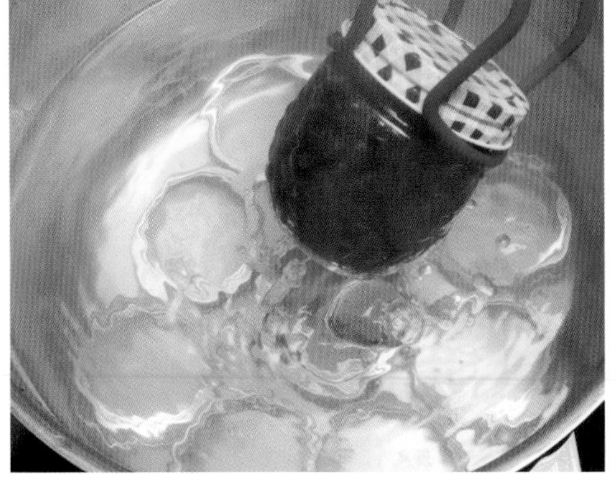

Step 9: *After 20 minutes, remove the jars from the canner with tongs.*

Step 10: *Set the hot jars on a clean, dry towel. Keep jars separated and not touching one another.*

Step 11: *Do not disturb jars until cool. A clicking sound and a depression in lid will announce the seal.*

Step 12: *Completed beet and cabbage relish displayed on a large deli-meat and jardinière platter.*

Vidalia Onion Relish

11½ cups diced Vidalia onions (8)
½ cup chopped red peppers
¼ cup salt
½ teaspoon turmeric
1 teaspoon mustard seed
2 teaspoons pickling spice
2 cups cider vinegar
2½ cups sugar

Mix the onions, peppers, and salt. Wait 40 minutes; drain/squeeze. Cook the turmeric, mustard seed, pickling spice, and vinegar for 10 minutes and cool, strain, and discard the spices. Cook the spiced vinegar, sugar, and drained vegetables until thick. JSP/RWB10(8OZ)15(16OZ)A.

Variation in technique: Eliminate the salt brining. Instead, pour hot water over the peppers and onions and drain/squeeze (like the Pepper Hash recipe). Proceed with the recipe, adding 1 tablespoon salt.

Pickles Du Jour

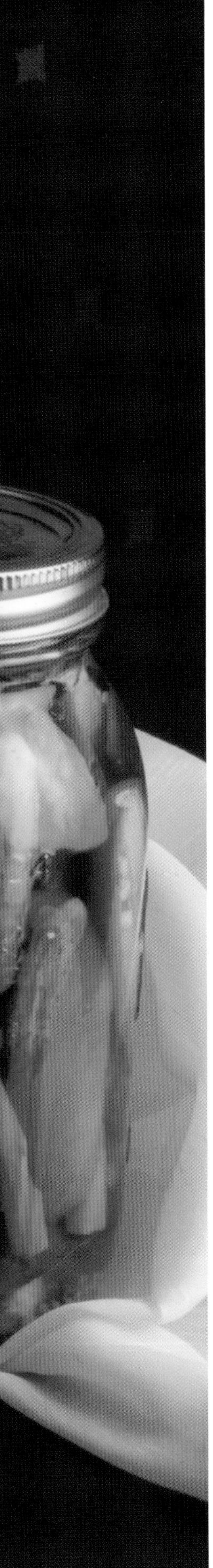

Chapter 4
Pickles

A pickle is a vegetable or fruit preserved in an acid. This acid might be lactic acid, lemon or lime juice, or vinegar. Meat may also be pickled. A fruit or vegetable may be pickled with only salt, but ultimately, the released water and the sugar from the fruit or vegetable changes into lactic acid, which becomes the preserver. Readers may not think of carrots, zucchini, beets, or peaches as appropriate vegetables or fruits for pickling, but they do become pickles when placed in acidic brine, with or without a sweetener. I am always amused when a market patron asks, "Where are the pickles?" Technically, one-half the inventory is pickles. Of course, I know buyers are usually referring to cucumber pickles.

Jamlady usually makes hermetically sealed pickles for market. This means Jamlady and I have not made a lot of crock pickles. Well-made crock pickles should not be classified with canned pickles. They are two different products. **Fermented pickles produce their own preserving acids over time, and fresh-pack or quick-process pickles are made with the addition of an acid, not by fermentation. Fermented pickles may also be canned.** Canned lime pickles and bread-and-butters are extremely popular at market as are canned dills. Still, some people prefer crock-fermented pickles, depending on what they "were raised-up on." In comparison to a canned pickle, some people think crock pickles are inconvenient. Many patrons want shelf-stable pickles for gifts. A hermetically sealed product is more convenient, efficient, and reliably uncontaminated. Jamlady and I will give you some recipes for crock-fermented pickles, canned pickles, and fresh refrigerator pickles. Personally, we love all kinds of pickles, but "quickles," quick-process, or zip-lock bag pickles are probably the best recipes for beginners.

The most popular market pickle is the bread-and-butter pickle. It's hard to keep **Aunt Frances Basten's Bread and Butter Pickles** around because so many people like them. These B&Bs are made with cucumbers and are iced during the brining stage. Uniced B&Bs are inferior to iced pickles. If you have extra refrigerator space, keep B&Bs refrigerated even after they are processed and sealed.

Make Aunt Frances' pickle with medium-sized cucumbers and no peppers. There should be no hard cucumber seeds in the final product. The completed color of this northern B&B pickle is usually lighter than a southern version with peppers.

Aunt Frances Basten's Bread and Butter Pickles (Kingston, New York)

4 quarts thinly sliced cucumbers
1/3 cup salt
3-4 cups thinly sliced onions (8)
4 trays ice cubes (non-hard water)
4 cups sugar
1/2 teaspoon turmeric
1 teaspoon celery seed
2 tablespoons mustard seed
2 3/4 cups vinegar*

Wash and scrub 5- to 6-inch pickling cucumbers. Salt the sliced cucumbers, onions, and ice cubes. Cover and weight down for 3 to 6 hours; drain/squeeze well. Mix the sugar, spices, and vinegar; boil for 30 seconds. Add the cucumber mixture; cook for 30 seconds. JSP/RWB10(16OZ)**R**A. **R** is optional, but recommended. Depending on the altitude, jars may need longer processing times, or refrigerate the pickles. pH = 3.5 to 4.0.

Variation: Lemon Bread and Butter Pickles—Lemon cucumbers make gorgeous B&B pickles.

Variation: Variegated Bread and Butter Pickles—Use 1/2 lemon cucumbers and 1/2 green cucumbers.

Variation: Curry Bread and Butter Pickles—No turmeric, but add 1 teaspoon curry powder. A less-sweet **Curry Bread and Butter Pickle** may be made with cucumbers but no onions. Brine 12 thinly sliced medium cucumbers for 4 to 6 hours with 1/4 cup salt and 4 trays ice cubes; drain/squeeze well. Mix 1/2 teaspoon curry powder, 1 1/4 cups vinegar, 1 1/4 cups sugar, 2 tablespoons mustard seed, and 2 teaspoons celery seed; boil. Add the drained cucumbers; heat to boiling and JSP/RWB10(16OZ)A. **Refrigeration is recommended for freshness and to maintain the color. This product is shelf-stable.**

Note: *In a canning recipe, it is better to overmeasure than undermeasure the vinegar.

In an effort to make better B&Bs than my Aunt Frances, I have made a lot of B&B pickles. **This pickle is an Aunt Frances B&B made with maple syrup instead of sugar:** 5 cups maple syrup to 2 3/4 cups vinegar with 16 cups cucumbers and 4 cups onions. Tastes good! **The only problem with the completed recipe is that it has an excessive pH of approximately 4.46.** This pickle may be made and refrigerated, but it is unsafe to can for the shelf. **What if you have a little more cucumbers in the recipe and a little less vinegar? This recipe illustrates why you cannot substitute maple syrup for sugar without testing.** For this same recipe, I doubled the vinegar to 5 1/2 cups, and the pickle was ground up and tested again. The pH with 5 1/2 cups vinegar was 4.25. Again, I added 2 3/4 cups vinegar, or 3 times the original amount of vinegar in the recipe, and it took the pH down to 4.10. Clearly, if you reduce the maple syrup and increase the vinegar, you will have a product that tastes okay, may be canned safely, and is shelf-stable. **Test your final maple-syrup pickle with a pH meter and adjust the acid level, or don't can it for the shelf.**

Many market patrons have indicated a preference for pickles made with "natural" sugars like maple syrup. The maple-syrup flavor is deliciously delicate. Considering the pH and cost issues, I recommend honey for a pickle made without sugar, or substitute only one-quarter of the sugar with maple syrup, increase the vinegar, and test the batch. **B&B pickles may be sweetened with honey or some other natural sweeteners like agave or brown rice syrup (see zucchini quickles).** Use a pH meter to check your honey pickles' pH or consult *Stocking Up*, by Carol Hupping (174), which uses 5 cups vinegar to 2 cups honey with 30 cucumbers and 10 onions. I have not tested this recipe but assume the author is credible.

Canners need to be careful and informed if they can anything using maple syrup. Just remember, when you see only 1 cup of maple syrup in Apple-and-Maple Preserves, in *The Jamlady Cookbook* (161), there is one or more reasons why. **The pH of maple syrup is 6.5 to 7.0! Do not can with maple syrup without first measuring the product's pH, or store it in the refrigerator.**

Left to right: *Hot Beekeeper's Bread and Butter Pickles and Aunt Frances' Bread and Butter Pickles.*

Maple Syrup Bread and Butter Pickles—Test Recipe

16 cups thinly sliced cucumbers*
1/3 cup salt
3-4 cups thinly sliced onions
2 or more ice cube trays**
5 cups Grade A medium amber maple syrup
2 tablespoons mustard seed
1 teaspoon celery seed
1/2 teaspoon turmeric
2 3/4 cups vinegar***

Do not can this recipe without first reading all of the instructions carefully. Wash and scrub 5- to 6-inch pickling cucumbers. Salt the sliced cucumbers, onions, and ice cubes. Cover, weight down for 3 to 6 hours, and drain/squeeze well. Boil the maple syrup, spices, and vinegar for 30 seconds. Add the cucumber mixture; **test the pH.** JSP/RWB10(16OZ)15(32OZ)**RA**. **R is optional for a pH of 4.25 or lower.**

* Recipe may be halved.
** Pickles need to be iced. More ice is needed in hot weather.
*** 2 3/4 cups vinegar equals a pH of 4.46, which may not be canned (refrigerate only) or use 5 1/2 cups vinegar for a pH of 4.25. Test and verify the pH.

Caution: A search for published maple-syrup-sweetened pickles netted two. If you make these recipes, test them or keep them refrigerated. ***Approach recipes like these cited below with skepticism. The size of the pepper and onions, as given, are not measured and could dramatically affect this recipe's pH.**

*Edna Smith Berquist's *The High Maples Farm Cookbook* (1971, 397-398) has a recipe for Maple Bread and Butter Pickles: 8 cups cucumbers, 1 pepper, 3 onions, 1/4 cup salt, 2 cups cider vinegar, 1 cup sugar, 1 cup maple syrup, 1/2 teaspoon turmeric, 1/4 teaspoon celery seed, and 1 tablespoon mustard seed. Mary Pearl's *Vermont Maple Recipes* (1952, 72) are made with all maple syrup and no sugar. Both publications are at the Conrad Hilton Library in Hyde Park, New York.

When we tested the Berquist recipe, the pH for this pickle was in the 3.75 to 3.85 range. We used a small pepper and 2-inch diameter onions for this Berquist recipe.

Probably few people look closely at formulations for B&B pickles. Over the years, I have observed Canadian B&B makers using little or no turmeric in their B&B's. New Englanders, as exemplified by Aunt Frances' B&Bs, use a little turmeric. Southern Illinois and Missouri picklers use even more turmeric. Finally, as seen in the terrific Southern B&Bs, there is more turmeric, cinnamon instead of mustard, and green peppers to darken and spice the pickle. **Jamlady's generalization is based on her observations: "the warmer the climate, the warmer the B&B pickle looks and tastes."**

This next five-star pickle is a variation of Hot Beekeeper's Relish, except the cucumbers and onions are sliced and turmeric is added. Both recipes are original Jamlady recipes.

Hot Beekeeper's Bread and Butter Pickles

11 1/2 cups sliced cucumbers
3 cups sliced sweet onions
1/2 cup salt
1 tray ice cubes
5 cups cider vinegar
4 cups clover-ginseng honey*
25 sliced jalapeño peppers
2 teaspoons mustard seed
2 teaspoons celery seed
1 teaspoon turmeric

Weep the pickling cucumbers and onions with salt and ice for 3 to 4 hours; drain/squeeze. Boil the cider vinegar, honey, jalapeño peppers, and spices for 5 minutes. Add the drained/squeezed cucumbers and onions. JSP/RWB10(8OZ)15(16OZ)20(32OZ)A.

* May substitute other honey

Terrific Southern Bread N' Butter Pickles

24 cups sliced cucumbers*
7 sliced medium onions
1 1/2 cups salt
1 tray ice cubes
9 cups sugar
6 1/4 cups cider vinegar
10 small bell peppers
2 1/2 tablespoons celery seed
2 tablespoons turmeric
6 true cinnamon sticks

Mix the thinly sliced cucumbers and onions with the salt and ice for 12 hours; drain/squeeze. Slice and seed the peppers. Cook the sugar, cider vinegar, bell peppers, celery seed, turmeric, and

true cinnamon sticks for 5 minutes. Add the drained vegetables; cook for 5 minutes. JSP/RWB10(8OZ)15(16OZ)15(32OZ)A.
* Small batch = 1/4 recipe.

Bread-and-butter pickles may be made from zucchini. Jamlady and I have made many recipes for zucchini B&B pickles. Some are a disappointment but not these. Intially, only the brown-rice-syrup pickles failed to wow us, but they tasted twice as good on day two as day one—less sweet and tarter. **A discussion about these different sweeteners has been included, because patrons often ask if they can use brown rice syrup or honey in pickling.** Well you can, but the product sweetened with honey or brown rice syrup may not win a taste test, and the product pH must be well under 4.6 for a canned shelf-stable product. The big surprise was how great agave tasted—better or as good as cane sugar.

Our **zucchini bread-and-butter quickles**' recipe is great for utilizing a bumper crop of zucchini. I investigated three different natural sweeteners: Aunt Patty's Agave Syrup, Lundberg's Sweet Dreams Brown Rice Syrup, and raw honey. For two trials, the pH of the **Agave Quickles** with Zucchini and Red Onion **tested 3.67 and 3.71.** The **Brown Rice Quickles tested 3.70,** and the **Honey Quickles tested 3.77.** With pH numbers this low, canning these pickles is not a problem, except the crunch and consistency may change some. Agave was the best of the three. These pickles lasted well in the refrigerator, so one may not be motivated to can them. **These B&Bs take very little total time to make, excluding the overnight salting time.** Make some quickles and use them for wonderful hostess gifts.

Another variation on this pickle, **Jelly Quickles,** uses **melted-down hot-pepper jelly instead of the sugar.** Jamlady and I know creative canners will be trying all sorts of jellies in other pickle recipes after seeing it here. Take a look at the 2005 winning pickle for the International Pickle Festival on page 91. Does it look like there might be jelly in this secret formulation? I don't know, but it looked and tasted like there might be. More experimentation and research needs to be done in both the area of using jams in pickles and relishes and in using different natural sweeteners.

Zucchini Bread and Butter Pickles

8 cups thinly sliced zucchini
1 1/2 cups thinly sliced onions
1/4 cup pickling salt
1-2 trays ice water
2 cups cider vinegar*
1 1/2 cups sugar
1 cup light corn syrup
1 tablespoon mustard seed
1 1/4 teaspoons celery seed
1 teaspoon turmeric
1/4 teaspoon dry mustard

Use 7-inch zucchini and small onions. For 2 hours, weep the zucchini, onions, salt, and ice water to cover. Drain, rinse, and drain/squeeze again. Boil the cider vinegar, sugar, corn syrup, mustard seed, celery seed, turmeric, and dry mustard for 5 minutes; add the drained vegetables and boil 3 minutes. JSP/RWB10(8OZ)10-12(16OZ)A.
* May substitute white wine vinegar

Jamlady's Mixed Squash Pickles

2 quarts sliced squash
2 medium onions
1 tray ice cubes
1/4 cup pickling salt
2 cups sugar
2 cups vinegar
2 teaspoons celery seed
1 teaspoon mustard seed
1 1/2 teaspoons dry mustard seed
1/4 teaspoon fennel seed
20 fresh oregano leaves
1 teaspoon turmeric

Use smaller unpeeled zucchini, pan pans, and/or yellow crookneck squash. Thinly slice the onions. Mix the squash, onions, ice, and salt in a stainless steel pot (conducts the cold) overnight. Rinse/drain twice. Rinse; drain/squeeze. Cook the sugar, vinegar, and spices and mix with the drained vegetables; cook for 5 minutes. JSP/RWB10(8OZ)10-12(16OZ)15-18(32OZ)A.

A Hawaiian cook sent me an interesting chayote squash (vegetable pear, mirliton, christophene, pipinolas, or *Sechlum edule*) recipe—stating, "It grows easily here. Most of the cultures steam or stew it. It has stickiness to the cut sides; we usually wear gloves to cut it up." **Pickled Pipinolas or Chayote Squash Pickles:** Brine one gallon unpeeled sliced pipinolas in 1/2 cup salt and ice cubes for 2 to 3 hours; drain. Boil 4 cups cider vinegar, 5 cups sugar, 2 teaspoons celery seed, 2 teaspoons mustard seed, 2 teaspoons turmeric, 6 whole clove, and add in the drained chayote slices. Cook for several minutes until all is thoroughly heated. Pour into sterile jars and process in a RWB for 15 to 20 minutes or JSR.

For more information on preserving with chayote, see **Chayote and Pear Relish** at www.uga.edu/nchfp/how/can_06/chayote_pear_relish.html.

Michael Pechman's Zucchini Quickles

3-4 pounds zucchini
1/2-3/4 pound white onions
1/4 cup pickling salt
1 quart cider vinegar*
3 1/4 cups brown sugar**
4 teaspoons mustard seed
1 1/2 teaspoons celery seed
1 teaspoon turmeric

Processor-slice the zucchini and onions or hand cut to 1/4 inch thick. Add the salt; weep the vegetables for 6 to 8 hours in a cool place. Rinse; drain well. Boil the cider vinegar, sugar (or other sweetener), mustard seed, celery seed, and turmeric, and pour over the drained zucchini and onions. Mix well. Refrigerate or can as other B&Bs.

* May substitute any type 5-percent vinegar

** May substitute white sugar, prepared jelly, agave (see other agave cite), or other sweetener like white grape juice concentrate. Sweeten with honey to taste.

Variation: Jamlady's Jelly Quickles—To add heat and fruit flavor to a pickle or relish, add hot pepper jelly or fruit jelly to the pickle recipe. Since the hot peppers in the pepper jelly have already been acidified for canning, this is especially useful when you don't have a pH meter. Just melt the prepared jelly with the receiving recipe's vinegar and complete the batch. **Here are three options:** melt the pepper jelly into an unsweetened pickle recipe, add it to any existing recipe without reducing the sugar in the recipe, or reduce the sugar in the existing recipe and keep the pickle refrigerated. The fourth option is to do as you like, but only can product with a pH of 4.2. or less. And, of course, the pickle still needs to taste good.

Michael Pechman's Zucchini Quickles—Blue-ribbon winner at the 2005 International Pickle Festival, Rosendale, New York.

Variation: Jamlady's Small-Batch Zucchini Quickles with Agave or Small-Batch Cucumber Quickles with Agave—6 ounces processor-sliced zucchini (1 medium zucchini or cucumber), 4 ounces sliced red onions, 1 tablespoon salt, and 1 tray ice cubes. Combine the sliced zucchini or cucumbers, onions, salt, and ice cubes in a bowl. Mix, cover, and weep for 6 to 12 hours; drain/squeeze. Boil ¼ cup red wine vinegar, ⅛ cup *Aunt Patty's Agave Syrup, ¼ teaspoon celery seed, ¼ teaspoon mustard seed, ¼ teaspoon turmeric; add the drained zucchini mixture. Stir and wait 1 minute. Place the pickles in a sterilized pint jar, cover, and refrigerate; makes 1 cup (pH = 3.70). JSP/RWB if you like. **Caution: *Aunt Patty's Agave Syrup is recommended, as all agave syrups may not have the same pH.**

Variation: Jamlady's Original Zucchini Quickles with Rice-Syrup—Use the same recipe as above only substitute ⅛ cup Lundberg's Sweet Dreams Brown Rice Syrup for the agave syrup. pH = 3.70. **Note:** One of the advantages of agave, rice syrup, and honey in pickles is they tend to thicken the chilled product naturally. In both recipes, we used red onion for color, but regular onion may be used. Any 5-percent vinegar may be used. Of the three variation of quickles made with alternative sweeteners, we deemed agave the best, honey second, and brown rice syrup third. All three sweeteners made acceptable pickles.

Pickled beets, B&B pickles, corn relish, and berry jams form the mainstay of any farmers' market. Some patrons believe a "proper" pickled beet should not be spiced. A handwritten recipe for **"small beet pickles"** was found in the back of the Conrad Hilton Library's 1894 copy of *Woman's Exchange Cookbook:* **"2 cups vinegar, 1 cup water, 1 cup sugar—Mrs. Milo Beau."** Some pickled beet recipes use spices, different cultivars, different vinegars, horseradishes, or hot peppers. One vendor makes them with rosemary, but I don't prefer them that way.

Some patrons believe pickled beets were not "spiced-up" in the "good old days." Although a recipe for **Beet-Root Pickles,** in *Preserving, Pickling, and Canning Fruit Manual,* demonstrates otherwise (Peterson, M. 1869, 21).

> **Beet-Root Pickles**—Boil the root till tender; then peel it, and (if agreeable), cut it into shapes; pour over it a hot pickle of white vinegar, a little ginger, pepper and horse-radish sliced.

The new processing times for beets have been greatly extended by our United States canning experts. It is better to partly cook the beets and peel them, so processing for 35 minutes will not result in a mushy pickle. Heat penetration studies evidently found that more processing time was needed, especially for flat, sliced beets. Do not stack slices neatly. A large solid mass of neatly stacked beets will not distribute heat evenly; alternate slices with some chunks.

Traditional Pickled Beets

3 quarts prepared beet pieces
3½ cups white vinegar*
2 cups sugar
1½ cups water
2 cinnamon sticks
1 tablespoon whole allspice
1½ teaspoons salt

Use any variety or shape of beet. Slip the skins off cooked beets or, preferably, partially cook the beets and peel. Fill the jar with irregular pieces or baby whole beets. Boil the vinegar, sugar, water, cinnamon, allspice, and salt for 15 minutes; pour over the beets. JSP/RWB35(16OZ)35-40**(32OZ)A.
* May substitute red wine vinegar
** Old times were about 20 to 25 minutes; new times are 35-40 minutes. Consult the USDA for current recommended times, as these times often change.

Variation: Hot Pickled Beets—Eliminate the cinnamon stick and allspice; add a hot pepper and optional spice.

Variation: Shredded Pickled Beets or **Shredded Mixed Pickles**—Peel the beets, processor-shred the raw beets; cook them in hot, spiced, or plain vinegar for 5 minutes. JSP/RWB30(8OZ)A. Some canners mix cabbage, carrots, onions, and beets together for a canned mixed salad. Use straight vinegar with these mixed pickles or pH test.

Variation: Pickled Three-Bean Salad—Cook all vegetable ingredients in brine (1 cup wine vinegar, ½ cup bottled lemon juice, 1½ cups sugar, 1¼ cups water, and 1 teaspoon salt) for 1 minute. Marinate 12 to 24 hours in the refrigerator. Then, JSP/RWB/15(16OZ)A. **If canning, test the pH of the completed salad for a pH of 4.2 or less** or JS**R. Label well.** Vegetables may include: 1½ cups blanched green/yellow beans, 1 cup canned/rinsed/drained red kidney beans, 1 part canned/drained garbanzo beans, ½ cup diced red onions, ½ cup diced celery, ½ cup canned red pimento (or diced red/green pepper or ¼ teaspoon paprika). If canning, do not add any oil to the canning jar. Instead, add 2 teaspoons oil per 8-ounce jar upon opening. Otherwise, add ¼ cup oil to the recipe and keep the pickles refrigerated. For a quick hot or cold **green bean salad** use freshly cooked beans dressed with some vinegar, sugar (to taste), soy sauce (dash), chopped parsley, diced onions, and grated ginger (to taste), or use French dressing with sugar (to taste). Corn, lima beans, or other beans may be added to this quick salad, but if canning, check the pH if adding any low-acid vegetable to the salad. Some salads may be canned or frozen. **Freezer coleslaw** is a frozen coleslaw containing a cup of each vegetable (cabbage, carrots, bell peppers, and onions), shredded together with 1 teaspoon salt. Weep 1 hour; drain, and combine with a heated syrup of 1 cup vinegar, ¼ cup water, 2 cups sugar, 1 teaspoon celery seed, and 1 teaspoon mustard seed. Mix. JSP/RWB or freeze. Check the pH of the completed salad or refrigerate. To serve this frozen salad, thaw and enjoy, or thaw, drain, and add mayonnaise. Jamlady has an old newspaper clipping that contains a recipe submitted by R. R. of Lake-in-the-Hills for freezing this mixture with1 cup sugar and a mango. **If you think this "mango" is a tropical fruit, read on and check all references for mango in the index.**

The next fun recipe, **Guess What Pie** or **Jamlady's Original Pickled-Beet Pie** evolved from Jamlady comments about using leftover pickle juice in a dessert. This recipe may be made with just the beet pickle juice but is arguably better with the addition of the shredded pickled beets. **This recipe was inspired by the early American recipe for mock lemon pie or vinegar pie.** This pie also "uses up" leftover yolks. When Jamlady, Doris, and I made Guess What Pie, we used the special tart dough from *The Jamlady Cookbook* (217) for the bottom crust, but you may use any regular unbaked 9- to10-inch pie shell.

Canned shredded beets are useful in this pie and in mixed salads of oranges, romaine lettuce, drained/shredded beets, and nuts/seeds (sliced almonds, pine nuts, or shelled pumpkin seeds) with

¼ cup beet pickle juice, ½ to ¾ cup olive oil, and ¼ cup fresh orange juice to form a dressing. How might you use pickled shredded beets? **Shredding peeled raw beets is easier and faster than precooking whole beets to make pickled beets, and it improves heat distribution during the canning process. Also, relish shredded pickled beets on pork chops or cottage cheese.**

Mock Lemon (Vinegar) Pie

1 cup granulated sugar
⅓ cup firmly packed light brown sugar
¼ cup sifted flour
⅛ teaspoon grated nutmeg
⅛ teaspoon cardamom
1 cup water
¼ cup cider vinegar
½ cup melted butter (1 stick)
3 large eggs or 6 yolks
1 unbaked 9- or10-inch pie shell

Guess What Pie?

¾ cup sugar
⅓ cup firmly packed light brown sugar
¼ cup flour
¼-½ teaspoon cinnamon
¾-1 cup strained, shredded pickled beets
⅝ cup water
¾ cup strained pickled beet juice
½ cup melted butter (1 stick)
3 large eggs or 6 yolks
1 unbaked 9- or 10-inch pie shell

Preheat the oven to 350 degrees F. Mix together the sugars, flour, and spice(s). Add the water, vinegar (or pickle juice), and melted butter. Mix well. Add the eggs; mix again. Place the strained beets inside the pie shell and add the pie mixture. Bake 1 hour or until the filling is puffed and lightly browned. Cool to cut. Serve with ice cream, and see if anybody can guess what they are eating.

Pickled Beets with Horseradish in Spiced Red Wine Vinegar

Spiced Red Wine Vinegar:
4 cups red wine vinegar
½ cup sugar
4 tablespoons grated horseradish
1 teaspoon salt

Per spice bag:
12-20 cinnamon sticks
1 teaspoon whole allspice
1 tablespoon mustard seed
1 teaspoon whole clove

Main ingredient:
Partly cooked, peeled beets

Boil the red wine vinegar, sugar, horseradish, salt, and spice bag for 10 minutes. Cook the beets, slip the skins, or, preferably, for a firmer pickle, cook the beets partway and peel. Place the cut beets, cinnamon stick, and hot-spiced vinegar in the jar. SP/RWB35(16OZ)35-40(32 OZ)A.

Many vegetables may be pickled solo. Jalapeño and Serrano peppers may be pickled alone or with carrot disks, whole garlic, or diced onions. Brussels sprouts, okra, and green tomato pickles are well liked and are used often in Bloody Mary's or Martinis. Green tomatoes may be pickled whole, sliced, or in wedges.

Hot Pickled Jalapeño Peppers

Per quart jar:
10 carrot disks
3-6 garlic cloves
1 teaspoon pickling spice
½ teaspoon mustard seed
5 peppercorns
1 bay leaf
1 teaspoon pickling salt

Vinegar Mixture:
4 cups water
5 cups red wine vinegar

Main ingredient:
Jalapeño peppers

Parboil or microwave the carrots in water for 2 minutes, or raw pack paper-thin carrots. Loosely raw pack the peppers, garlic cloves, and spices with the carrots and cover with the hot vinegar mixture. SP/RWB15-18(16OZ)20(32OZ)A.

When canning, sweet peppers are interchangeable with hot peppers. Peppers, hot or not hot, have the same approximate pH. Years ago when Jamlady and I first met, we searched in all the canning books for the answer. **May we substitute hot peppers for regular peppers?** Many so-called experts said, "Don't change the recipe." So, the answer to this question is: 1 cup hot pepper may be substituted for 1 cup sweet peppers and visa versa. **And yes, 6-percent-acidity vinegar may be used instead of 5-percent acidity, but not 4-percent acidity, or homemade vinegar.** Presumably, the pH is unknown for homemade vinegar. However, **if the pH of the homemade vinegar is established at 5-percent acidity or above, the homemade vinegar may be used in canning recipes.**

Peter Piper's Pickles

Per quart jar:
15-20 oregano leaves
1 rocoto/manzana hot pepper
2 chili chilaca peppers
2 jalapeño peppers
6-8 peppercorns
1 teaspoon pickling spice
½-1 teaspoon salt
2 garlic cloves

Main ingredient:
Red/green sweet peppers

Vinegar mixture:
1 part water
1 part 5- or 6-percent vinegar

Line the jar bottom with oregano leaves, hot peppers, and spices. Fill the jars with red and green sweet pepper; add the brine and leave a ½-inch headspace (pint) or ¾-inch headspace (quart). JSP/RWB15(16OZ)20(32OZ)A.

Oregano leaves with garlic and spices on the bottoms of pickle jars.

Hot Pickled Brussels Sprouts.

Hot Dilled Brussels Sprouts

Main ingredient:
Brussels sprouts
Per quart jar:
5 peppercorns
1 garlic clove
½ teaspoon dill weed
1 teaspoon pickling salt
½ teaspoon mustard seed
3 Serrano peppers (optional)

Vinegar mixture:
4 cups water
5 cups cider vinegar

Clean and trim the Brussels sprouts, raw pack them with the spices, and then add the hot vinegar mixture. Leave 6-percent headspace. SP/RWB20-25(32OZ)A.

Note: Vegetables may be precooked in brine, packed into jars, and processed; this is called hot packing.

Okra or **Gumbo,** *Hibiscus esculentus,* is a tall, annual African herb whose long-ribbed pods may be pickled or used to thicken soups, ketchups, or stews. **Okra pods can be canned, dried, or cooked fresh. Pick whole okra pods when small; larger okra pods are too tough to pickle. Shell larger pods, and cook them like peas** (see E.L.D. Seymour's *The Wise Garden Encyclopedia* 1970, 869). The okra flower is a yellow red-centered hibiscus blossom and may be used ornamentally in flower beds. **Okras are often grown in southern states for pickles and gumbo!** Very small okra pods may be pickled for use in martinis.

Hot Okra Pickles

Main Ingredient:
12 pounds small okra pods
Per pint jar:
3 pieces garlic
¼ teaspoon mustard seed
¼ teaspoon dried hot pepper*

Brine:
1 quart white vinegar
1 quart red or white wine vinegar
2 quarts water
1 cup pickling salt

Wash and air-dry the okra pods. Jar them with the garlic, mustard seed, and hot pepper; cover with hot brine. SP/RWB15(16OZ)A.

* May substitute 1 to 3 fresh hot pepper pods

Dilly Okra

Main Ingredient:
2 pounds baby okra pods
Per pint jar:
1 garlic clove
1 dill head
5 whole peppercorns
1 celery stalk/leaves

Brine:
2 cups water
2½ cups white wine vinegar
2 tablespoons pickling salt

Wash the okra pods; pack them with garlic cloves, dill, peppercorns, and celery. Cover the okra with hot brine, leaving ½-inch headspace for 16-ounce jars and ⅜-inch for 8-ounce upright jars. SP/RWB6-10(4OZ)15(16OZ)A.

Cajun Pickled Okra Pods

2 pounds 1-3-inch okra pods
20 garlic cloves
5-10 hot peppers

Brine:
2 bay leaves
5-10 hot peppers
1 tablespoon celery seed
1 teaspoon white peppercorns
1 teaspoon black peppercorns
½ cup pickling salt
1 cup water
4 cups white wine vinegar

Wash the okra pods. Jar the washed pods with the divided garlic cloves and hot peppers. Boil the hot brine of bay leaves, spices, salt, water, and white wine vinegar; pour over. SP/RWB15(16OZ)A. Cure for 30 days.

Note: Some folks pickle larger okras, but discriminating chefs cook and juice the stringy, tough pods for soup stock.

Clockwise from right: *Flute of champagne with pickled kumquats, vodka gimlet with minted lime pickles, Bloody Mary with dilly beans and hot pickled carrots, martini with pickled onions and hot pickled baby okra, wine with pickled orange slice, and Damson-infused vodka with orange lime-pickle and lemon lime-pickle garnish.*

Sweet and Sour Okra Pods

4 garlic cloves
1-2 tablespoons mustard seed
1 teaspoon whole clove
1 teaspoon whole allspice
1 teaspoon black peppercorns
3 pounds small okra pods
3 seeded red bell peppers
1 sliced parboiled Texas onion*
1 cup water
3 cups 5-percent vinegar
1 teaspoon pickling salt
1¾ cups sugar or honey

Distribute the garlic cloves, spices, pods, pepper slices, and parboiled onions in 4 sterilize pint jars. Avoid overpacking the jars or the jars can transpire. Refrigerate any low-liquid jars horizontally. Boil the water, vinegar, salt, and sugar or honey; pour it over the okras. Leave 6-percent headspace. SP/RWB15(16OZ)A.

* May substitute small pearl onions

Kosher-Style Dilled Green Tomatoes

Per quart jar:
Fresh, firm green tomatoes
2 garlic cloves
½ teaspoon dill seed
¼ teaspoon celery seed
5-10 peppercorns
1-10 Serrano peppers

Brine:
5 cups white or cider vinegar
8 cups hot water
1 cup pickling salt
2 tablespoons pickling salt

Pack the jars with green tomatoes, garlic cloves, spices, and peppers; cover with hot brine, leaving 6-percent headspace. SP/RWB5-10(32OZ)**RA**. **Label—"Keep Refrigerated".**

According to one expert, shelf-stable, green-tomato-pickle quarts must now be processed for 15 minutes. JSP/RWB15(32OZ)A. Her recipe has 1 cup less vinegar and 2 tablespoons less salt than Jamlady's recipe. Cooking this pickle longer makes it softer but shelf-stable. Older processing times were 5 to 10 minutes per quart, but this is now. So, increase the processing times or use shorter times, and keep the product refrigerated. Label it **"Keep Refrigerated."** Alternatively, JSP/180dF/30(16OZ)A.

Green tomatoes may be made into "quickles." In light of new processing times, I recommend "refrigerated quickles." The following recipe is another Michael Pechman ribbon winner from the 2005 International Pickle Festival. This young high-school student showed the judges his culinary talents by garnering several blue ribbons at the 2005 festival.

Wall of pickled green tomatoes in quart jars.

End-of-Summer Pickled Green Tomatoes

1 quart green tomato slices
15 garlic cloves
¼ cup small hot red peppers
2 chopped red peppers
5 tablespoons kosher salt
4 cups white vinegar
2 chopped Bermuda onions
3 cups sugar
5 celery hearts (2-inch pieces)

Prepare ¼-inch tomato slices; split in half the garlic cloves and peppers. Weep the tomatoes in the salt for 12 hours, covered and cold stored. Then, drain and rinse. Simmer the vinegar, hot peppers, onions, garlic cloves, and sugar for 2 minutes; pour over the tomatoes, onions, celery, and red peppers. JS**R.**

Traditional dill pickles or quickles may be made with petite cucumbers like tindoras small Kirbys, or other unique cucumbers like lemon cucumbers. **This basic recipe may also be used with other 5.12 to 5.78 pH vegetables.**

Green Tomato Quickles—a superb refrigerator pickle.

Hot Harkema Dills

Per quart jar:
1-3 garlic cloves
Sprig of dill
1-20 Thai or Serrano peppers
1 teaspoon pickling spice

Main ingredient:
Baby pickling cucumbers

Brine:
2 quarts cider vinegar
2 quarts water
1/4 cup pickling salt or more

Pack the spices and baby cucumbers in each jar. Pour the boiling-hot brine into the jar, leaving 6-percent headspace. SP/RWB10-15(16OZ)15-20(32OZ)A. **Processing times should increase with increased product thickness (larger cucumbers or tighter packing)** or **JSP/180dF/30(16OZ)A.** Start timing with thc first rolling boil. **Prcliminary bubbles rising from the bottom of the pan do not constitute a full-rolling boil.** Refrigeration is recommended for extra safety and firmness for pints processed 10 minutes or quarts processed for 15 minutes. **Check the processing times currently recommended by the USDA, Canadian Food Inspection Agency, United Kingdom, and/or Australian food agencies.**

The artful pickle maker is aware of the synergetic nature of safe pickling. All the parts, flavors, textures, balanced ingredients, and visual appearance need to work together. Even the placement of the dill and other accents contribute to the overall appreciation of the adroitly crafted pickle or *jardinière*.

Hot Harkema Dills with Serrano peppers.

Kosher Dills

1 quart water
1 pint vinegar
½ cup pickling salt
2 large dill heads
2 teaspoons pickling spice
1-2 garlic cloves
2-6 small Serrano peppers (optional)
3 pounds small Kirby cucumbers

Boil the water, vinegar, and salt. Per quart jar: pack the dill, spices, garlic cloves, and peppers with small, clean Kirby cucumbers. Pour the hot-boiled brine into the jars, leaving 6-percent headspace. SP/RWB15(16OZ)20(32OZ)A or JSP/180dF/30 (16OZ)A.

Sweet Dills

1½ pounds cucumbers
⅜ cup brown sugar
¼ cup pickling salt
2¼ cups cider vinegar
2 cups water
4 dill heads*
¼ teaspoon mustard seed (optional)
2-4 garlic cloves**
1-4 Serrano peppers

Use baby or small cucumbers. Boil the sugar, salt, vinegar, and water. Jar the cucumbers with the dill, garlic cloves, mustard seed, and peppers; pour the hot brine over, leaving 6-percent headspace. SP/RWB10-15(16OZ)15-20(32OZ)A or JSP/180dF/30(16OZ)A. **Increase the processing times for larger pickles, or "Refrigerate Only."**

* May substitute equivalent dill seed/weed

** May substitute ½ teaspoon cumin

Sweet Gherkin Pickles

7 pounds 1½-inch cucumbers
Boiling water
½ cup pickling salt
8 cups sugar
6 cups vinegar
1 teaspoon turmeric
2 teaspoons celery seed
2 teaspoons pickling spice
1 drop oil of cinnamon*

Step 1: Keep notes in a notebook; check off each step. Scrub the cucumbers. Cut off the bloom end; discard it. Do not remove the stem. Drain the cucumbers, place them in a glass jar or crock, cover them with boiling water, and wait 8 hours.

Step 2: Drain, adding ¼ cup salt, recover with boiling-hot water, and wait 24 hours.

Step 3: Drain, adding ¼ cup salt, recover with fresh boiling-hot water, and wait 12 to 18 hours.

Step 4: Drain, prick the cucumbers with a sterile fork.

Step 5: Boil the syrup: 3 cups sugar, 3 cups vinegar, turmeric, and spices. Pour over the cucumbers. Mix well; wait 6 hours. Cucumbers may not be totally covered.

Step 6: Drain syrup from the cucumbers. Reserve it and add 2 cups sugar and 2 cups vinegar. Boil the syrup; pour over the cucumbers.

Step 7: Drain the syrup from the cucumbers and add 2 cups sugar and 1 cup vinegar. Boil the syrup, pour it over the cucumbers, and wait 8 hours.

Step 8: Drain the syrup, add the last 1 cup sugar,

and heat. Some recipes add 2 teaspoons pure vanilla (optional). Compare to similar recipes and observe spice variances. Pack the cucumbers in sterile jars; cover with the syrup. Remove any trapped air; leave 6-percent headspace. SP/RWB10-15*(16OZ)A.
* Thicker cucumbers

Many New Yorkers are familiar with fermented sour pickles and love them. Midwestern or Southerners tend to like half-sours, which aren't fermented as long. **These pickles (below) aren't fermented, but they are sour.** Make these pickles with small whole cucumbers or with thick cucumber slices.

Sour Pickle Chunks

16 cups cider vinegar
4 cups water
1 cup salt
1 cup sugar
1 cup mustard seed
Cucumbers

The number of cucumbers is determined by availability and size. If brine runs out, make more. Boil the vinegar, water, salt, sugar, and mustard seed; pour it into the jars of cucumbers. SP/RWB5-10(16OZ)**RA**. **Label "Keep Refrigerated."** Process longer for a shelf-stable product: JSP/RWB15(16OZ)20(32OZ)A. **A good beginner's recipe!**

Pennsylvanian 24-hour Cucumbers

2 quarts water
1 cup white vinegar (Heinz)
½ cup sugar
½ cup iodine-free salt (kosher or pickling)
Kirby cucumbers
Fresh dill heads and weed
Garlic buds*

Boil the water, vinegar, sugar, and salt for 5 minutes; cool. Wash the Kirby cucumbers; rinse the garden-fresh dill. Place the dill and garlic "buds"* in the bottom of the jar. Add the cucumbers. Pour cooled brine over the cucumbers. Place more dill and garlic buds on the top. Refrigerate 24 hours.
* The term **"buds"** can be misleading, as some people call cloves buds. I recollect my aunt using the budding tops of chives or garlic for these pickles. Recipe from Frances Basten, Kingston, New York.

Pickled Garlic Buds (garlic cloves or single garlic bulbs with tops) may be made by cooking the bud spears in water for about 2 to 3 minutes and marinating them in the refrigerator with equal measures of rice vinegar, soy sauce, and honey (or sugar). **Keep refrigerated.**

Freezer Pickles are made, frozen, and eaten later. **Freezer Pickle Recipe:** 8 cups thinly sliced cucumbers, 2 cups thinly sliced onions, ⅓ cup salt, and water to cover. Wait 3 hours, drain/squeeze, and then cover with a warm vinegar solution: 2 cups sugar, 1 cup cider vinegar, and ½ teaspoon celery seed. Mix; freeze the 4 pints. Thaw 4 hours prior to serving.

FERMENTATION PICKLING

Certain vegetables or fruits are unsuitable for fermentation because they don't contain enough sugar. In the fermentation process, the bacteria generate lactic acid from the sugar contained in the fruit itself. Asparagus, corn, snap beans, and spinach, for example, do not have sufficient sugar for fermentation to take place. **The whole idea in fermentation pickling is to create a hospitable environment for the creation of lactic acid, while inhibiting any spoiler organisms.** A salt concentration of around 8 percent is best, or about ¾ pound salt to each gallon of water. The best temperatures are around 75 degrees F, except for kraut (60 degrees F). **Lower temperatures slow the process, and higher temperatures accelerate it.**

When fermenting, bubbles will rise in the brine, and this gas will need to escape. All the vegetables being fermented must stay under the level of the brine—usually submerged by a stone or weight. There should be at least 2 inches of brine above the weight. Each day, remove all scum that forms. When fermentation has stopped, the escape route for the gas must be sealed. Make sure the fermentation has ceased, or pressure may pop corks or lids.

Barrels of pickles or crocks, may be sealed with ⅛ to ¼ inch of paraffin wax to prevent spoilage. Usually two layers of paraffin are used to close any questionable seals. If the fermentation is still going, make a small hole in the paraffin, so it may be sealed when the fermentation has stopped. Instead of sealing pickles in a large container, they may be canned in jars. If you wish to make large barrels of pickles, I suggest you consult Clyde H. Campbell's *A Manual on Canning, Pickling and Preserving.* I have never made a large commercial barrel of pickles. The temperatures and brines need to be carefully controlled. The instructions in Campbell's manual are quite specific. Even the way water is added to the bottom of the barrel, as opposed to the top, can affect the outcome of large-barrel batches.

Plastic Bag Pickles: For those folks interested in actual long fermentation, first try **the reclosable plastic-bag-pickle technique.** Start with sterile and clean materials. Boil 1 cup water and mix in ½ tablespoon pickling salt. **Cool the brine; hot brine will not work.** Add ½ tablespoon vinegar (garlic vinegar or fresh lemon juice), ⅛ teaspoon mustard

Reclosable plastic bag pickle.

Making half-sours!

seed, 5 peppercorns, 1/8 teaspoon dill seed, and 1/8 teaspoon pickling spice. Garlic is optional; keep the cloves submerged. Put 1 fresh Kirby cucumber inside the bag with the spices and acidifier (vinegar or lemon juice). **Avoid wax-coated cucumbers.** Wrap a rubber band loosely around the bag so that the cucumber will not rise above the liquid level when adding the brine. Seek to create an hourglass-shaped bag. Close the bag, removing as much air as possible. Use a binder clip to hang the bag up—so the liquid level covers the pickle at all times. **Optimal room temperature is 75 degrees F, but a cooler environment turns a twenty-four-hour experiment into a two-day trial.** This experiment is a variation of the technique suggested by David A. Katz in "Zip-Lock Pickle" (1977). The rubber band was Jamlady's idea. Run more experiments and develop your own technique, or just make a pickle or two a day. Larger bags will accommodate several pickles. Keep records of experiments, noting the temperature, amount of salt used, types of acidifiers, spices, and other vegetables or fruits added. Add some bread or garlic croutons on top of the batch. Starting small is a good way to learn, and there might be a family science project here too.

Tums® appear to be an ingredient in some sour pickles. The initial brine is made with 1 crushed non-flavored Tums® tablet, 1 cup vinegar, 3/8 cup salt, and room-temperature water to fill a 1/2-gallon container. For smaller experiments, spices, garlic, and dill may be added to a jar or plastic bag and covered with the same brine. Keep notes. **Keep the cucumber under the brine, and provide the gas an escape route.** This can be achieved in a plastic bag by unzipping the bag a tiny bit. This pickle's optimal room temperature is 82 degrees for 6 to 8 days. You'll know when the pickle is ready because it turns color. Refrigerate to stop the fermentation.

After mastering small-batch production, it's time for a bigger batch. Locate a crock with weight stone and lid. A Harsch Fermenting Crock or a similar crock will do, or devise your own.

This next pickle changes over time and may be eaten at almost any stage in its development. A 2 to 3 day old pickle is undercured, but is edible and crunchy. Some folks prefer half-cured or fully cured pickles, and the resourceful chef uses pickle juice and soft overcured pickles in soups and stews. **Pickles go well in tomato-based soups, stews, potato soup, potato salad, and in tomato fish chowders.**

Fermented Polish-Dill Pickles

Step 1—Wash 4 pounds of 3- to 4-inch, just-picked cucumbers. Crock larger ones first. Soak any older cucumbers in ice water for 2 hours; wash, dry, and scald them in boiling water, drain, and dry them.

Step 2—Place 6 fresh dill heads and 2 green oak leaves or wild grape leaves (optional: wood flavor) in the bottom of the crock. Use no reactive metal containers. Try some of these spices: bay leaf, mustard seed, ginger, chili pepper, horseradish leaf, chive, clove, cinnamon stick, peppercorns, coriander seed, juniper berry, or allspice as flavorings.

Step 3—Put the cucumbers in the crock, standing up.

Step 4—Boil 6 cups water with 3 tablespoons salt. Cool the brine to lukewarm; pour it over the pickles. Cover the crock top with a plate; weight it down. Keep the pickles submerged. Place cheesecloth over the crock top. Sample pickles at will. A fully cured pickle takes 6 to 10 days. Refrigerate the crock when the desired pickle is created, or JSP/180dF/30(16OZ)A.

Note: Some cooks use 1 cup vinegar and 1/2 cup salt per gallon of water. One to two gallons of water will do 2 to 3 pounds of cucumbers, depending on their shape and size. Use about 4 tablespoons pickling spice per 1- to 2-gallon batch, plus 6 garlic cloves and 1 teaspoon celery seed. Vinegar in brine speeds up the pickling process and deters the growth of bacteria, but this isn't how the real old-timers did it. **Try to keep a crock of pickles in a 55- to 75-degrees environment; 80 degrees is too warm. Some pickle makers cut off the bloom ends and pack pickles stem-side down.** Intermittently remove any surface scum. **Some pickle makers place a crust of bread atop their pickles; others make them in glass jars and set them outside in the sun.**

A Hungarian friend of mine, Mrs. Maria Kaup, uses a gallon glass container of cucumbers (with an X cut in the bottom of each pickling cucumber). Maria

Fermented half-sours in the crock.

covers the cucumbers and 5 garlic cloves with cool pre-boiled brine (made from about ½ cup salt to 1 gallon water). Maria wraps a slice of rye bread in cheesecloth, sets it on the top of the pickles with some fresh dill (optional), and sets the jar in the sun by day and inside by night. Maria uses no other spices and says the pickles are ready when the brine is cloudy (2 to 3 days), but cautions picklers to pack the pickles tightly "so they don't move above the brine." Refrigerate the pickles to stop the process. As you can see, most good pickle makers have worked out their own system over time.

Sauerkraut may be made in glass jars. This method uses brine, but kraut may also be dry-salted with weights. Shred 2 pounds room-temperature cabbage to 1/16 inch, and put some in a sterile quart canning jar. Press the cabbage down until the jar is half-full. Add 1 teaspoon pickling salt, and complete the jar with cabbage. Press down, add 1 teaspoon pickling salt, pour in room-temperature water, and push the cabbage under the water level. Attach the lid loosely. Keep the brine level to the top by replacing it daily with brine of 1½ tablespoons salt per quart water. Keep the kraut under the water level. Arrange the lid so it can be screwed down or opened some; put a small pin hole in the top and cover it with tape. For a similar technique, see *kimchi*—airlock with Ziploc® of brine. **The best kraut is made at 60 degrees F and ferments in 5 to 6 weeks.** Ten degrees warmer makes inferior kraut in 3 to 4 weeks, and kraut made at 75 degrees will likely be soft and disappointing. Taste the kraut to know when to stop. Bubbles stop rising when the fermentation is done. A small batch of kraut, like dills, may be made with a rubber band and a Ziploc® plastic bag. Run small trials. Small successes and small failures are better than a 4-gallon crock of bad kraut. Learn as you experiment. When the kraut is done, paraffin seal it or heat the kraut to 180 degrees, correctly pack it firmly in hot jars, add kraut juice or weak brine (1 tablespoon salt to 2 cups water), and SP/RWB15(16OZ)20(32)A or JSR (lasts 1 to 2 months).

Sampling the half-sours.

Atjar Bening

2 cucumbers*
2 small onion
2-3 minced garlic cloves
2-5 small hot peppers
½ teaspoon kosher salt
½ cup vinegar
2½ tablespoons sugar

For this Indonesian mixed-vegetable pickle, peel, seed, and cube the cucumbers; slice the onions (if used, shred the cabbage and carrot). Salt all the vegetables in an iced, stainless-steel pan for 2 to 3 hours. Seed and slice the hot peppers and boil with the water, vinegar, and sugar; cool. Pour the vinegar solution over the drained vegetables; salt to taste. Refrigerate and serve with rice dishes. Shelf life = +/-10 days.

* May substitute 1 thinly sliced carrot and some shredded cabbage for 1 cucumber

Variation: Quick Atjar—Prepare the cucumbers, onions, garlic cloves, and peppers. Skip the salting step, carrots, and cabbage. Combine all ingredients together and refrigerate. Serve in 2 to 3 hours.

LIME PICKLES

Lime pickles are vegetables made crunchy by soaking them in a solution of pickling lime and water. Pickling lime, a firming agent, is also called calcium hydroxide, hydrated lime, dehydrated lime, $Ca(OH)_2$, or slaked lime. Always thoroughly rinse pickling lime from processed vegetables. **Other firming agents are alum, calcium chloride, as ice, and salt. Alum isn't used much anymore; it may cause nausea.** Calcium chloride is a firming agent and is sometimes used commercially. Salt and ice are often used in pickle making; see B&B pickles.

The following pickles are examples of lime pickles made with cucumbers and tomatoes. Pickled watermelon rinds may be made as lime pickles. Market patron Star Blaz e-mailed Jamlady:

> I am almost 60 years old and would be hard-pressed to name a year wherein I have not put up a couple dozen jars of various items . . . Now I'm hanging up my apron, in honor of what I consider to be the best most delicious item to ever grace the table—your lime pickles. The sweet-tangy, incredibly snappy-crunch is unbeatable.

In 1995, Mrs. Joan Anderson, owner of the brickyard in Crystal Lake, Illinois, gave me this next lime pickle recipe. Since then I've created many new variations. This crisp, crunchy pickle is a favorite with children and often graces our holiday dinner table. Each jar is packed with at least 24 pieces so everyone can share equally.

Green lime pickles are a crunchy pickle to love!

Mrs. Anderson's Green Lime Pickle Chunks

Step 1—Day 1:

1½ gallons mature cucumbers
2 cups pickling lime*
Water to cover

Dissolve the pickling lime* in enough soft water to cover the cucumbers. Use only fresh cucumbers. Peel, seed, and cut the cucumbers into chunks, donuts, or sticks. Soak the pieces for 24 hours in a cool place, or ice them in a non-reactive stainless, steel container.

Caution: *Wear goggles; don't breathe in lime or allow lime to make contact with your eyes. Do not mistake food-grade pickling lime for quicklime.**

Caution: **Do not mistake edible *calcium hydroxide* **(pickling lime, hydrated lime, or $Ca(OH)_2$) for the dangerous *calcium oxide* (quicklime or CaO), which is a white, caustic alkaline solid. Always buy food-grade chemicals for cooking.**

Step 2—Day 2:

8 cups sugar
1½ quarts vinegar
1 tablespoon salt
½ teaspoon oil of clove
½ teaspoon oil of cinnamon

Drain the cucumber chunks, and rinse them 4 times. No short cuts allowed—4 times. Let the cucumbers soak in the last icy-cold rinse water for 3 hours. **To make syrup, cook together the sugar, vinegar, salt, oil of clove, and oil of cinnamon.** Drain the pickles; add them to the clear-colored syrup. Heat the syrup with the pickles until they turn transparent; refrigerate overnight.

Step 3—Day 3:

1 cup sugar
½ bottle green (or red) food coloring

Pour off the syrup; add 1 cup sugar and a ½ bottle (½ ounce) of food coloring to the syrup. Heat again and pour over the pickles; refrigerate overnight.

Step 4—Day 4:

1 cup sugar

Pour off the syrup; add 1 cup sugar to the syrup. Heat; pour into pickle-packed wide-mouth tapered jars. SP/RWB10(4OZ)10(8OZ)15(16OZ) 20(32OZ)A. **For Jamlady's three new versions of this lime pickle, page 109.**

Sealed jars of green lime pickles.

Variation: Crunchy Lemon Pickles—Flavor this pickle with ½ teaspoon oil of lemon and ½ teaspoon oil of cinnamon and no oil of clove. Color with ¼ bottle yellow food coloring.

Variation: Crunchy Orange Pickles—Flavor with ½ teaspoon oil of orange and ½ teaspoon oil of cinnamon and no oil of clove. Color with ¼ bottle orange food coloring.

Variation: Crunchy Spearmint Pickles—Flavor with ½ teaspoon oil of clove, ½ teaspoon oil of cinnamon, and ¼ teaspoon oil of spearmint (or to taste). Color with a scant ½ bottle green coloring with some yellow food coloring (light green color).

Variation: See the variation for **Old South Cucumber Lime Pickles** on a bag of Mrs. WAGES® Pickling Lime for 7 pounds unpeeled sliced cucumbers: 1 cup lime to 2 gallons water, 8 cups vinegar, 8 cups sugar, and 2 teaspoons pickling spices. Yes, of course, pickling spices may be used with Mrs. Anderson's recipe too!

Red-hot cinnamon-stick lime pickles were first given to me by Mrs. Jane Cunningham when I taught art in Woodstock, Illinois. Jane said they were great, and so they are.

Mrs. Cunningham's Red Cinnamon Pickles

Step 1—Day 1:

2 gallons cucumbers
8½ cups water
2 cups pickling lime*
1 tray ice cubes

Prepare 2 gallons cucumber sticks. Remove all peels, seeds, and soft inners, using only firm cucumber meat. In a stainless-steel pot, add the cucumbers to the lime, water, and ice cube mixture; wait 24 hours.

* **See cautions on page 108**

Step 2—Day 2:

water to cover
1 cup vinegar
1 tablespoon alum (optional)
1 ounce red food coloring

Drain and rinse the cucumbers 3 times in fresh cold water. Soak them in cold water for 3 hours; drain. Cover the cucumbers with fresh soft water, 1 cup vinegar, alum (optional), and food coloring. Simmer 2 hours; let sit 1 hour. Sticks should be red; drain.

Step 3—Day 2:

8 cups sugar
2 cups white vinegar
2 cups water
16 ounces red-hot candies*

Heat sugar, vinegar, water, and candies, and pour over the drained cucumbers; refrigerate.

* E.J. Brach's Cinnamon Imperials (if allergic to corn, avoid and see Mrs. Anderson's recipe)

Step 4—Day 3:

Drain the syrup off, reheat, and pour back over the pickles. Refrigerate.

Step 5—Day 4:

Drain, reheat the syrup, pour it back over the pickles, and wait 6 hours. Pack the pickle sticks in 16-ounce, wide-mouth tapered jars and cover with the reheated syrup. All syrup should be used. If not, consider cooking the syrup down more or repacking the pickles more loosely. SP/RWB10(8OZ)15(16OZ)A.

Crystal Green Tomato Raisin Pickle is not an easy pickle to make well. The tomatoes need to be thin and cooked until tender. Beginners should try to reduce tomato breakage by starting with a quarter-batch. Add the raisins near the end. Perfectionists—this recipe provides free therapy! This recipe was published in *Comfort,* an old newspaper (c. 1850).

Crystal Green Tomato Raisin Pickle

5 pounds green tomatoes
1 vial Lilly's lime*
2 gallons water
3 pounds sugar
7 cups cider vinegar
2 tablespoons whole clove
2 tablespoons allspice
2 cinnamon sticks
1 teaspoon grated gingerroot
1 pound seedless raisins

Slice the tomatoes thin. The original recipe said slice to "1/12 inch thick." Do your best. Protect your nose and eyes (see previous cautions). Put the tomatoes in an iced, flat and long stainless-steel steamer tray with the pickling lime and water for 24 hours. Drain/rinse the tomatoes 3 times in fresh water. Soak the slices in cold water for 1 hour; drain. Try not to break the tomato slices. Cook the sugar, cider vinegar, spices, and gingerroot together to make syrup; cool. Add the tomato slices to the vinegar syrup, bring to a boil, and cook until the tomatoes are transparent and tender and the syrup is thick and clear. Add the raisins near the end. Some cooks prefer not to cook the pickle, but instead, take several days heating the syrup back up and pouring it over the pickle as is done with the cucumber lime pickles. When completed, the pickle should be crunchy, but still tender. This pickle is something special. JSP/RWB15(16OZ)A.

* The original recipe called for "a vial of Lilly's Lime", which was probably 4 cups, if the next recipe is any indicator. I believe I used 3 cups once and 4 another; both worked. I have asked Eli Lilly and Company for the exact amount of lime in a vial of Lilly's Lime, but they were unable to confirm the amount.

Variation: Crystal Tomato Pickles—Slice 7 pounds green tomatoes into 1/4-inch pieces and cover with 2 gallons water and 4 cups pickling lime. Wait 24 hours. Remove; rinse many times. Mix, boil, turn off heat, and infuse for 1 hour 9 cups sugar, 8 cups vinegar, 6 true cinnamon sticks, and a spice bag (1 teaspoon grated nutmeg and 1 tablespoon freshly ground gingerroot or 1 teaspoon ground ginger). Add the tomato slices, cooking rapidly. When done, the syrup should coat the spoon. JSP/RWB12-15(8OZ)15(16OZ)A.

MUSTARD PICKLES

Two interesting handwritten recipes were found in the back of a copy of *The Woman's Exchange Cook Book* (1894).

"Cucumber Pickles"

1 cup of ground mustard
1 cup sugar
1 cup salt

Mix while dry. Add 1 cup vinegar. Wash cucumbers fresh from vine. Drop into the vinegar. Cover and place weight on them. They require no cooking and will keep indefinitely. Lill."

Note: Keep these pickles refrigerated.

Variation: a similar pickle, called **"Lazy Day Pickles"** or **"Mustard Cukes,"** may be made by packing small 2½-inch cucumbers into a sterile, widemouth tapered jar and pouring this mixture over them: 1 cup salt, 1 cup dry mustard, and 1 gallon vinegar. SP/RWB5(16OZ)**R** or SP/RWB10-15*(16OZ)A or JSP/180dF/30(16OZ)A. Wait 5 weeks to open.

* For thicker pieces

"Mustard Pickles"

1 quart ripe cucumbers cut into small pieces
1 quart green cucumbers cut into small pieces
1 quart onions cut into small pieces
1 quart cauliflower cut into small pieces
1 large or 2 small peppers cut into small pieces

For the dressing:
2 quarts vinegar
1 cup sugar
½ cup flour
3 tablespoons mustard
½ ounce turmeric

Let stand in weak brine 24 hours. Then cook in same brine until soft.

Cook until it thickens and then mix thoroughly with [drained] vegetables[*]. Mrs. C. H. Hosford"

* **Keep refrigerated**

To can **Jamlady's Mustard Pickles,** cut up 1 quart small green tomatoes, 5 bell peppers, 1 quart small pickling onions, 2 quarts baby cucumbers, and 1 small head cauliflower. Brine all overnight in 2 cups salt to1 gallon ice-cold water. Then, heat the vegetables in the brine to scalding; drain. Mix 6 tablespoons dry mustard, 1 tablespoon turmeric, 1 cup flour, 1 cup sugar, and add enough white vinegar to equal 2 quarts. Cook the dressing until thick, add the pickles, and pack them in sterilized jars. SP/RWB10-15-20*(16OZ)A or JSR.

* For thicker pieces

SPECIAL PICKLES

Asparagus, *Asparagus officinalis,* native to Europe, Asia, and North Africa, is a perennial vegetable. **Grown from seed or plants, asparagus stalks should not be harvested until the third year.** "Dear" asparagus pickles are highly regarded, probably because regular grocery stores don't sell comparable products. Asparagus pickle may be made with *sugar, honey, agave, no sweetener, or with an artificial sweetener (best added after opening). Please note: I do not recommend any artificial sweeteners but realize some people choose to use them.

Italian-Style Asparagus Pickle

Main ingredients:
Asparagus tips/spears
Carrot sticks
Onion slices

Vinegar mixture:
5 cups red wine vinegar
2 cups water

Per quart jar:
2 tablespoons fresh oregano leaves
1 tablespoon sugar* (above)
1 tablespoon pickling spice
1 teaspoon salt

Cut the asparagus about 1-inch shorter than the jar. Blanch all the vegetables for 1 minute in hot water and shock in ice-cold water or just raw pack, cutting the carrots and onions thin. Pack the jars attractively, but not tightly. Add the hot vinegar mixture, leaving approximately ¾-inch headspace for a quart. Process raw packed jars: SP/RWB20-25**(32OZ)A. Wrap the pickle with *prosciutto* to serve.

** For fatter asparagus

Hot Dilly Asparagus or Hot Pickled Asparagus

Per quart jar:
- 5-20 Serrano peppers
- Thin carrot accents
- Raw celery stalks
- 1 teaspoon dill seed or pickling spice
- 1 teaspoon mustard seed
- 1-3 peeled garlic cloves
- 1-2 teaspoon(s) salt
- 5-10 black peppercorns
- Oregano leaves (optional)
- Fresh dill (optional)

Main ingredient:
- Asparagus spears

Vinegar mixture:
- 5 cups red wine vinegar
- 2 cups water

Use oregano leaves for the Hot Pickled Asparagus recipe, or use fresh dill weed, dill head, or seed for the Hot Dilly Asparagus recipe. Jar the asparagus with the indicated spices and vegetables. Boil the hot vinegar mixture for one minute and pour into the jars. SP/RWB20-25*(32OZ)A. A spear is delicious in a Bloody Mary.

* For fatter asparagus

Pea pods or sugar peas, *Pisum sativum* var. *saccharatum,* are edible. They are not **dehiscing (di his′ing), meaning they do not burst open to discharge their seeds as a regular pea pod does.** Sugar peas have a thicker, softer, sweeter, less fibrous pod and are delicious to eat raw, steamed, stir-fried, or pickled.

Jamlady and I first pickled pea pods as a solo vegetable on June 30, 1998, and ever since we have been enjoying their culinary impact on our hors d'oeurves, sandwiches, and salads. **Split-open pickled pea pods make magnificent, little green boats that may be stuffed with cream cheese or goat cheese and topped with crabmeat, red salmon, or black caviar. "Out-rig" them with bright red pepper floats for a colorful appetizer. Put honey pods in salads, lay them flat on sandwiches, or just eat them right out of the jar!**

Honey Pods

- 10 pounds pea pods
- 5 quarts white wine vinegar
- 5 cups soft water
- 3 cups raw clover honey
- 1/4 cup pickling salt
- 7 tablespoons pickling spice

Steam the pea pods for 5 minutes; then plunge/shock them in ice-cold water. Meticulously stack drained size-graded pods in sterile canning jars. Cook the vinegar, water, honey, salt, and pickling spice for 15 minutes; strain and pour over the pods. SP/RWB12-15(8OZ)15-20*(16OZ).

* For thicker or tighter pack

Variation: Peppery Pods—Follow any of the hot *jardinière* recipes.

Broccoli, *Brassica oleracea* (**the Italica group** or cultivar is broccoli, as opposed to the **Botrytis group** or cultivar, which is cauliflower), does not form a solid head but grow in a cluster of flower buds. **Flower buds, stems, and attached leaves are all edible.** Broccoli is a cool weather crop, best started in early spring or mid-July.

Few published canning recipes exist for broccoli, possibly due to broccoli's stronger flavor and high pH of 6.30 to 6.52, which is in line with the pH of cabbage at 5.20 to 6.80. Make good use of the broccoli and sage in your garden with this unusual pickle (DOB = June 30, 1998). **Serve aromatic broccoli pickles with meat, Indian curry, and rice. Eat it when you have a sore throat or wish to stimulate your appetite.** The taste of this aromatic pickle is totally earthy and unlike most other pickles. The tart taste is refreshing for several mouthfuls, but this is not a pickle to consume by the jar-full. Also, **sage does contain *thujone*** and should only be consumed in culinary/spicing quantities.

Jamlady's Aromatic Broccoli Pickles

Main ingredient:
Freshly picked broccoli

Per pint jar:
5 juniper berries
5 sage leaves

Spiced vinegar:
5 quarts vinegar
3 cups raw honey
7 tablespoons pickling spice
5 cups water

Pick fresh and tender broccoli clusters; soak them in a bowl of highly salted water to eliminate elusive green worms. Loosely pack the sterile jar with broccoli, juniper berries, and sage leaves. Cook the vinegar, honey, and spices together; strain and pour into jars. SP/RWB15(16OZ)**R**A. Matures in 5 weeks. pH = 3.45 to 3.55, but refrigeration is still recommended. The vinegar in this recipe might be reduced to achieve a product pH of 3.9; be sure to test the final product's pH before consuming it.

Note: Notice the ratio of vinegar to water; 20:5 or 4:1 is a huge increase from the normal *jardinière* ratios of 1:1, and the ratio is increased to compensate for the high pH of broccoli. Vinegar might be reduced to 21:7 or 3:1, but the final pickle would have to be tested or kept refrigerated.

Broccoli may be used in *jardinières* or in combination with other vegetables. This pickle combines peppers and broccoli and may be made hot or not hot.

3-9 V Italian Style Pickles

Spiced vinegar:
1 quart red wine vinegar
1 cup sugar
1½ cups non-hard water
2 tablespoons pickling spice

In each jar:
fresh basil leaves
fresh oregano leaves
3 garlic cloves
6 whole black peppercorns
1-2 okra pods per jar (optional)

Main ingredients:
Raw sweet peppers
Raw hot peppers (optional)
Raw small broccoli flowerets
Parboiled onion slices
Parboiled carrot discs
Parboiled cauliflower flowerets
Raw celery slices

Boil together the vinegar, sugar, pickling spice, and water for 15 minutes; strain. Jar the other spices and selected vegetables. Pour the hot-spiced vinegar into the jar. SP/RWB20(16OZ)**R**A

Note: Only use broccoli as a minor vegetable in this *jardinière*; test the pH of the final product, or refrigerate the final product.

Garlic, *Allium sativum* L., may be pickled solo in straight vinegar. Two products result: a flavored vinegar and pickled garlic. Unpeeled garlic may also be pickled. Persian Sweet Garlic may be made by boiling individual garlic cloves in a sweet vinegar-water solution for 10 minutes and JSR. **This next recipe is a "Refrigerate Only" recipe, as less than**

full-strength vinegar is used. Combine 40 separated, peeled or unpeeled garlic cloves with 2 cups vinegar, 2 cups water, 1 cup sugar, 8 whole clove (or other spice), and 2 tablespoons peppercorns and refrigerate. Supposedly, this garlic improves with age. ***S-allyl cysteine*** (SAC) is the active ingredient in pickled garlic, which studies show "lowers cholesterol, blood pressure and sugar levels, and inhibits platelet aggregation as well. While SAC has some anti-tumor properties, the odorous sulfides that circulate in the lymphatic system have greater anti-cancer properties. The wonderful thing is that the longer you leave the garlic in the vinegar, the more SAC is formed—for over 4 years—it just gets better with age—up to about 5 years!" (http://www.gourmetgarlicgardens.com/pickle.htm). Alternately, cloves of garlic may be peeled and canned (see next recipe).

The Australian Food Safety Centre of Excellence states on its website that oil and spices have no preserving effect on garlic, and garlic must be preserved with vinegar before any oil is added to the garlic. "Vinegar should be added to the vegetable component of these preserves before any oil is added so that the ratio of vegetables to vinegar by weight is not greater than three to one. For example: to make 400 grams of preserved garlic, one would mix 300 grams of garlic with 100 grams of vinegar. The resultant mixture will then contain approximately one percent acetic acid, which would ensure a final pH below 4.6. This will not guarantee the products will not spoil if not kept properly refrigerated, but it will ensure they do not become toxic." To be safe, weigh all ingredients.

Hot Dilled Garlic with Carrot Accents

Per 8-ounce jar:
- 5-10 peppercorns
- ½ teaspoon pickling salt
- ½-1 teaspoon sugar (optional)
- ½ teaspoon pickling spice
- 1 dill head*
- Peeled garlic cloves
- 1-15 Serrano/Thai peppers
- Several thin carrots sticks
- Red or white wine vinegar

Jar the spices. Loosely pack the garlic, hot peppers, and carrot sticks and cover with hot vinegar, SP/RWB15(8OZ)20(16OZ)RA. **Keep refrigerated for extra safety. The juice is garlic-flavored vinegar.**

* May substitute ½ teaspoon dill seed

Variation: Sweet Persian Pickled Garlic—Add the optional sugar; eliminate the hot peppers and dill.

Variation: Not-Hot Pickled Garlic—Use sweet peppers and white wine vinegar or cider vinegar. **Refrigeration is highly recommended.**

Caution: Although properly formulated, pickled vegetables such as garlic should be shelf-stable; it is prudent to keep pickled garlic refrigerated at all times due to its pH, density, and known association with botulism. Remember, botulism is of utmost concern for foods that will be eaten without reheating, as the botulism toxin is killed with heat. Since pickled cloves of garlic are used in cold salads, it is recommended all pickled garlic be refrigerated (at all times) and only coated with oil after opening.

Green beans, *Phaseolus vulgaris,* are native to tropical America. Included in the group are: green beans, snap beans, French beans, string beans, wax beans, kidney beans, and pinto beans. **Most beans can be eaten in immature stages, but lima beans are only eaten when mature and removed from the mother pod.**

One of the most popular bean pickles is the dilly bean.

Dilly beans may be made hot or not hot. There are recipes for pickling green beans with lemons, spices, and honey, but they are not popular in the United States. **Be sure to tip the green beans.** Tipping the green beans helps the vinegar to penetrate the green bean, makes the jars of beans look tidier, allows for more edible product in the jar, and eliminates stem removal later.

Small French beans or regular green beans may be canned, but French beans make especially tender dilly beans. Thin French beans may need less processing time than thicker or overgrown beans. In Crystal Lake, Illinois, I have always processed quarts of smaller (thinner), loosely packed regular-bean dilly beans for 20 to 25 minutes, pints for 15 to 20 minutes, depending on the thickness of the bean. One expert consulted uses 10 minutes for pints of dilly beans at 0 feet altitude, but Crystal Lake, Illinois, is at 900 to 940 feet altitude. Consult local canning experts for times, and check your altitude.

Extra Hot Dilly Beans

Main ingredient:
Green beans
Per quart jar:
2 garlic cloves
1 scallion (optional)
2 red bell pepper strips
½ teaspoon dill weed*
½ teaspoon dill seed*
¼-½ teaspoon pickling salt
10 habanero peppers
½ teaspoon mustard seed
5-6 peppercorns
Vinegar mixture:
5 cups red wine vinegar
4 cups water

Tip the green beans. Loosely and vertically pack the green beans in the jar with spices and accents, or cut each bean into 2 to 3 pieces. Pour the hot brine into the jar and SP/RWB15-20(16OZ)20-25(32OZ)A900FT. These are Crystal Lake, Illinois, processing times at 900-940 feet of elevation. Dilly beans may be used in Bob Aicher's Hot Beef for hot beef sandwiches (see recipe).

* May substitute fresh dill head

Caution: Do not jam-pack or crowd the jars; water may be forced out of the canning jar during processing.

Variation: Mild Dilly Beans—Change the number or variety of hot pepper used.

Depending on one's budget and sensibilities, some canners might consider substituting high-quality red wine vinegar for distilled white vinegar to improve the overall taste of the product. Another canner, needing to feed many, might place cost considerations above taste and improved visual effects. Jamlady suggests a compromise.

Medium Hot Dilly Beans

Main ingredient:
Tipped French green beans
Per quart jar:
5 Serrano peppers
1 jalapeño pepper
2 yellow pepper accents
2 garlic cloves
½ teaspoon pickling salt
1 fresh dill head
Vinegar mixture:
3 parts white vinegar
2 parts red wine vinegar
3 parts water
or
5 parts red wine vinegar
3 parts water

Loosely pack the beans, peppers, and spices in jars; cover with the hot vinegar mixture. SP/RWB15-20(16OZ)20-25(32OZ)A900FT.

Note: Many *jardinières* may be made with a 50 to 50 ratio (vinegar to water), but Jamlady considers a ratio of 60 to 40 to be safer, especially with reduced salt formulations. Salt may be increased but not reduced.

Bob Aicher's Italian Beef

- 3½-4 pounds* boneless chuck-eye roast or beef chuck blade roast
- 1 jar (15.5 ounces) mild vegetable antipasto (i.e. "*giardiniera*" or *jardinière*)
- 1 envelope Good Seasons Zesty Italian Salad Dressing mix
- 1 8-ounce jar of hot or medium hot dilly beans
- 1 can (10¾ ounces) beef broth or beef stock
- 2 sliced/seeded green bell peppers
- 2 tablespoons olive oil
- 10 rolls
- 10 thin slices of mozzarella cheese

Place the roast in a 3½-quart slow cooker. Add the drained antipasto and dilly beans (substitution: *pepperoncini*** or pickled peppers), salad mix, and broth. Cook covered on low for 18 hours. Sauté the green bell peppers in the oil and set aside. Remove the roast, reserving the vegetables and defatted gravy. Discard all bone and fat. Open a roll, add the beef, cheese slice, reserved vegetables from the gravy, sautéed green peppers, and finally drench it all with some gravy.

* Substitute a 6-pound roast. Increase all other ingredients by half, and increase the total cooking time to 21 hours. Serves 10 to 12. For a 10-pound roast, oven bake at 225 degrees F in a foil-covered roasting pan with 3 dressing mixes, 8-ounces hot-pickled okra, 2 cans beef broth, 24-ounces *pepperoncini,*** and an 8-ounce jar of drained pickled yellow pepper rings. Bob says you may vary this basic recipe with different pickled vegetables to produce tasty beef sandwiches. What a great way to cook with canned pickles!

** ***Pepperoncini* are a pickled Tuscan variety of pepper that is slightly hot.**

The vegetable **cauliflower,** *Brassica oleracea,* is native to coastal Europe. **The clustered flower buds of this plant are found in white, yellow, purple, or green.** Cauliflower is a cool-weather crop and may be seeded twice a year. **White cauliflower is not self-blanching and requires leaf tie-backs to protect the heads from the sun.** The purple and green culivars need not be blanched.

There are some very different looking varieties or cultivars of cauliflower, but **Romanesco ("pyramid cauliflower")** from Italy is especially awesome. Naturally dyed cauliflower is also impressive and colorful. For this photo, we used half the amount of beet normally called for in the recipe below, so the liquid in the jars of pink-colored cauliflower wouldn't be too dark. We wanted viewers to be able to see the beautiful color and the product. Consequently, the cauliflower is less intensely dyed in the photograph than in the Pickled Pink Cauliflower recipe below. It also takes time for the intensity of the color to penetrate the cauliflower; therefore, allow a few weeks for the color to enrich.

Pickled Pink Cauliflower

- 1 small to medium beet
- 1 head white cauliflower
- 2 cups red wine vinegar
- 1½ cups water
- 2 teaspoons pickling salt

Still life with pickled cauliflower.

Peel and cook a beet; cut it into ½-inch cubes. Blanch the cauliflower in boiling water for 2 minutes. Pack a few beet cubes and cauliflower in a jar; pour in a hot brine of vinegar, water, and salt. Voilà! Fuchsia! SP/RWB15(8OZ)15(16OZ)20(32OZ)A. pH = 3.4 to 3.5. Origin: Middle-Eastern.

Many people like cauliflower in soups, casseroles, and salads. Try **Chinese cauliflower pickle *P'ao Ts'ai.*** Boil a cauliflower head and 2 peeled carrots in water for 10 minutes. Drain; break the cauliflower into pieces. Dice the carrots; add 2 diced and seeded chili peppers, 3 sliced bell peppers, ½ head shredded cabbage, and 1 peeled, seeded, and diced cucumber. Boil together: 2 cups rice vinegar (or red wine vinegar), ½ cup sugar (or honey or agave), and 1 teaspoon salt. Add the vinegar mixture to the prepared vegetables. Serve hot or cold.

The Japanese add vinegar to stir-fried vegetables. For a quick pickle, or ***tsukemonos,*** stir-fry (in order) in oil: 1 sliced carrot, 6 sliced okra, and 1 broken-up head of cauliflower. Add 2 tablespoons rice vinegar, 1 teaspoon salt, and a pinch of spice (like dill weed or curry powder). Add a lid to the pan; steam for 3 minutes and refrigerate.

The topic of Japanese pickles is extensive and beyond the scope of this small book, but here is the short course. ***Shiozuke*** is a salt pickle. Vegetables are salted in earthenware and pressed with a stone or "pickle press" for several days. Purchase a **pickle press,** or use a big, flat, heavy stone. A one night salt pickle is an ***ichiyazuke.*** Long-term pickles are ***umeboshi,*** which are tart and salty pickled plums or apricots. ***Umeboshi*** are often eaten daily and are considered a folk remedy for colds. Their origins are rooted in tenth-century Japan. ***Suzuke*** are pickles cured in rice vinegar. ***Nakazuke pickles*** may be made by mixing 2 pounds ***nuka*** (rice bran), ¼ pound salt, and 2½ cups water in a covered earthenware pot.

Some vegetable peels are added for two days and removed. After stirring daily for a week, the mixture may be used to submerge salt-rubbed vegetables like eggplants, cucumbers, cabbage, and radishes. The crock is best kept refrigerated. To enjoy this pickle, remove and wash pickle pieces. (see "The Pickle Pot," by Elizabeth Andoh, in the Japanese recipe index at www.bento.com/taste./tc-pick.html).

Takuan is a Japanese radish that is preserved in rice bran. ***Kasuzuke*** is pickled in a white liquor called ***sakekasu,*** which is mixed with sugar and salt. ***Misozuke*** is made by burying garlic, pumpkin, and other vegetables in *miso paste* and *sake*. Some of these *misozuke* pickles take years to mature, or from another perspective, are stored or preserved for two years. ***Koji*** (rice mold) is used as a pickling base to make ***kojizuke*** and is also used to manufacture ***sake, miso, mirin,*** and ***soy sauce. Shoyuzuke*** are vegetables pickled in ***shoyu,*** soy sauce, and sweet liquid *mirin.* ***Fukujinzuke*** is a soy-sauce pickle of vegetables like white radishes, eggplants, lotus root, ginger, ***shiso*** buds, turnips, ***shiitakes, udo,*** sword beans, and ***shirouri*** and is eaten with curry and rice. ***Senmaizuke*** is a famous turnip pickle, salt-pickled with ***konbu*** seaweed, sugar or *mirin*, and chili peppers. ***Iburi Gakko*** is a dried and smoked radish, which is pickled with salt and rice bran for three months.

Korean ***kimchee*** or ***kimchi*** or "pickles" is the national dish of Korea and is eaten often with rice. Did you have any idea there were so many pickling techniques practiced in Asian countries? See Chapter 2 for more information on the evolution of pickles.

Korean-Style Kimchi

¼ head Nappa cabbage
3 thin slices red onion
1½ tablespoons pickling salt
2 cups water
10 ice cubes
3 sliced green onions
1 teaspoon sugar
1 minced garlic clove
⅛ teaspoon minced hot pepper*
½ teaspoon minced gingerroot
¼ teaspoon fish sauce (optional)
Salted shrimp (optional)

Weight down the shredded Nappa (Chinese cabbage), red onions, pickling salt, water, and ice cubes with a weighted plate. Wait 10 to 12 hours or longer. Drain; **reserve the brine.** Combine the green onions, sugar, minced garlic, hot pepper (to taste), gingerroot, and fish sauce with the drained (not squeezed) Nappa cabbage mixture. Pack the *kimchi* in a pint or quart canning jar, pack down, and pour in enough of the reserved brine to cover. **Add a reclosable plastic bag into the neck of the jar and some reserved brine.** This will form an air lock. Screw the lid on loosely, or leave it as is. Refrigerate 2 to 14 days. Sample the pickle after day two. Optional: add ¼ teaspoon fish sauce (*garum*) or some salted shrimp.

* May substitute ⅛ teaspoon dried hot pepper

Dilled Cauliflower Pickles

Per pint jar:
1 thinly sliced onion
2 garlic cloves
1 hot pepper (optional)
1 accent piece red bell pepper

Main ingredient:
Cauliflower flowerets

Brine:
1 quart water
½ quart cider vinegar
¼ cup pickling salt

This is not a shelf-stable recipe. Jar the spices and cauliflower; cover with hot brine. SP/RWB15(16OZ)**R.** Label well and **"Keep Refrigerated"** or increase the vinegar and test the pH. **See Pickled Pink Cauliflower with a pH of 3.4.** This pickle is shelf-stable.

Spiced Pickled Cauliflower may be made by preblanching the cauliflower. Plunge the cauliflower in boiling water. Cover; wait 2 minutes. Drain; pack the jars with cauliflower. Cook 1 quart vinegar with 1 cup sugar (or ½ cup honey), 2 tablespoons mustard seed, 5 whole clove, 5 cinnamon sticks, 10 whole allspice, 1 broken nutmeg, and 1 teaspoon salt for 15 minutes. Pour the strained brine over the cauliflower; adjust headspace to 6 percent and SP/RWB20(32OZ)A. Vary the spices; select from mustard seed, celery seed, whole clove, whole allspice, turmeric, cinnamon sticks, hot peppers, and broken nutmeg. **Instead of blanching, the cauliflower may be dry-salted with ¼ cup salt and one tray of ice cubes for 2 to 3 hours. Then drain, rinse, drain, and mix the cauliflower with the brine and process.** Some recipes call for dry-salting both the cauliflower and onions (*The Ball Blue Book* 1995).

The **artichoke,** *Cynara scolymus,* is native to the Mediterranean and is also grown in California. For **pickled artichokes:** cut small artichokes down, remove the outer leaves, and leave a 1½-inch stem. Add the artichokes to a citric-acid or lemon-juice solution (2½ teaspoons citric acid or 1 cup lemon juice to 2 quarts water). Simmer the trimmed artichokes 3 to 5 minutes, according to size. Jar the drained artichokes, cover them with vinegar, and leave them for 12 hours in a cool place. Drain; cover with fresh vinegar for 4 hours. Drain; add vinegar-soaked spices and fill with oil. SP/RWB30(16OZ)**R**A. **Caution: Refrigerate and label "Keep Refrigerated."** Suggested spices per pint are: 2 bay leaves, ¼ teaspoon basil or fresh leaves, ¼ teaspoon oregano or fresh leaves, 1 garlic head, peppercorns, and mustard seed. **Alternately, process in vinegar without the oil (shelf-stable). See previous comments on canning with oil.**

Eggplant, *Solanum melongena,* may be pickled in mixed *jardinières* or with red bell peppers. Serve pickled eggplant with pastas or sandwiches.

Hot Pickled Eggplant

Main ingredients:
- Split baby eggplant or small pieces
- A tad lemon juice
- Red and green bell peppers

Per quart jar:
- 1-2 garlic cloves
- 15-20 fresh oregano leaves
- 1 teaspoon pickling spice
- 5-10 peppercorns
- ½ teaspoon pickling salt
- 1 sliced jalapeño
- ⅓ hot finger pepper
- 1 fresh chili

Vinegar mixture:
- 3 parts red wine vinegar
- 2 parts water

Parboil the eggplants in salted lemon water. Loosely pack the parboiled eggplants, raw bell peppers, and spices, and pour the hot vinegar into the jars, leaving ¾-inch headspace. SP/RWB20(32OZ)**R**A. This recipe should be shelf-stable, but testing the first batch is recommended. Don't overpack the jars. For extra safety, use a 4:1 vinegar to water ratio.

Although eggplant was cultivated in 600 B.C. China, there are very few eggplant recipes in old United States cookbooks. *The Everyday Cookbook* includes only one recipe, stuffed eggplant (Neil, E. 1892). After 1900, and through 1930s and even up to the 1950s, there just wasn't that much eggplant eaten in America, but new immigrants changed all that.

Honey-Sweet Eggplant Nuggets is an excellent

side pickle for roasted lamb or hot curries. Unlike many eggplant recipes, which chop the eggplant as a relish, this recipe calls for larger more uniform-sized pieces of peeled eggplant. These eggplant nuggets are best made with rich, full-bodied red wine vinegar or spiced herbal vinegar. Don't miss this pickle!

Honey-Sweet Eggplant Nuggets

6 medium eggplants
1 large red onion
1 tablespoon lemon juice
1 tablespoon salt in water
1½ cups red wine vinegar
2½ cups raw clover honey
1 cup water

Spice bag:
1 teaspoon allspice
½ teaspoon clove
½ teaspoon white or green peppercorns
1 true cinnamon stick

Peel the eggplant. Cut it into ¾-inch x ¾-inch x ½-inch pieces. Add equal-sized onion pieces, 1 tablespoon lemon juice, and 1 teaspoon salt and cover with water. Boil for 5 minutes; drain. Cover with water, wait 2 minutes, and drain again. Cook the spice bag with the vinegar, honey, and water. Discard the spice bag; add the eggplant and onion. Cook until the vegetables are tender. JSP/RWB15(8OZ)20(16OZ)A.

In recent years, fewer people ask for peppers packed in oil. Nevertheless, some people still want peppers preserved in oil. Commercially jarred or preserved peppers, those not processed at 240 degrees F, have first had a pretreatment with some acid before the oil is added. Otherwise, the pepper in oil need to be kept refrigerated. To can peppers in oil, by the RWB method, follow the directions carefully. It is just as easy (and safer) to can the peppers in vinegar and a little water (see recipe) and add the oil after opening. **Alternately, if making peppers in oil, just keep them refrigerated. Label "Keep Refrigerated."**

Pickled Peppers in Oil

1 pound hot peppers
¼ pound red or yellow peppers
⅙ pound sliced onions
Garlic cloves
Dried oregano and/or parsley
Pickling salt
Olive oil

Please see cautions below. Layer all of the peppers, onions, and garlic in a 5-percent-acidity cider vinegar for 24 hours. Keep cool. Sterilize the jars, rings, and lids. Use a thermometer. Heat the peppers and onions in the vinegar to 140 degrees F. Drain and discard the liquid. Soak the dried spices in a little hot vinegar for several hours. Place ½ inch of oil in each jar. Add the pepper mixture, presoaked oregano flakes and parsley leaves, and ¼ teaspoon pickling salt per pint. Remove the air bubbles. Add new vinegar to complete the jar, leaving ½-inch headspace for pints. SP/RWB30(16OZ)**RA**. **Refrigeration is highly recommended.**

For pickling peppers without oil, follow the various recipes in the *jardinière* section. Oil may be added to *jardinières* after opening.

The next **carrot recipe has oil and tomato puree** as a dressing on the pickle. There is no need to can this pickle; it may be pickled and kept in the refrigerator. Before the worries of oil trapping botulinum in air pockets of vegetable cell walls, we used to can these pickles and take them on camping trips. Now the recommendation is to **refrigerate** all products canned with oil.

Golden Slices of Carrots

4 pounds carrots
3 medium green peppers
5 green onions
2 cups thick tomato puree
½ cup olive oil
1½ cups sugar
1½ cups cider vinegar
2 teaspoons prepared mustard
2 teaspoons white vinegar Worcestershire sauce

Peel and thickly slice the carrots; parboil until al dente.* Seed and slice the peppers. Slice the green onions, using a few light-green tops. Cook all ingredients except the oil and carrots until al dente.* Add the carrots; refrigerate 12 hours. Before serving, add the oil and refrigerate for 12 hours more. Plate with fresh parsley and dill. Keep refrigerated or check the pH, adjust the acidity if necessary and JSP/RWB15(16OZ)RA. **Label "Keep Refrigerated."**
* If this product is being canned, the range cooking time may be reduced a little and the processing times extended.

I am not recommending processing times (with or without the oil) for shelf-stable tomato product because Montana State University's Extension website shows revised times (April 2006) that are longer than I have used successfully for years. Their processing times for tomato juice in pints is 40 minutes (hot packed) and 90 minutes (raw packed). Information on the website www.fao.org/ denotes 25 to 35 minutes for mixed vegetables in tomato juice, depending on the jar size. The pH of this pickle is 4.13 to 4.20. My experience tells me 25 to 35 minutes should be sufficient processing time, but in light of an expert stating otherwise, I will just leave it up to canners themselves to determine what processing times they will use for shelf-stable vegetables in tomato sauce. Whatever you do, it is safest to keep the product refrigerated after canning. For a shelf-stable product, the critical point to check is the pH of the total product. It must be well under 4.6 (4.2).

Pickled Mushrooms in Truffle Oil—a quick to make refrigerator pickle.

Pickled Mushrooms in Truffle Oil

2½ cups white vinegar	5 garlic cloves
1¾ cups water	¼ cup jalapeño strips
3 tablespoons salt	3 pounds small button mushrooms
⅓ cup chopped onions	1 teaspoon truffle oil

Simmer the vinegar, water, salt, onions, garlic cloves, and peppers in a saucepan; stir. Wash the mushrooms. Add the washed mushrooms to the saucepan for 6 to 8 minutes, or until slightly softened. Remove the heat; strain solids from the brine. Cool to stop the cooking. When the mushrooms and brine have cooled, add together and mix in the truffle oil. Keep Refrigerated. Recipe from Michael Pechman.

Pickled Mushrooms with Shrimp

4 teaspoons salt	⅛ teaspoon black pepper
6-7 cups water	½ teaspoon fresh or dried thyme
1 pound fresh button mushrooms	2 cups white Zinfandel or Chardonnay
½ cup sliced red onions	2 cups white vinegar
1 minced garlic clove	½ cup virgin olive oil
¼ cup chopped parsley	2 tablespoons fresh lemon juice
2 bay leaves	1 pound large cooked, shelled shrimp

Add the salt to the water. Wash the mushrooms in salted water; drain, retaining the mushrooms. Cook all ingredients (except the shrimp) with the mushrooms for about 8 to 9 minutes. Cool; add the shrimp. **Refrigerate.** Serve after 6 hours on a bed of greens or in radicchio leaves with lemon wedges. This is a great make-ahead recipe.

Hot Dilled Mushroom Caps

1¼ teaspoons citric acid*	10 peppercorns
1 teaspoon salt	2-6 garlic cloves
1 quart water	2 Thai peppers
6 cups small mushroom caps	2 Serrano peppers
Fresh dill weed	1 quart cider vinegar
½ teaspoon dill seed	

Recipe is per 8-ounce jar. Add the citric acid and salt to the water. Add the washed and trimmed mushroom caps; simmer 5 minutes. Drain. Put fresh dill weed, dill seed, peppercorns, garlic, and peppers in each jar. Then add the drained mushrooms. Pour cider vinegar over the mushrooms, SP/RWB20(8OZ)A. To serve, stuff the mushrooms with goat cheese and caviar or salmon cream cheese.

* May substitute ½ cup lemon juice.

Variation: Dilled Pickled Mushroom Caps—Use without hot peppers.

Variation: Pickled Mushroom Caps or **Hot Pickled Mushroom Caps**—Substitute pickling spice for dill. For the hot version, use hot peppers.

Pickled Cocktail Onions

8 cups boiling water
8 cups ½-inch to ¾-inch onions
4 cups vinegar
1 cup sugar
½ cup pickling salt
2 tablespoons mustard seed
1 tablespoon black pepper
Minced red pepper*
1 teaspoon celery seed (optional)
2 tablespoons grated horseradish
Several bay leaves**

Cover the small onions with boiling water to prepare them for peeling, and wait 5 minutes. Drain and rinse with cool water. Peel the onions, discarding the peels. Reserve the onions. Simmer the vinegar, sugar, salt, spices (except bay leaf), and horseradish for three minutes to make the brine. Add the onions, bring to a boil, and reserve the brine separately. Jar the onions with 1 bay leaf per jar; pour the brine into the jars. SP/RWB20(8OZ)A. Increase the processing time for larger onions.

* May substitute hot pepper flakes
** May substitute juniper berries

JARDINIÈRES

Small pickling cucumbers may be made into *jardinière* (French), *giardiniera* (Italian), or garden pickles (English) when combined with baby garlic, onions, carrots, or other garden vegetables. Various types of vinegar may be used, but use at least 5- or 6-percent-acidity vinegar. Substituting for some of the basic vinegar, try 1 to 2 tablespoons balsamic vinegar.

Many foreign words have been adopted into the English language. If you think only a few words like *jardinière* or *giardiniera* have been adapted into the English language, take a second look at words like chow-chow (Chinese), chutney (Indian), guacamole (Mexican), gyro (Greek), gelato (Italian), and ketchup (Chinese). **No better examples of the "melting pot" phenomenon can be seen than the absorption of foreign culinary words into the American-culinary vernacular.**

A *jardin* in French is a garden, and *jardinières* are pickles of garden vegetables. Any of the following vegetables may be used in a *jardinière* (mixed garden vegetable pickle), but the final pH must be comfortably under 4.6. Wash and cut the vegetables into desired shapes. The most common shapes are disks, sticks, or chunks, but more special shapes like stars are doable. **Cucumbers may be**

This jar of jardinière was used to make the mixed pickle and cold-cut platter featured on page 127.

peeled and sliced; their centers may be cut out with a star-shaped or heart-shaped cookie cutter. Some vegetables are raw packed, and others are parboiled or blanched first (hot packed). The spice or vinegar may be varied, but use at least 5-percent-acidity vinegar. Use no less than a 50 to 50 water to vinegar ratio, erring on the side of more vinegar and less water. **When using high pH vegetables, the ratio of vinegar to water should be increased, or straight vinegar should be used.** Test the product's final pH. If you have no pH meter, keep the product refrigerated. Label it **"Keep Refrigerated."**

Vegetables	How to pack or prepare to pack	pH range under 4.3	Need to acidify pH range above 4.6
Baby corn	parboil		5.90-7.30
Beans (green/waxed)	raw or parboil		5.60-6.50
Small French beans	raw		5.60-6.50
Bell peppers pieces	raw		5.20-5.93
Broccoli flowerets	parboil		6.30-6.52
Brussels sprouts	parboil		6.00-6.30
Cabbage pieces	blanch		5.20-6.80
Capers	canned capers are usually packed in salt brine		6.0
Carrot slices or sticks	parboil or cut thin		4.90-5.30
Cauliflower flowerets	parboil		5.60-6.00
Celery pieces or sticks	pack raw		5.70-6.00
Cucumber slices or sticks	pack raw		5.12-5.78
Eggplant pieces or very small eggplants	parboil with a little lemon juice		4.75-5.50
Garlic	only use a few with these formulations		5.30-6.30
Green tomatoes, small or pieces	pack raw		4.42-4.65
Hot peppers	pack raw		5.20-5.93
Husk tomatoes	pack raw	4.21-4.30	
Jerusalem artichoke pieces	pack raw		cooked, 5.93-6.00
Mushrooms	use previously canned mushrooms or can in full strength vinegar		6.00-6.70
Okra pods	raw (small ones) or blanch before packing		5.50-6.60
Olives, green fermented	raw pack	3.50-4.60	
Olives, ripe	use previously canned olives		6.00-8.00
Onions, small whole onions or pieces	blanch before packing		5.40-5.80
Pea pods	parboil before packing		6.22-6.88
Shallots	blanch before packing		5.30-5.70
Summer squash, small whole, pieces, or blossoms	pack raw		5.00-6.20
Zucchini sticks or slices	pack raw		5.69-6.10

Do not use very low-acid vegetables unless pickling them in full-strength vinegar or unless the product's pH is adjusted using a pH meter. Don't use too much cabbage (low-acid) or other pH vegetables in *jardinières;* they will pull the pH up over the 4.6 botulism line. When making experimental pickles, test the pH or continuously refrigerate the pickles. Otherwise, follow approved recipes.

Per quart jar:

1-2 teaspoon(s) pickling salt
2 garlic cloves (pH = 5.30 to 6.30)
3-10 peppercorns
½ hot pepper
½-1 teaspoon spice(s)*
2 slivers fresh horseradish root (optional)
* May use: pickling spice or mustard seed, juniper berries, fresh oregano leaves, or other herbs

Vinegar to Water Ratio

Vinegar	Water	Percentage Vinegar
1 part	0 parts	100%
1 part	1 part	50%
2 parts	1 part	66.7%
3 parts	1 part	75%
3 parts	2 parts	60%
4 parts	1 part	80%
4 parts	3 parts	57.1%
5 parts	1 part	83.3%
5 parts	2 parts	71.4%
5 parts	3 parts	62.5%
5 parts	4 parts	55.6%
7 parts	1 part	87.5%
8 parts	1 part	88.9%

There are an infinite number of *jardinière* combinations possible. Select the strength of the vinegar solution, considering the acidity of the vegetables used in the *jardinière.* The average dill pickle has a completed pH of around 3.2 to 3.6. Observe the amount of vinegar and salt in dill pickle recipes, which lead to a final pH of around 3.2 to 3.6. Note the average pH shown for some recipes in this book.

Snap Pea Jardinière

Main ingredients:

Carrot sticks, pack raw (pH = 4.90-5.30)
20 (only) sugar snap peas, pack raw (pH = 6.22-6.88)
2 (only) peas shoots, pack raw (pH = 6.22-6.88)
Zucchini slices, pack raw (pH = 5.69-6.10)

Per quart jar:

4 garlic cloves
25 oregano leaves
6 peppercorns
2 teaspoons pickling spice
½-1 teaspoon salt
1-2 hot Thai peppers

Vinegar mixture—80%:

4 cups vinegar
1 cup water

Limit the number of snap peas to 20 per quart and pea shoots to 2. Parboil the carrots. Loosely jar-pack the pea pods, pea shoots, zucchini, carrots, garlic, hot peppers, and spices. Pour the hot vinegar mixture into the jar, SP/RWB20(32OZ)**RA**. Test the pH or **refrigerate.**

It is impossible to pack duplicate jars. Don't overpack jars; err on the side of underpacking. Most novice canners want to get as much in the jar as possible. This is not a good thing. Make one jar of *jardinière,* grind it up with its juice, test it, and if 3.8 to 4.0 or under, follow the same procedure again. Or, alternately, just refrigerate the product, labeling it **"Refrigerate Only."**

Not Hot Jardinière

Main ingredients:
- Carrots, parboiled (pH = 4.90-5.30)
- Green beans, pack raw (pH = 5.60-6.50)
- Sweet peppers, pack raw (pH = 5.20-5.93)
- Cucumbers, pack raw (pH = 5.12-5.78)
- Tomatillos, pack raw (pH = 4.21-4.30)

Per pint jar:
- 30 oregano leaves
- 2 garlic cloves
- 6 black peppercorns
- 3 white peppercorns
- ¼-½ teaspoon pickling salt

Vinegar mixture—60%:
- 1 part red wine vinegar
- 2 parts white wine vinegar or white vinegar
- 2 parts water

Review the pH of the main ingredients. If practical, pack more of the lower pH vegetables. JSP/RWB20(16OZ)**RA**. Test the completed *jardinière,* or refrigerate it and label **"Keep Refrigerated."** This recipe is formulated for shelf-stability, but it still should be checked—especially if you are a novice canner.

Hot Jardinière with Oregano Leaves

Per quart jar:
- 3 garlic cloves
- 1-12 Serrano or Thai peppers
- 6-8 peppercorns
- 1 teaspoon mustard seed
- ½-1 teaspoon pickling salt
- 20 oregano leaves

Main ingredients:
- Sweet peppers, pack raw (pH = 5.20-5.93)
- Celery, pack raw (pH = 5.70-6.00)
- Eggplant, parboil with water and a little lemon juice (pH = 4.75-5.50)
- Tiny green tomatoes, pack raw (pH = 4.42-4.65)
- Foot-long green bean, pack raw (pH = 5.60-6.50)
- Small cucumbers, pack raw (pH = 5.12-5.78)
- 3 (only) Chinese pea pods, pack raw or blanched (pH = 6.22-6.88)
- Jalapeño peppers, pack raw (pH = 5.20-5.93)

Vinegar mixture—62.5%:
- 5 parts vinegar
- 3 parts water

Pack the spices and main ingredients in a sterile jar, and pour the hot vinegar mixture over. SP/RWB20(32OZ)**RA**. Test the pH or **R (refrigerate).** Again, this pickle should be fine to can if the directions are followed, and if it is packed correctly.

Note: Throughout this book, I hesitate to recommend canners formulate recipes unless they use a pH meter. I am not suggesting beginners, without a pH meter, refrain from making these pack as you go *jardinières*, but it does mean the final product must be labeled "Refrigerate Only," and the jars should be stored at temperatures under 39 degrees F. Just don't be nonchalant about proper storage or labels. An experienced canner should know what has worked before and, hopefully, can be relied upon to pack the jars in some consistent manner, staying within the margins of error. From an author's perspective, I can't know how attending to these details you might be, so I must recommend refrigeration or testing of processed jars. Of course, one might also increase the vinegar to increase the margin of allowable error. If you are uncertain about something in this book, please e-mail me, consult multiple sources, and try to initially work with an informed and experienced canner.

Hot Dilled E-C Jardinière

Per quart jar:
- 1 teaspoon dill seed
- 1 garlic clove
- 8 peppercorns
- ½-1 teaspoon pickling salt
- ½ teaspoon dill weed

Main ingredients:
- Eggplant, parboiled with water and a little lemon juice (pH = 4.75-5.50)
- Carrot disks, cut thin or parboil (pH = 4.90-5.30)
- Serrano peppers, pack raw (pH = 5.20-5.93)

Vinegar mixture—60%:
- 3 cups or 3 parts red wine vinegar
- 2 cups or 2 parts water

Loosely pack the jars with spices, main ingredients, and the hot vinegar mixture. Leave a 6-percent headspace or scant 1 inch from the quart's top. SP/RWB20-25*(32OZ)**R**A. Test the completed product for shelf-stability or refrigerate. This recipe is formulated for canning if packed and processed correctly.

* For thicker and larger pieces, process longer (25 minutes).

Delicious display of jardinières with rolled delicatessen meats.

Hot Garlicky Jardinière

Main ingredients:
Golden zucchini, pack raw (pH = 5.69-6.10)
Baby cucumbers, pack raw (pH = 5.12-5.78)
Assorted sweet/hot peppers, pack raw (pH = 4.65-5.45)

Per quart jar:
6 garlic cloves (pH = 5.30-6.30)
3 cardamom seeds (optional)
½-1 teaspoon pickling salt
10 green peppercorns
20 oregano leaves*

Vinegar mixture—66.7%
2 parts red wine vinegar
1 part water

Raw pack the vegetables with spices, and pour in the hot vinegar mixture. Leave 6-percent headspace, SP/RWB20(32OZ)RA. This recipe should be shelf-stable if the jars are packed and processed properly; pH testing is recommended or **refrigerate.**

* May substitute 5 juniper berries and sprig rosemary or 5 whole allspice and 2 bay leaves

Hot Jardinière with Balsamic

Per quart jar:
2 sliced garlic cloves
20 oregano leaves
1 teaspoon mustard seed
1-2 bay leaves
½-1 teaspoon pickling salt
5 green peppercorns

Main ingredients:
Eggplant, parboiled in water with lemon juice (pH = 4.75-5.50)
Cauliflower, parboil (pH = 5.60-6.00)
Carrots, slice thin or parboil (pH = 4.90-5.30)
Okra pods, pack raw (pH = 5.50-6.60)
Peppers, pack raw (pH = 4.65-5.45)

Vinegar mixture—61.9%:
3 cups or 3 parts red wine vinegar (5-percent acidity)
2 cups or 2 parts water
¼ cup balsamic vinegar (6-percent acidity)

Add the spices and selected main ingredients to the jar. Pour in the hot vinegar solution, leaving 6-percent headspace. SP/RWB20(32OZ)**RA**. For a shelf-stable product, pack the canning jars loosely, and pH test the ground-up end product.

Pickled Dilled Eggplants & Peppers

Per quart jar:
½ teaspoon dill weed
½ teaspoon dill seed
½ teaspoon salt
8 peppercorns
3 garlic cloves

Vinegar mixture—55.5%:
5 cups or 5 parts red wine vinegar
4 cups or 4 parts water

Main ingredients:
Eggplants, parboil with water and a little lemon juice (pH = 4.75-5.50)
Sweet green and red pepper accents (pH = 5.20-5.93)

Cut the vegetables into 1-inch x ½-inch x ½-inch pieces. Place the spices and vegetable pieces in the jar. Pour in the hot vinegar mixture and SP/RWB20(32OZ)**R**A. **Please pH test for shelf-stability or "Keep Refrigerated."**

Hot Jardinière with Basil Leaves

Per quart jar:
3 Serrano peppers
3-4 jalapeño peppers
15 basil leaves
3 garlic cloves
8 peppercorns
1 teaspoon mustard seed
1 teaspoon salt

Vinegar mixture:
4 parts red wine vinegar
3 parts water

Main ingredients, select from:
Carrots, parboil (pH = 4.90-5.30)
Green beans, pack raw (pH = 5.60-6.50)
Small cucumbers, pack raw (pH = 5.12-5.78)
Cauliflower**, blanched (pH = 5.60-6.00)
Okra pods**, blanched or raw (pH = 5.50-6.60)
Yellow sweet peppers, raw (pH = 5.20-5.93)
Ripe olives** (pH = 6.00-8.00)
Green fermented olives (pH = 3.50-4.60)

Build the *jardinière* in the jar with spices and selected main ingredients. Pour the hot vinegar mixture into the jar. SP/RWB20(32OZ)**R**A. For a shelf-stable product, pH test the end product or keep your product refrigerated. If oil is desired, add it after the jar is opened.

** Use just a few; note the pH.

Hot Sandwich Jardinière/Dial-a-Scoville Unit

Main ingredients:
- Sweet green and red peppers (pH = 5.20-5.93)
- Red Hungarian hot peppers (pH = 5.20-5.93)
- Jalapeño peppers (pH = 5.20-5.93)
- Scotch bonnet peppers (pH = 5.20-5.93)
- Serrano peppers (pH = 5.20-5.93)
- Thai peppers (pH = 5.20-5.93)
- Habañero peppers (pH = 5.20-5.93)
- Celery sticks or tops (pH = 5.70-6.00)
- White or red onions (pH = 5.30-5.80)
- 1- to 3-inch long cucumbers (pH = 5.12-5.78)

Per quart jar:
- 2 garlic cloves
- 20 oregano leaves
- ½ teaspoon mustard seed
- 1 bay leaf
- 6 juniper berries
- ½-1 teaspoon salt
- ½-1 tablespoon sugar (optional)
- 3 asparagus spears (pH = 6.0-6.7)
- 2 Chinese pea pods (pH = 6.2-6.8)

Vinegar mixture—62.5%:
- 5 cups or 5 parts red wine vinegar
- 3 cups or 3 parts non-hard water

Caution: Do not increase the number of asparagus spears or pea pod accents (pH = 6.0-6.8) without increasing the vinegar to water ratio.

Cut the vegetables pieces to sandwich size (smaller than regular *jardinières*). Pack the jars; pour the hot vinegar mixture over. Leave 6-percent headspace. SP/RWB20(32OZ)**RA**. Test the pH to establish shelf-stability or **"Keep Refrigerated."**

Hot Baby Jardinière

Main ingredients:
- Baby carrots
- Pearl onions
- 2-inch pickling cucumbers

Per 8-ounce jar:
- 3-5 baby garlic bulbs with stems*
- 2 fresh Serrano peppers
- ½ teaspoon pickling spice
- 3 green peppercorns
- 1/16 teaspoon pickling salt

Vinegar mixture:
- 5 parts red wine vinegar
- 4 parts water

Peel the carrots and onions and parboil them in water in the microwave for about 2 to 3 minutes. Scrub the cucumbers. Fill the jar with garlic bulbs, peppers, spices, cucumbers, carrots, onions; cover with the hot vinegar mixture. Leave 6-percent headspace. SP/RWB20(8OZ)A.

* May substitute garlic cloves

PICKLED FRUITS

Pickled peaches are by far the most popular pickled "fruit" at farmers' markets. Of course, if you get technical, this statement is not correct because tomatoes, peppers, and cucumbers are very popular. Restating, "Of the fruits people think readily of as being fruits, peaches are the most popular!" You smart gardeners and market goers know tomatoes are fruits, as are peppers, because they have seeds inside them and, of course, are pickled extensively. **Cucumbers are also fruits. So are pea pods, acorns, and grains of wheat.** So actually, peaches are not the most popular pickled fruit at market, and it's hard to pick between cucumbers, peppers, and green tomatoes.

Pickled peaches may be canned whole, sliced, halved, or stuffed with honey, raisins, nuts, cinnamon, and nutmeg in place of the pit, which has very carefully been removed through the stem end. Jamlady saw a recipe for stuffed peaches (Elliott 1870, 219) with the same stuffing as used for melons (219) and larger cucumbers.

> **stuffing of cabbage cut fine, mustard seed, few celery seeds, pickled cucumber cut fine, onion if you like it, horse-radish scraped, allspice, clove, pieces of cinnamon, teaspoonful of sugar to each melon, and few grains of pepper.**

Mrs. Elliott instructs on peach mangoes:

> Use the same stuffing and open them carefully to extract the seed, after being in salt and water two days. Boil the vinegar with a teacup of sugar and pour on them.

See Mrs. Grant's Apple and Tomato Relish (61) for further discussion on mangoed fruits and vegetables.

Peaches may be pickled in combination with mangoes (tropical fruit) and apricots. The same recipe may be used for mangoes (tropical fruit) or apricots as is used to pickle peaches. This recipe is enhanced with brandy or Grand Marnier!

Brandied Peach Pickles

Syrup:
- 5 cups sugar
- 2 cups cider vinegar
- 2 true cinnamon sticks
- ½ teaspoon oil of clove

Per quart jar:
- Peaches without skins
- 1 true cinnamon stick
- 1 tablespoon XO Brandy or Grand Marnier (optional)
- 1 clove

Boil the sugar, cider vinegar, cinnamon, and oil of clove for 2 to 3 minutes; strain. Plunge each whole peach in hot water, then cold. Slip off the skins or peel the peaches. Sometimes the skins won't slip off easily if the peaches are underripe. Don't fret, slightly underripe peaches hold together better and taste fine. Pack the peaches in the jar, but don't overpack them or **"geyseric activity"** will result and some syrup will be forced out of the jar. Underfilling will cause the peaches to float up in the jar. **Avoid blocking the neck of the jar with peach pieces too large to allow for proper syrup movement.** After packing the peaches in each jar, pour the syrup into the jar, leaving 6-percent headspace. SP/RWB10(32OZ)**RA** or JSP/RWB20-25*(32OZ)A or follow recommended times of 25 to 30 minutes by other experts.

* Time depends on the size of the whole peaches or peach pieces.

Variation: Pickled Apricots, Pickled Pears, Pickled Mangoes—Use whole or sectioned apricots, pears, mangoes, or a combination of all three.

Variation: Dutch Ginger Pears—Spice with lemon rinds, lemon juice, and gingerroot. Use 5 cups brown or white sugar to 2 cups vinegar, no cinnamon or clove. Cook pears with the syrup or cold pack the pear, adding the syrup, gingerroot, and lemon.

Mrs. Winslow's Domestic Receipt Book for 1878 (Jeremiah Curtis & Sons and John I. Brown & Sons 1877) is a pamphlet at the Conrad Hilton Library, Hyde Park, New York. A recipe on page thirty for stuffed or "mangoed" pickled peaches instructs:

> Take out of free-stone peaches the pits; fill with large and small mustard-seeds, mixed with some grated horse-radish; tie them up with a thread; pour over them a hot syrup, made of one pound of brown sugar to a quart of vinegar. The peaches must not be too hard to pickle in this way.

On a relish plate, **Pickled Whole Crab Apples** are often seen as gewgaws or useless ornamentals. Not everyone wants to eat around the seeds of these small fruits, and few people will eat the seeds. To make whole picked crab apples: wash the crab apples, and cook them tender in a syrup of 6 cups sugar, 3 cups vinegar, 3 cups water, 1 cinnamon stick, 1 tablespoon clove, and 1 tablespoon mace or allspice. Pack the apples and syrup in a sterile jar and SP/RWB15-25(16OZ)A. Time by size. Try pickling cored crab apples if you have patience, or use the same recipe for **Pickled Apple Quarters** (with or without skins). The water in this recipe and some of the spices may be substituted with fruit juice (under 4.6 pH) or herbal tea or infusion (under 4.6 pH).

Years ago, Jamlady worked the Crystal Lake, Illinois, Farmers' Market and was positioned next to the melon man. **Melon man sold muskmelons, *Cucumis melo,* which some folks here in the Midwest mistakenly call cantaloupe.** After every market, underripe and cracked melons would be entrusted to Jamlady if she could only find a way to use them. Having never made pickled muskmelons, Jamlady decided it was worth a try and began making all sorts of muskmelon ("cantaloupe") recipes, including pickled muskmelons. One day, an old-timer from Tennessee came by Jamlady's stand and bought the pickled muskemelon. He said the pickled muskemelon was for a friend with emphysema, and "It was good for clearing the throat and for colds." After that, Jamlady related the story to others. Before long, several patients with a variety of lung ailments started buying the pickled muskemelon, espousing its benefits. If you check out some of the purported medicinal values of vinegar, mace, clove, and cinnamon, it is understandable why this formulation may have helped some emphysema patients.

The recipe by Mrs. J. in *Peterson's Preserving, Pickling & Canning* (Lemcke, Gesine 1899, 57) for Spiced Cantaloupe states:

> Take 6 pounds of sugar, to every twelve pounds of cantaloupes; one-half ounce clove; one-quarter ounce each, mace and allspice. Boil the fruit tender in water; drain off the water; then boil 1 quart of vinegar, add the sugar and spices, and while hot, pour over them, and set away in a cool place.

Preserving and Pickling (Lemcke, Gesine 1899, 77) gives a recipe for Cantaloupe Pickle.

> Pare and cut in small pieces 8 medium-sized muskmelons. Boil 3 quarts of vinegar with 6 pounds of sugar, pour over the melon, let stand overnight; next morning drain off the vinegar, let it come to a boil, add 1½ ounce celery seed, 1 ounce white mustard seed, ½ ounce whole clove, 1 ounce whole cinnamon, 3 pieces fine-cut ginger. Put in melons and cook slowly 5 hours, then put away in jars. The seeds and spice may be put in small bags if not liked in the pickle.

Classic Pickled "Cantaloupe"*

2 peeled and cubed underripe melons
1 quart hot vinegar
2 cups brown sugar
2 cups white sugar
2 sticks true cinnamon (broken)
Oil of clove (to taste)**
1 teaspoon mace*** (optional)
2 cups water****

Prepare the melon *(Cucumis melo)*; drop it in the hot vinegar, marinate 1 hour, and refrigerate overnight. Then, drain off the vinegar. Combine it with the sugar, spices (spice bag), and oil of clove (if used). Oil of clove is very strong. Do not mix it directly into the entire batch. Dilute it in some batch juice and slowly add it (to taste). Boil the vinegar mixture until clear syrup is formed. Put the melon in the syrup; cook for ½-hour or until transparent. JSP/RWB10-15(16OZ)A.

* May substitute muskemelon
** May substitute 2 teaspoons clove
*** May substitute 2 tablespoons whole pickling spice
**** Not needed unless the melons are very hard

Note: The extra juice produced may be canned separately to use in tea or for clearing the throat.

Red Watermelon, *Citrullus vulgaris* L., may be pickled to make **Watermelon Pickle** or **Watermelon Preserve** from the same melon used for **Pickled Watermelon Rind.** Soak 2 to 3 quarts balled or cubed watermelon fruit in 2 quarts water with ½ cup salt overnight. Drain the fruit; mix it with 4 to 5 cups sugar, 4 sliced lemons, and 3 tablespoons crystallized ginger or peeled ginger sticks. Cook it slowly until the fruits are transparent. Jar the watermelon; cook down the syrup (until it spins a thread), and cover the watermelon with the syrup. SP/RWB10(8OZ)A.

Pickled Watermelon Rinds

4 quarts prepared rind
3 tablespoons pickling lime
Non-hard water
8 cups sugar
5 cinnamon sticks
2 tablespoons whole clove
2 tablespoons fresh ginger
1 thinly sliced lemon
1 quart vinegar

A 7-pound watermelon nets about 4 quarts prepared rind. Eat the fruit, pickle it, or make Chokoloskee Island Chutney. To prepare the rind: cut off the outer dark-green part and most of the red part. Leave some firm, pink flesh; 1-inch squares are perfect. Put the prepared rind in 2 quarts cold water with 3 tablespoons pickling lime for two hours. **Do not breathe in powered lime or get it in your eyes.** Rinse and drain the rind 3 times; cook it tender in water (cook about 1 hour, then drain). While cooking, mix in 8 cups sugar with a spice bag (5 cinnamon sticks and 2 tablespoons whole clove). Add fresh-grated ginger (or 5 pieces minced candied ginger), 1 lemon sliced thin, 1 quart vinegar, and 1 quart water. Cook for 10 minutes. Add the watermelon rind when tender. Cook until clear. Add water if the syrup becomes too thick. Remove spice bag, put the pickles in the jar, lid, and wait 6 hours. P/RWB10(8OZ)15(16OZ)A.

Pickled sour cherries are another old-time favorite. **Jamlady's recipe uses no sugar, but a recipe in *Mrs. Beeton's Household Management: A Complete Cookery Book*** (1907, 1128) and in

The National Cook Book, by a Lady of Philadelphia (1850, 117), for pickled cherries, is made with a pound sugar to a quart vinegar, poured hot over the cherries twice, once on day one and again on day seven. Sugar may be added to the Jamlady's recipe if a sweet pickle is desired. Look over the cherries carefully, selecting only firm and slightly underripe cherries.

Pickled Whole Sour Cherries

Sour cherries
1 quart red wine vinegar
1 quart non-hard water
2 tablespoons pickling salt

Raw pack stemmed (stems removed) sour cherries. Cover the cherries with a brine of 1 quart good red wine vinegar, 1 quart non-hard water, and 2 tablespoons pickling salt. SP/RWB5-10(16OZ)**RA** or SP/180d/30(16OZ)A or SP/RWB20(8OZ)A. The expert canning sites don't appear to give times for this exact recipe. The "with-sugar-syrup" recipe calls for RWB20-25(16OZ) or 30-35(32OZ). Lots of older canning books show processing of pickled cherries as RWB5(16OZ). But, this is now. Sour cherries have a pH range of 3.20 to 4.20, and other cherries max out at around 4.2; pH is not a big issue here, but cyanide in the pits might/should be reduced by the longer cook time. (**Note:** Use the index to see other discussions on cyanide.) Serve pickled cherries with meats, and use the juice as cherry vinegar in salad dressings. Please review the note below.

Variation: Pickled Royal Ann Cherries or **Pickled Black Cherries**—To raw pack and pickle Royal Ann or black cherries, prick the cherries with a needle. Fill sterile, 8-ounce jars with stemmed cherries. Add per jar: ½ teaspoon pickling salt and ½ teaspoon sugar (or honey or agave [test the pH or **Keep R**]). Fill the jar with a hot 50:50 or 60:40 vinegar-to-water solution.

Variation: Pickled Cherries with Hyssop or **Tarragon**—Add 1 herb sprig per jar.

Variation: *Maraschino* Cherries—Soak the raw cherries in 1 quart water, 1 tablespoon salt, and ½ teaspoon alum for 12 hours. Drain and rinse. Heat to boiling: 2 to 2¼ pounds pitted cherries, 1½ cups water, 2½ cups sugar, 1 tablespoon lemon juice, and ½-ounce red food coloring; keep cool for 1 day. Drain off the juice and heat to boiling. Add ½-ounce almond extract or other flavoring. JSP/RWB20(8OZ)20-25(16OZ)A.

Please note: Prior to pitting, the cherries should be washed in water containing 1 pinch ascorbic acid crystals. Use 1 teaspoon ascorbic acid crystals (not powder) to a full bowl of water.

Variation: *Maraschino* Cherry Recipe #2—Wash 2 to 2½ pounds firm, unblemished Royal Ann cherries in ascorbic acid water (1 pinch ascorbic acid crystals in the prep water). Cook 3 cups sugar, 1½ cups water, and 2 tablespoons food coloring. Add the washed cherries; simmer 2 minutes. Remove the cherries from the heat, and store them in a cool place for 1 day. Jar the cherries, reheat the strained syrup, cover the cherries with the hot syrup, and SP/RWB20(8OZ)A.

The word "*maraschino*" comes from the European cultivar of the sour cherry tree, *Prunus cerasus marasca,* **bearing the common name *maraschino* cherry. The distinctive taste of this cherry is due to the *hydrogen cyanide* that tastes like almonds. *Hydrogen cyanide* in small quantities is not very harmful. Some say it stimulates respiration and improves digestion. In excess, it can cause respiratory failure and death** (*Prunus cerasus marasca,* Cultivation Notes: www.gardenbed.com/p/6635.cfm). When making these recipes, it is your choice to pit or not pit the sour cherries. The added almond flavoring will approximate the flavor of unpitted cherries. An Italian cordial, ***maraschino*** is made from this marasca cultivar of sour cherry. If ever in Venice, Italy, check out this cherry cultivar and the liqueur.

By the way, I received a very cordial e-mail from

Mr. Franco Luxardo (pun intended). The Luxardo Family owns and operates a 20,000 *marasca* cherry tree orchard in Italy and are the leading world producer of *Maraschino liqueur*. They have been producing this liqueur for over 176 years (six generations). Try *Maraschino liqueur* in gelatin molds, puddings, ice cream, candy, buttercream icings, jams, and drinks. To make your own sour cherry liqueur: Mix 1½ cups sour cherries, 1 cup sugar, 1 cinnamon stick, 2 clove, and 2 cups vodka in a quart canning jar; rotate and store the jar for a couple of months in a cool place. For more information on homemade liqueurs, see *The Jamlady Cookbook* (126-127).

Most of the *maraschino* cherries in the United States are made from Royal Ann cherries. Prior to 1896, most *maraschino* cherries were made in Yugoslavia and Northern Italy where a liqueur was added to the local *marasca* cherry. **Over time the liqueur was reduced and finally eliminated from jarred *maraschino*** cherries.

For **chocolate-covered cherries:** Mix 1 pound (3½ to 3¾ cups) unsifted powdered sugar, ½ cup margarine, 1 tablespoon vanilla (or other flavoring), and ⅛ teaspoon salt; form around the *maraschino* cherry. Dip these prepared cherries in a heated chocolate mixture (double boiler) of semi-sweet chocolate squares mixed with a little paraffin to allow the chocolate coating to harden properly. Place the coated cherries on waxed paper. Refrigerate.

Besides making liqueurs and pickles from cherries, Damson plums may likewise be used. Damson plums may be preserved in vodka (see the drink photo on page 97). Damson plums may be pickled like blueberries, bananas, lemons, oranges, kumquats, grapes, and other fruits.

Spiced Damson Plums

2 quarts Damson plums
3 cups sugar
½ cup red wine vinegar
3 cinnamon sticks
1 tablespoon whole allspice
1 teaspoon whole clove

Pinprick the plums twice. Boil the sugar, wine vinegar, and spices for two minutes; pour over the plums and cold store overnight. Strain off the juice and reheat and pour over the plums again. Keep cool overnight. Strain the juice again, reheat it, and pour into the plum-packed jars. Leave 6-percent headspace or ⅜ inch for an 8-ounce jar. SP/RWB15(8OZ)A. Spiced plums are good with bread pudding.

As seen from the recipe below, these pickled fruit recipes do not have to be canned. Make and use them over a period of weeks. This same basic recipe may be used with other fruits such as apples and pears for **Pickled Apples** and **Pickled Pears.**

Miss Neil's recipe in *The Every-Day Cook Book and Encyclopedia of Practical Recipes (1892, 157) for* ***Pickled Plums*** instructs:

> To seven pounds plums, four pounds sugar, two ounces stick cinnamon, two ounces clove, one quart vinegar, add a little mace; put in the jar first a layer of plums, then a layer of spices alternately; scald the vinegar and sugar together, and pour it over the plums; repeat three times for plums (only once for cut apples and pears), the fourth time scald all together, put them into glass jars and they are ready for use.

Let's talk about blueberries versus huckleberries. **Blueberries have small soft seeds. Huckleberries, while related to blueberries, have ten larger and harder seeds.** Wild blueberries grow profusely in Maine and Nova Scotia. Many regions in the United States have one variety of these berries or another. **Black huckleberries,** *Vaccinium canadensis* and *V. pennsylvanicum,* **grow on low-growing shrubs** (1 - 3 feet tall). **In New England, a "huckleberry"**

refers to a species of *Gaylussacia;* "blueberries" are from the low-growing species. Notice these two genus names are completely different, but both are called "huckleberries." The black huckleberry is spicy and sweet, but the seeds are tough. If you are lucky enough to live where the blueberries are plentiful, this recipe for **Spicy Pickled Blueberries** or **Spicy Pickled Huckleberries** will enable the quick conversion of perishable berries into shelf-stable product. In addition, you may freeze pies, pie fillings, or make preserves or jams, but those recipes probably won't use up the blueberries as quickly as this recipe. If you really have a lot of blueberries and can't process them all, make **blueberry vinegar.** Combine equal berries to vinegar (lemon zest or herbal flavoring optional). Leave on the counter, wait 4 weeks, strain, and process pints for 10 minutes.

Spicy Pickled Blueberries

2 quarts blueberries
1½ pounds white/brown sugar
2 teaspoons whole allspice
2 cinnamon sticks
5 whole clove
1 cup red wine vinegar

Wash, pick over, and stem the blueberries. Boil the sugar, spices, and vinegar for 2 minutes. Simmer the berries in the syrup 1 to 2 minutes until tender, cold store for 8 hours. Remove the berries from the syrup, and place them in a sterile jar. Reboil the syrup; pour it over the berries. SP/RWB20(8OZ)A. Use with game or cottage cheese salads.

Since bananas are inexpensive, this pickle recipe is an appropriate recipe for beginners. Banana pickle need not be canned. Just cook the pickle and serve it on ice cream, yogurt, or cottage cheese or refrigerate it.

Banana Pickle

1 cup brown sugar
¾ cup red wine vinegar
¾ teaspoon ground mace
½ teaspoon ground cinnamon
¼ teaspoon ground clove
6 peeled and diagonally sliced bananas

Make the sugar syrup by boiling the sugar, vinegar, and spices for 8 minutes. Add the sliced bananas, and cook for 2 minutes. Pack the mixture into sterile, 8-ounce wide-mouth tapered jars. SP/RWB10(16OZ)**RA** or SP/RWB15(8OZ)20 (16OZ)A.

Variations: Substitute lemon juice or lime juice for vinegar. Use white sugar for brown; change the spices by using fresh-grated ginger, nutmeg, or cinnamon or all three spices together. Some spiced banana recipes call for butter. A few raisins may be added to the pickle. Try making the pickle with only whole clove and ground mace.

Use any variety of stemmed or unstemmed, firm, slightly underripe, seeded or unseeded grapes for pickled grapes. Heat 2 cups vinegar and 8 cups sugar with 1 teaspoon nutmeg, ground ginger, cinnamon, or clove. Fresh gingerroot and another spice (like clove) may be used instead of ground ginger. Pour the hot syrup over the grapes; cook until tender. JSP/RWB10-15(8OZ). With one version of this recipe, the syrup is cooked down until thick, poured over the grapes, and processed for a longer time. This method probably leaves more trapped air in the grapes. Some pickle whole bunches of grapes with this hot syrup of 2 cups vinegar, 3½ cups sugar, and 3 whole clove. Pour the syrup into the grape-filled jars. Process or cook until the skins are tender. Some chefs cook the grapes in 1 part sugar, 2 parts water, and 1 part vinegar (with spices) until the skins are tender, and JSP/RWB15(16OZ)20(32OZ).

In Trinidad and Tobago, I've seen island women making "Pickled Limes" with limes, peppers, vinegar, salt, and spices. Many of these pickles had no oil in their ingredients but some did. A jar of Forro's hot pickled limes, canned in Plymouth, Tobago, had no oil. It was made with limes, hot peppers, vinegar, salt, and spices and was a wonderful embellishment for stews, meats, rice, and other Indian dishes. Trinidad and Tobago have a large Indian population, and the pickles, sauces, and chutneys there reflect the Indian influence.

Pickled Lemons or Limes

1½ pounds lemons or limes*
⅓ cup sea salt or canning salt
3 cups water
Several cinnamon sticks (optional)
1 teaspoon peppercorns (optional)
2-3 hot peppers (optional)
A few clove**

Add the lemons to boiling water for 3 to 4 minutes, remove, and plunge into cold water. Discard the liquid. Cool and cut the lemons into wedges or cut partly in wedges, leaving the lemon attached at the base. Brine: boil ⅓ cup salt, 3 cups water, and the spices. Jar the lemons, pour in the spiced brine, and SP/RWB15(16OZ)A. Older books show 10(16OZ).

* **Note: Caribbean varieties of lemons and limes are often different from varieties commonly seen in the United States.**

** May substitute coriander, garlic, mustard seeds, fenugreek seeds, ginger, mace, nutmeg, horseradish, currants, raisins, cumin, nigella seeds, or asafetida.

The classic Moroccan side pickle, Preserved Lemon, is easy to make as no canning is required. Select thin-skinned lemons or limes; score them in quarters, leaving bottoms attached. Salt the inside bottom of a quart jar. Squeeze some lemon juice into the jar. Salt each lemon section and place in the jar. Salt the top again and push down. Pour olive oil on top of the lemons, keeping all lemons covered with oil. Refrigerate the preserved lemons for a minimum of two weeks. Use in Moroccan cooking, in marinades, and in meat and fish dishes. Globally, there are other fermented pickles made with oil. Research more on Indian pickles or *achar*.

Pickled Oranges: Wash and boil 6 water-covered whole oranges until tender. Drain, reserving the liquid. Ice to cool the oranges and slice thin. Combine 1¾ cups vinegar, 2 cups sugar, 1¼ cups reserved liquid, and a spice bag (1 mace blade, 2 cinnamon sticks, and 10 clove); boil for 10 minutes. Add the orange slices; simmer for 30 minutes. Turn off the heat; leave the mixture at room temperature for 24 hours. Discard the spice bag, drain the oranges, and pack them into 8-ounce, widemouth tapered jars. Boil the syrup until thick, pour into the jars, and cool. SP/RWB10(8OZ)A. Cure for two months.

Pickled Kumquats: Wash 2 quarts kumquats; drain. Place the kumquats in a bowl, sprinkle with 2 heaping tablespoons baking soda, and cover with

Fresh Kumquats

Pickled kumquats in a flute of champagne or carbonated fruit juice.

boiling water. Wait 10 minutes; drain and rinse with cold water. Slit each kumquat on a side, boil 10 minutes in water to cover, and drain. Mix 4 cups sugar, 4 cups water, 1 cup vinegar, and a cinnamon stick. Add the fruit; cook until transparent and the syrup is thick. JSP/RWB10(8OZ)A.

Spiced Mangoes: Cook 4 cups sugar, 2 cups cider vinegar, 1 cup non-hard water, and a spice bag (2 tablespoons whole clove, 2 cinnamon sticks, and 1 tablespoon allspice). Add the peeled mango slices (8 pounds mangoes) and simmer to achieve some slice transparency. Jar, and add 1 tablespoon Grand Marnier per jar. SP/RWB15(8OZ)20(16OZ)A.

Hot Pickled Mangoes: Loosely pack peeled firm (underripe) mango slices in jars. Boil 4 cups red wine vinegar with 1/3 cup sugar and 1 tablespoon salt. Add 1 minced garlic clove and a spice bag (2 tablespoons mustard seed, 1-inch minced gingerroot, 3 tablespoons freshly grated horseradish, 1 teaspoon black peppercorns, and 1 optional hot pepper). Pour the hot vinegar solution into the jar. SP/RWB15(8OZ)20(16OZ)A. Cure 3 weeks.

Pickled Papaya: For 2 pints, peel 1 green papaya. Use papaya just prior to ripening as too-green papaya will impart a "bitter-milky flavor."(Agromisa Foundation, Wageningen Agricultural University). Measure 4 cups sliced papaya. Boil the papaya in water for 2 minutes; drain. Mix and simmer: 2 cups sugar, 1 cup vinegar, a spice bag (4 clove, 2 cinnamon sticks, and 10 peppercorns). Add the papaya; cook slowly for 10 minutes. JSP/RWB20(16OZ)A.

Note: A study by Vongsawasdi, P., et al. at KMUTT, Bangkok, Thailand, entitled "Maturity and fermentation periods as affecting on qualities of pickling papaya," discusses how to make **fermented papaya pickle** with 200 grams (0.441 pounds) diced papaya at 28 degrees C, plus or minus 2 degrees (78.7 degrees F to 86 degrees F), in a three-percent brine solution (by weight), with the papaya flesh protected from air, and the gas being allowed to leave the glass container. Research results showed fourth month papaya has sufficient sugar for fermentation in 4 days to a pH below 4.0, but younger papayas, lacking the optimal amount of sugar, took 6 days to ferment to a pH below 4.0. **The starting pH of the fourth month papaya was 6.66.** This is a higher pH than is generally listed for papaya, so further confirmation of papaya's range of pH (or maximal pH) should be investigated. **This research showed lactic acid activity substantially increased during the first 4 days of fermentation but remained constant thereafter.** Papaya's flesh pH decreased from 6.61/day 0 to 4.59/day 2 to 3.99/day 4 to 3.74/day 6 to 3.69/day 8 with slightly lower numbers in the brine.

Note: Dry the latex from tapped papaya plants for 4 days; powder the papayas and use the powder as a meat tenderizer or rub directly on meats.

Baked Papaya: Underripe papaya may be halved, seeded, dusted with sugar and cinnamon, and baked skin down in a 3/4-inch-deep water bath at 350 degrees F for 35 minutes.

Quick Pickled Papaya: Cover papaya chunks and hot peppers with straight vinegar or fresh lime juice; wait a few minutes and taste (**beginner's recipe**). **Filipino *Achara (Atsara)*** is similar to cabbage-based salads or pickle. Mix 1/4 cup salt with the shredded flesh of a 2-pound papaya (4 to 4 1/2 cups) for 1 hour; drain/squeeze. Boil a brine of 1 cup vinegar, 1/2 to 1 cup sugar, and 1 tablespoon salt. Pour the brine over the drained papaya, 1/2 cup cut red pepper, 1/4 cup sliced mild onion, 1 sliced garlic clove, 1/4 cup shredded carrot, 1-inch piece minced gingerroot, 1/4 cup raisins (optional), 1 hot pepper pod (optional), 1/4 cup fresh pineapple chunks (optional), and pepper to taste. Jar and store in the refrigerator; wait 1 day to serve.

Experiments: substitute shredded green papaya for cabbage (about the same pH) in some experimental recipes. To can, check the final pH.

Caution: When working with hot peppers, don't wipe your eyes with your hands. Use milk or beer, not water, to wash out eyes burning from contact with hot peppers.

FIGS

Pickled Figs: Dust 5 pounds fresh figs with baking soda; cover them with boiling water. Wait 10 minutes, drain in colander, and rinse. Boil 2 cups red wine vinegar or white vinegar, 7 cups sugar, 2 to 3 cinnamon sticks, and 1 teaspoon clove for 10 minutes. Wait 10 minutes. Add the figs, bring the mixture to a full boil, and keep a low boil for 15 minutes. Remove the fig mixture from the heat; wait 24 hours. Boil the mixture again for 15 minutes more on day 2 and 3. JSP/RWB10(4OZ)10(8OZ)15(16OZ)A or JS**R** for near future use.

Fresh figs on a red charger.

Pour hot water over the figs and baking soda.

Allow the figs to cool off.

Drain the hot water.

Cook the figs in the sweet syrup.

Pickled figs plated with cheesecake and mint leaves.

PICKLED HARD-BOILED EGGS

Pickled eggs in a jar fascinate many people. A reported incident a couple of years ago caused some concerns about pickled eggs. As reported in the *Journal of the American Medical Association* article "Foodborne Botulism From Eating Home-Pickled Eggs" (2000, 284:2181-2182).

> The picked eggs were prepared using a recipe that consisted of hard-boiled eggs, commercially prepared beets and hot peppers, and vinegar. The intact hard-boiled eggs were peeled and punctured with toothpicks then combined with the other ingredients in a glass jar that closed with a metal screw-on lid. The mixture was stored at room temperature and occasionally was exposed to sunlight.

This article is not clear on whether or not the product was actually canned and sealed in a RWB. However, other sources consulted maintain the eggs were not hermetically sealed but just put into vinegar and left at room temperature. Clearly, that is quite different from canning an actual product. Pricking a hard-boiled egg with a toothpick (or any unclean instrument) is likely to inject botulinus or other unwanted substances into the yolk (pH = 6.8) and should be avoided. Pickled eggs, if canned, should be kept refrigerated. **In light of the lack of research regarding the penetration of vinegar into the yolk, it is best to make all pickled eggs as a refrigerated item, even if canned. Label "Keep Refrigerated."**

Pickled Chinese Eggs utilize cooled hard-boiled eggs and a salt-mordant dye bath of strong black tea or other food dyestuff (like beet or cochineal). Lightly roll the eggs on the counter to crack the shell. Simmer the eggs in the dye bath for about an hour. I usually leave the eggs soaking in the refrigerated dye bath overnight. Then, shell the eggs and eat or pickle them in refrigerated brine.

Pickled Eggs: Place the hard-boiled and shelled eggs in sterile jars. Cover them with hot preboiled (for 15 minutes) brine (1 quart vinegar, 4 to 5 hot peppers [optional], 1 teaspoon "spice of choice," 1 teaspoon black peppercorns, 1 teaspoon salt, and 1 teaspoon mustard seed). Select the "spices of choice" from allspice, cardamom, garlic, gingerroot, horseradish, pickling spice, coriander, or clove. JSP/RWB10(16OZ)**RA**. **"Keep Refrigerated"** and label appropriately.

Refrigerated Pink Eggs: Cook 2 beets, slip their skins, and slice. Add 1 diced onion, slivered horseradish (optional), and 8 hard-boiled and peeled eggs. Brine: Boil 3 cups water, ½ cup red wine vinegar, 2 tablespoons sugar, and a pinch salt and pepper. Pour the brine over the eggs, onions, and horseradish; refrigerate.

Spiced Pickled Eggs or **Garlic Pickled Eggs** are made with 2 cups hot, uncut vinegar. Add 6 hard-boiled and peeled eggs (4 to 5 clove for spiced eggs only, and don't stud the eggs with the whole clove), 1½ tablespoons sugar (optional), ½ teaspoon allspice (spiced eggs only), 8 diced garlic cloves (garlic eggs only), ½ teaspoon salt, ½ teaspoon pepper, and ½ teaspoon ground mustard or mustard seed. **"Keep Refrigerated."**

FIDDLEHEADS

Maine is a great state. Anyone spending some time in Maine knows they have wonderful natural products, such as maple syrup, fresh seafood, wild blueberries, stone-ground mustards, and *Matteuccia struthiopteris,* **fiddleheads** (ostrich ferns). **Blooming only once a year in April and May, these spiraled fern heads are harvested, cooked for a minimum of 10 minutes, and served with butter, lemon Dijon sauce, and hollandaise. They are also used in other gourmet dishes like**

quiche or Fiddlehead Pie. To make **Fiddlehead Pie:** Sauté onions and coarsely chopped fiddleheads in butter or olive oil, mix the vegetables into a standard cheese-quiche filling, and bake in a precooked piecrust. Visit www.fresh-fiddleheads.com for their recipe. If you don't have a source for fiddleheads, www.fresh-fiddleheads.com can ship some to you.

Fiddleheads may be pickled solo or made into mixed pickles or bread-and-butter pickles (El-Begearmi, Mahmoud. "Facts on Fiddleheads." University of Maine Cooperative Extension, Bulletin #4198. 1-4).

Caution: Avoid food-borne illness associated with fiddleheads by cooking them for a minimum of 10 minutes.

Look for 4- to 5-foot fiddleheads in Connecticut, New York, and in other areas; they grow in symmetric clumps and in moist thickets along streams and riverbanks. Last spring, we bought the fiddleheads shown in the photograph at Emanuel's Market in Stone Ridge, New York.

Pickled Fiddleheads: Wash the fiddleheads, and pack them in sterile jars with garlic, peppercorns, and choice of spice(s): mustard seed, celery seed, dill sprig, allspice, ground nutmeg, and cinnamon stick. **Cover them with brine of 16 parts vinegar to 4 parts water to 1 part salt to 1 part sugar and JSP/RWB12-15(8OZ)A.**

Pickled Sweet Fiddleheads: May be made with 4 parts vinegar to 5 parts sugar plus ½ **teaspoon salt per pint; JSP/RWB12-15(8OZ)A.** Of course, fiddleheads may be canned in straight vinegar with sugar. See similar recipes for false capers and radish pods. **Unlike the average *jardinières*,** fiddleheads need a least 80-percent vinegar to 20-percent water. If using fiddleheads in *jardinières*, raise the brine's vinegar to water ratio to 4 or 5 parts vinegar to 1 part water—plus ¼ part salt and ¼ part sugar. Parboil the fiddleheads first.

Caution: Always check the pH of newly formulated product or "Refrigerate Only." Put up a 4-ounce jar first, grind up the contents of the entire 4-ounce jar, test the pH, and throw out the tested food. Beware of recipes with insufficient vinegar, salt, and sugar.

Green Olives in Brine: Raw olives are bitter and inedible. They must be cured. There are several methods for curing olives. One recipe calls for 2 pounds well-washed, dark-green olives. With a hammer, hit each individual olive to split them. Soak them in water for 10 days, changing the water daily, or until the bitterness leaves the olives. Heat a brine of 1 cup pickling salt to 2 quarts water, slice of lemon zest, slice of orange zest, several garlic cloves, some bay leaves, and 1 tablespoon coriander for 15 minutes. Cool. Drain the olives. Place them in sterile jars, and pour the strained brine over. Close the containers and wait a month to eat. Some recipes call for hot water instead of regular water during the first 1 to 3 days; then cover the olives with brine and vinegar in 3 to 1 by volume. Top the jars with olive oil and refrigerate.

Lye-Treated Green Olives: Olives may also be made by covering the olives with a lye solution (4 level tablespoons of lye to each gallon of 65 degree F water) in a stoneware crock or glass container. Never use a metal container (poisonous). When the

Fiddleheads

olives turn a yellowish-green color and have absorbed the solution to the pit (cut to check—in 12 hours), drain, and flush the lye solution down the drain, following it with fresh running water. If after 12 hours the progress is not sufficient, drain off the lye solution and use a new lye solution for 12 hours more. Twice rinse the olives in cold water and leave covered. Change the water daily until no brownish color exists (5 to 8 days). Heat and cool a brine of 1 gallon water with 6½ tablespoons salt and pour over the drained olives. Wait 2 days to taste. Refrigerate. These olives keep for two weeks. They need to be processed further for a longer storage time. For more recipes like **Oil Cured Greek Style Olives** check out U.C. Davis Publication 2758—"Home Pickling of Olives."

PICKLED NUTS

Nuts may be pickled. **The British are especially fond of pickled immature green walnuts.** Pickled nuts are good with Indian food and on salads.

Hot Pickled Green Walnuts (or Pickled Immature Butternuts): Locate green unripe walnuts; prick each walnut with a skewer 3 times and soak 6 cups prepared nuts in a brine of 1 gallon water with 1 cup salt (for 6 to 7 days). Some cooks change to a fresh brine after 3 days. Rinse the nuts, put them in new brine, and simmer for 10 minutes. Drain; lay the nuts out to blacken. Boil 2 quarts cider vinegar with 4 tablespoons ground black pepper, 2 tablespoons salt, 1 tablespoon ground allspice, 2 teaspoons cayenne, and 2 small minced hot peppers. Add the walnuts. Wait 5 minutes; pack the nuts in jars and cover with the spiced vinegar. SP/RWB15(16OZ)A.

Variation: The recipe in *Mrs. Mary Randolph's*

Filet Mignon with green pickled walnuts. Serve on Kentucky Derby Day.

Virginia Housewife (1831) uses whole black peppercorns, garlic, mustard seed, and horseradish. *Pickles and Preserves* (Brown, M. 1955, 130) and *Chamber's Cookery and Domestic Economy for Young Housewives* (1876, 117) recommend "pepper, ginger, mustard seed, or other spices according to taste."

If you want to sample pickled green walnuts and have no English walnuts, contact A Taste of Britain by Post (www.tobbp.com) to buy them already made. **Place pickled green walnuts on venison steak or filet mignon for Kentucky Derby Day.** And, don't listen to critics about pickled green walnuts; we love them! Have some shipped to the discriminating gourmet on your gift list. Serve pickled green walnuts with red cabbage salad, venison-prune casserole, mashed potatoes, duck pâté, stir-fry, sharp cheese, or cold meat.

Pickled Green Almonds: In an interview with Chef Scott Boggs of the French Laundry Restaurant in Yountville, California, I learned the chefs there shave fresh green almonds over pastas and salads. Green almonds are considered a rare delicacy. They may also be pickled by pouring a hot spiced mixture of 2 parts water to 1 part vinegar to 1 part sugar over the green almonds; refrigerate them. Try spicing with star anise, peppercorns, coriander, or ginger. To can green almonds, try canning them in 100-percent vinegar after you have brined them a little, but don't can them using the French Laundry's recipe (given above) unless you store them in the refrigerator and mark all jars—**"Keep Refrigerated."** If anybody has an interesting recipe for canned pickled green almonds, I'd love to see it. For more information, see Jamlady's column in the March/April 2007 issue of *Fruit Gardener* magazine.

Hot-and-spicy peanuts are lovely with Indian curries or salads. Vary some of the spices, keeping the vinegar, sugar, and salt ratios the same. The peppers may be decreased but not increased.

Hot Pickled Peanuts

5-6 cups roasted, unsalted peanuts
2 minced, seedless hot peppers*
6 sliced garlic cloves
2½ cups red wine vinegar**
¼ cup sugar***
½ cup non-hard water****
5 bay leaves or other spice
1½ teaspoons chili powder
1-1½ teaspoons cayenne pepper
¾ tablespoon mustard seed
1 tablespoon pickling salt

Jar the nuts, peppers, and garlic. Cook the vinegar, sugar, water, and spices; pour over the nuts. SP/RWB20(8OZ)A or JS**R**.

* For not hot peanuts, substitute mild peppers
** May substitute another 5-percent vinegar or part lemon juice
*** May substitute light brown sugar, honey, or agave (test the pH or **Keep Refrigerated**)
**** May substitute herbal infusion or tea (test the pH)

Sweet Pickled Nuts

2 cups white vinegar
2 cups raw clover honey
½ tablespoon salt
½ teaspoon whole clove
½ tablespoon minced gingerroot
2 cinnamon sticks
5 cups assorted nuts

Cook the vinegar, honey, salt, and spice bag (clove, gingerroot, and cinnamon sticks). Select the nuts from walnuts, pecans, cashews, peanuts, macadamia, pistachios, almonds, Brazil nuts, or hazelnuts. Add the nuts and simmer 10 to 15 minutes; discard the spice bag. JSP/RWB20(8OZ)A.

Variation: Pickled Pecans—Use 4 cups pecans, the juice and grated outer peel of 2 lemons, plus 1 orange or 2 Clementines, ½ cup dried currants, ½ cup dried raisins, 1½ cups wine vinegar, 2½ cups brown sugar, ½ teaspoon salt, 1 tablespoon grated nutmeg, and 1 teaspoon cinnamon.

Variation: Pickled Walnuts—Use 6 cups walnut halves, 2 cups vinegar, 2 cups brown sugar, 1 cinnamon stick, 1 teaspoon clove, and ½ teaspoon salt. Cook all ingredients except the walnuts. Add the walnuts; cook for 10 minutes. JSP/RWB20(8OZ)A.

Note: Wide-mouth tapered jars work well for pickled nuts.

PICKLED GRAPE LEAVES

Pickled Grape Leaves: Young, spring grape leaves from wild or domestic grapes may be pickled or frozen. Everyone can help pick and pack the young vine leaves. **Make a brine with 1 overflowing tablespoon salt per gallon of water.** Heat the brine. Blanch the grape leaves for 30 seconds; pat the leaves dry with a towel. Roll the leaves into logs around each other; pack them vertically in a canning jar. **Cover the leaves with a solution made from 2 cups lemon juice or 1⅔** tablespoons citric acid per gallon of brine. Pour this acidified brine into the jars of leaves and SP/RWB15(16OZ)A. Attach a recipe for *Dolmades* or Greek-stuffed vine leaves to a jar of preserved grape leaves and use it as a hostess gift.

One expert recommends blanching the grape leaves in 1 quart boiling water with 2 teaspoons pickling salt. The leaves are then rolled in stacks and put into the canning jars. A hot acidified mixture of 1 cup water plus ¼ cup lemon juice is poured over them. SP/RWB15(16OZ)A (Ingham, B. 1999, 1-9). **The Ingham recipe is probably safer as the concentrations of salt and acid are higher, but it is also easier, cheaper, and truer to the natural flavor to use citric acid instead of lemon juice.** To freeze: blanch light-green leaves in a strong brine of 1 cup salt to 4 cups water. Plunge them in cold water, pat them dry, stack 6 together (roll or leave flat), and freeze them in reclosable freezer bags. **Leaves may also be preserved in the same 1:4 salt brine but are saltier (Mallos, T. 1993. *The Complete Middle East Cookbook*).**

A bundle of pickled grape leaves.

PICKLED DAY LILY BUDS

Dilly Day Lilies: Day lily buds may be pickled and spiced with celery seed, clove, whole allspice, cinnamon, hot peppers, and garlic. Pack washed and drained lily buds plus spices in a canning jar. Make the brine: 1 quart vinegar, honey or sugar (about 3/8 cup per quart, optional), 1/2 cup water, and 6 tablespoons salt. Pour the hot brine over the buds, SP/RWB15(16OZ)A.

Caution: Day lilies, *Hemerocallis genus,* have bulbs. Do not confuse them with the genus *Lilium* growing from rhizomes.

FALSE CAPERS

Capers are flower-bud pickles from caper bushes or caper berries, *Capparis spinosa,* which are a common, spiny shrub found in Mediterranean countries and India. *C. spinosa* may be grown in the no-frost zones of Florida and California. **Historically, substitute capers or false capers have been made from flower buds of nasturtiums, elderberries, dandelions, hibiscuses, and calendulas (daisy-looking marigold).** Many of these buds, like the hibiscus, may be cooked as a vegetable, tossed in soup, included in aspic, fried in tempura batter, cooked in breads, put in ranchero eggs, or used in bread puddings and fritters. Pickled buds may be used in tuna salad, tartar sauce, herbal cream-cheese spreads, pasta salads, or as a garnish for broiled rosemary tomatoes or lemon-and-pepper scrod.

Caution: Please remind children that not all buds may be eaten.

Pickled Nasturtium Buds: Cover green nasturtium buds with a salt water brine (1 cup salt to 2 quarts water), and weigh them down for 1 to 3 days. Remove the buds, rinse them, and soak them in cold water for 1 hour. Drain the buds, cold pack them, and pour the hot vinegar over. SP/RWB15(16OZ)A (Peterson, M.E. 1869, 30).

Japanese Gari

2-3 pieces gingerroot
1 teaspoon salt
1 cup rice wine vinegar
1/3 cup sugar

Peel and cut the gingerroot into thin pieces; weep in salt for 1/2 hour. Jar the ginger; pour over the boiling vinegar-sugar solution. JS**R** for 1 week. When pink, serve with sushi. Shelf life = 1 month plus.

RAT-TAILED RADISH PICKLE

One interesting pickle from yesteryear is pickled, young radish pods, as found in *Mrs. Beeton's Household Management, A Complete Cookery Book,* (Beeton, I. n.d. 1138). The young radish pods were placed in strong brine for 12 hours; the brine was drained, reheated, and poured over the pods again and allowed to sit for 48 hours. This processing cycle was repeated. "Repeat again and again until the pods are perfectly green." The drained pods were packed in a jar with grated horseradish, covered with hot vinegar, closed, and cold-stored.

Another recipe for **Radish Pods** comes from *The Art of Cookery* (1882, 378):

> Gather the pods when quite young, put them into salt and water all night, boil the salt and water they were laid in, pour it on the pods, and cover close. When cold, make it boiling hot and pour it on again, and do till green; then drain and make a pickle for them of white wine vinegar, with mace, ginger, long pepper, and horse-radish. Pour it on boiling hot, and, when almost cold, boil up the vinegar again, and pour it upon them.Tie them down with a bladder, and put them by for use.

If you know a lot about radishes, you might know about the pods on radishes. In *L. H. Bailey's The Standard Cyclopedia of Horticulture* (1930, 2910), there is a picture of a **rat-tailed radish,** *Raphanus sativus* var. *caudàtus.* This radish is grown for its enormous pods, which are similar to a foot-long string bean.

> The rat-tailed or serpent radish, var. *caudàtus* (*Raphanus caudàtus,* Linn.) has enormous, long pods . . . which are eaten either pickled or raw, as are radish roots. Frequently the pods are 1 ft. long. The root is slender and hard. This is a cultural variety, coming true from seed. L.H.B.

World-famous mango chutney.

Chapter 5

Chutneys and Sauces

The word chutney comes from the Hindi word *chatni,* meaning a condiment or pickle. Chutney may be made from many different vegetables or fruits in consort with ingredients like sugar, ginger, turmeric, cinnamon, salt, seeds, nuts, and an acid like lemon juice or vinegar. In East Indian Hindu homes, many of the *chatnis* served are fresh and uncooked. While this book's main focus is cooked, canned chutneys, I do want to increase the reader's awareness regarding the long, historical, and culinary tradition in India and Pakistan of fresh *chatnis* and of *salsas* in Latin American countries.

A **quick and fresh chutney** may be made with 1 cup yogurt and freshly chopped herbs. A seasoned chutney of mint, coriander, minced shallots, garlic, hot peppers, and a little fresh lemon juice makes a nice side for cocktail meatballs, curries, rice, fried bread, and garlic toast. Nuts, such as walnuts, hazelnuts, or macadamia nuts, may be stirred into hot, seasoned yogurt and served in lamb-filled pita sandwiches. Try an uncooked yogurt dip with mint and coriander on spicy meatballs. Combine 1/2 pound ground lamb, 1/2 pound ground beef, 1/4 to 3/8 cup bread crumbs or gram flour, 1/2 small onion, 1 egg, 1 teaspoon grated gingerroot, 1/16 teaspoon cumin, 1/16 teaspoon cardamom, 1/16 teaspoon cinnamon, and 1 pinch pepper. Bake the meatballs at 350 degrees F on release foil until done.

At Chicago farmers' markets, some patrons approach a jar of chutney with bewilderment and ask, "What is it?" To which Jamlady usually replies, **"A chutney is a sweet-and-sour condiment with a kicker!"** And, just as soon as the definition is spoken, Jamady has to admit there's an exception, and that exception is sweet-apple chutney, which has no vinegar or lemon juice!

If you believe you have never had chutney, think again! **Salsa is technically chutney, and so is Chinese sweet-and-sour sauce.** Salsa has tomatoes, lemon juice, hot peppers, and cilantro. The **tomato,** *Lycopersicon lycopersicum,* native to the Andes, is somewhat sweet; the lemon juice is sour, and the hot peppers and cilantro are the kickers. Salsa is served as a relish or condiment for tacos, nachos, or chips. Indian *chatnis* are used in the same manner with fried vegetables and fried breads.

As with naturalization of plants, which is caused by wind, animals, and bird migration, people travel, and when they do, they spread food traditions and culinary ideas. Just look where the pickle has been. **It is Jamlady's philosophy that learning from another normally follows along two planes—up and down and sideways—and only fails to do so because of bias, arrogance, prejudice, or a lack of openness.**

Basically, the opportunity for learning can occur anywhere and at anytime if you are open-minded enough to see it.

The British citizens in the Commonwealth territories were superior in many ways to the indigenous peoples of these territories. Certainly, they had more money and education. Yet, the British of these colonial areas were faced with scarcity of certain goods and forced to make due or substitute for commodities not readily available to them. Because of the adaptability of the British people and the openness generated and driven by exposure to many distinctly different cultures, the British today now embrace chutney in the same way Americans embrace cranberry sauce for holiday turkey. As one British patron put it, "It would not be proper to have a fancy meal without several chutneys on the table."

Americans do eat chutney, but many are unaware of it because most American chutneys have individualized names. A1 Steak Sauce® is a ground-up chutney. It is a sweet-sour condiment with a kicker. Canned salsa is "simple chutney." For fairly obvious reasons, the British have been more open to accepting the word *chatni* or chutney and the food it names—because their exposure to the Indian culture has been greater than ours. The average American wants to call raspberry chutney raspberry salsa. This is due to the Latin influence in America. There are those who will disagree with Jamlady or state her opinions as an over simplification, and that's okay. Jamlady's point is: resistance to new foods and ideas is complicated and has to do with being open to learning from everyone. While almost everyone agrees with that concept in theory, it is in the application where we sometimes run into difficulty.

As Manfred, a Buddhist, once said, "Africans just cook a big pot of food and eat when hungry. Maybe they eat once a day; maybe they eat more. American's run to the fast food place and 'have to have' three or more meals a day." Both get their food quickly and on demand. One seems more primitive, but when considering the fats, nutrition, and lifestyle, which mode of living is the most efficient, least stressful, most cost efficient, and healthiest?

Safeid Til ki Chatni or **White Sesame Chutney** is made with sesame seeds, salt, green chili, adafoetida powder (1 pinch), white cumin seeds, raw cane sugar, tamarind juice, and shredded mint leaves. **Aalu Chatni** or **Potato Chutney** is made with cooked potatoes, sugar, gingerroot, onions, sultanas, pistachio nuts, cider vinegar, salt, and red chili powder (Pandya, M. 1986. *Indian Chutneys, Raitas, Pickles and Preserves.* 51, 55).

Both recipes have combinations of culinary ingredients that most Americans don't normally experience. The combination of a raisin or pistachio nut with a potato is not normally seen in American cooking nor is mint and hot chili with sesame seeds. Let us think about these combinations for a minute. To be a creative cook, let us use what we have just learned. Evidently, pistachio nuts, raisins, and potatoes do taste good together. Even if you will not make potato chutney, try putting pistachio nuts or raisins in an American potato dish. How about pistachio nuts and raisins in potato candy (see *The Jamlady Cookbook,* 218)? The same goes for chili and mint. Maybe we need to make hot mint jelly with sesame seeds infused with the mint. And no, Jamlady and I have not made these dishes yet, but in writing this passage and analyzing these combinations this possibility did come to mind.

When the British were in India, the British officers wanted ketchup, a condiment foreign to the Indian cooks. So, as the historical tale goes, the British officers requested the Indian cooks make some ketchup. **Bengal Chutney** was the final condiment. It was not ketchup, but the officers liked it and accepted it as a substitute. Supposedly, ever since, the marriage of the British subject to the Indian chutney has been apparent, and slowly but surely, Americans are gusting chutney on their cottage cheese, rice, fried eggplant, hamburgers, fried green tomatoes, barbecued chicken, fried alligator, and grilled porterhouse steak. Even the Hawaiians add a tablespoon of chutney to sour cream and serve it with fried shrimp chips.

If you do not know what **shrimp chips** are, try to get some from your local Chinese market. Shrimp chips look like transparent or plastic potato chips. When dropped in hot oil, these chips expand into crunchy chips. Hawaiians and Asians use shrimp chips with chutney dip. Our family discovered them when researching Hawaiian foods for a school project. We actually served these chips and dip to the elementary-school children. There are several versions of the chips. Some are wheat-flour chips; others contain shrimp flavors and rice. To make **chutney dip,** just mix a little chutney with sour cream and dip away.

Bengal Chutney was originally made at the Bengal Club during the British reign in India. This particular recipe should age for at least three months. Some Bengal Chutney recipes do not contain any tomatoes. For example, **Two-Year Bengal** has more spices and no tomatoes and may be aged for two years (so it is said) like a fine wine (15 apples, 1/2 pound onions, 20 garlic cloves, 2 chilies, 1 1/2 cups raisins, 2 2/3 cups light brown sugar, 3 1/4 cups vinegar, 1/3 cup mustard seed, and 1/2 cup fresh gingerroot). The apples are baked for 20 minutes with their skins and seeds removed; then add the other ingredients, and cook until thick. JSP/RWB10(4OZ)15(8OZ)20(16OZ)A.

This recipe is a Jamlady variation of Bengal Chutney. It includes tomatoes, but there are more apples than tomatoes. Jamlady's second variation, **Crocodile Chutney,** has more tomatoes than apples.

Bengal Chutney

4 cups plum tomato meats	2 1/2 cups brown sugar
3/4 cup grated gingerroot	2 cups malt vinegar
2 cups diced onions	5 whole chilies
6 large minced garlic cloves	3 tablespoons mustard seed
8 cups chunked apples	1 tablespoon pickling salt
4 cups red wine vinegar	1 1/2 cups raisins

Peel the tomatoes (plunge method), ginger, onions, and garlic. Cook all ingredients together—except the raisins and ginger. Cook the ginger in a microwave with some of the juice of the tomatoes and add to the batch. Cook by the on-off method*; allow the product to evaporate and thicken. Stir well. Add the raisins at the end; wait 15 minutes. JSP/RWB10(4OZ)15(8OZ)20(16OZ). Age 3 to 12 months.

Note: *Cooking with the heat on and then off hastens the evaporation time. The method is called the "on-off method" or the "switch method."

This next version of **Bengal Chutney** was created in appreciation of the large number of Americans who grow their own tomatoes and to recognize American's love of the tomato and tomato ketchup. **As you can see, Crocodile Chutney has more tomatoes than apples, and Bengal Chutney has more apples than tomatoes.** Either chutney may be used with hamburgers, rice, meats, broiled fish, fried vegetables, and dips. Alligator Chutney is good on crocodile, alligator, chicken, beef, or fish.

The price of alligator meat varies with the quality of the cut as it would with beef. The best cuts sell at prices similar to fine cuts of filet mignon or other exotic meats. Generally speaking, the tail and the jaw meats are the best and can be purchased mail order if you do not live where this meat is locally available. Alligator meat may be wild or farmed. Recipes for alligator meat may be found on the Internet with the search terms "alligator meat" or "alligator recipes." Gatorboys or Gator guides will take you hunting for gators. If you do catch a gator, remove all the fat from the meat prior to freezing it. Alligator is a mild-tasting meat and can be used in recipes as a substitute for chicken or veal. This gator topic is interesting to many, and Crocodile Chutney is as good on fried eggplant or fried green tomatoes as it is on a burger.

Hot Crocodile Chutney

10 cups red tomato meats
$1\frac{1}{2}$ cups diced onions
10 sliced garlic cloves
6 cups chopped organic apples
Juice of organic apple peels (optional)
$3\frac{1}{4}$ cups red wine vinegar
3 cups brown sugar
$1\frac{3}{4}$ cups diced jalapeño peppers
4 tablespoons minced gingerroot
1 tablespoon cinnamon
1 tablespoon cumin seeds
1 tablespoon mace
15 ounces dried raisins or currants
2 teaspoons pickling salt

Peel the tomatoes (plunge method), onions, garlic, and apples. Juice the peels, reserving only the juice. Slowly cook all ingredients, except the raisins, until slightly thick. Add the raisins and cook 10 minutes. JSP/RWB10(4OZ)15(8OZ)20(16OZ). pH = 4.0 or less.

In case you don't have any alligator or crocodile, try fishing, where legal, for baby crocodiles with flashlights or torches at night. In New Guinea, we went out in small boats, shone lights on baby crocodiles, and scooped up the stunned critters. After natives catch baby crocodiles, they raise them up in pens like pigs. We caught two babies the night we went out. Hides from the big crocodiles are sold and the meat eaten, presumably with chutney if you're British or Australian and living in the environs.

Two other Bengal variations are shown here. Chinese 5-Spice is a great spice, but it is usually used in making Chinese food. This Bengal offspring crosses ethnic lines. Bengal is good with rice, meats, and fried vegetables. Make half the recipe if these quantities are too large.

Crocodile Chutney on a hamburger with sweet dills, Aunt Frances' B&Bs, and an extra side of crocodile chutney.

Chinese 5-Spice Tomato Chutney

20 cups chopped tomato meats
12 chopped medium onions
28 peeled cubed apples
16 cups diced bell peppers
16 cups vinegar
7 cups light brown sugar
3 cups sliced celery
1 cup dried currants
4 tablespoons Chinese 5-spice
2½ tablespoons pickling salt
3 cups raisins

Peel the tomatoes (plunge method); retain the meats. Peel the onions and apples. Cook all ingredients (except the raisins) until almost thick. Add the raisins. Stir frequently. JSP/RWB10(4OZ)15(8OZ) 20(16OZ)A.

Many chutney recipes have raisins or dried currants, but Garam Masala Chutney does not and is modified to be more like an American chili sauce with garam masala spice. The complexities of flavors in this original Jamlady chutney are simply wonderful.

Garam Masala Chutney

14 cups tomato meats*
5 cups diced green peppers
2 pounds dark brown sugar
4½ cups vinegar
1 pound light brown sugar
2 cups chopped onions
3 ounces minced gingerroot
4 tablespoons garam masala**
10 chopped Serrano peppers
3½ tablespoons mustard seed
1½ tablespoons celery seed

Cook down all ingredients slowly until thick. JSP/RWB10(4OZ)15(8OZ)20(16OZ)A.

* Tomato meats should have no seeds, excess juice, or skins.

** Orkay® brand of garam masala (recommended) is an exotic Indian spice blend of coriander, cumin, red chilies, black pepper, turmeric, poppy seeds, cinnamon, clove, para cress, annanas flowers, cassia, stone flower, nutmeg, cardamom, caraway, mace, and salt.

Jamlady's experimental path branched in several directions. One path was to change the spices and ratios of the original recipes, and the other was to change the type of tomato and the complexity of the recipe—moving it to the more complex and back to its simplest form. The first four chutney recipes below were made with Lemon Boy tomatoes, heritage tomatoes, and other colorful tomatoes. The Hot Green Tomato Chutney utilizes unripe, green tomato and is a great way to make use of a prefrost glut of green tomatoes. Serve it with fried eggplant, Brie cheese, or grilled chicken.

Remember to always check pH values if changing recipes. Crocodile Chutney usually has a pH of 4.0 or less, counting from the 6 or 7 times Jamlady and I have made and measured it. Fall Tomato Chutney has a pH in the 3.5 range. Do not reduce the vinegar or sugar in any of these recipes. When salt is lower in many of Jamlady's recipes, the increased acidity compensates.

If you are a wannabe canner, try to measure ingredients carefully and watch the clock precisely to obtain accurate processing times for canned products. Successful canners are usually quite tidy, organized, accurate, artistic, and time-orientated. Also remember, quarts need more processing time than pints or 8-ounce jars. Thicker product may need more time than watery product.

Hot Green Tomato Chutney

6 cups chopped apples
12 cups chopped green tomatoes
4 cups vinegar
6 medium onions
2½ cups sugar
15 Serrano peppers
2 tablespoons gingerroot
½ tablespoon pickling salt
1 cup sliced dates*
1 cup raisins

Peel and chop the apples and tomatoes. Cook all ingredients, except the dates and raisins, until almost thick. Add raisins and dates; stir well. Cook until thick. JSP/RWB10(4OZ)15(8OZ)20(16OZ)A or JS**R.**

* **Do not add extra dates (4.8 pH); they are low acid. Do not use extra-high-pH dried fruits like dried papayas at 5.2 to 6.0.** Check the pH of fruits and vegetables chart in the back of this book.

Note: If the dates are added too early, they will not maintain their shape, and a different product will result.

Fall Tomato Chutney

24 cups tomato meats
20 cups red wine vinegar*
10 cups peeled pear chunks
9 cups brown sugar
6 cups diced bell peppers
5 cups diced onions
4 cups peeled apple chunks
3 tablespoons pickling salt
6 cups raisins
1 cup dried currants

Peel the tomatoes (plunge method). Retain only the meats. Cook all ingredients together (except the currants and raisins) until slightly thick. Stir well. Then add the currants and raisins; cook until thick. JSP/RWB10(4OZ)15(8OZ)20(16OZ)A. pH = 3.55. Age 3 to 6 months.

* May substitute white vinegar

Potpourri Chutney was formulated by making several changes to the basic apple-tomato chutney, yet still utilizing common garden vegetables.

Jamlady's Original Potpourri Chutney

4 cups cubed cucumbers
2 cups diced green tomatoes*
2 cups diced, yellow, sweet banana peppers
8 cups chopped tart apples
4 cups tomato meats
4 cups dark/light brown sugar
4 cups cider vinegar
2 cups diced onions
1 minced Serrano pepper
1 minced garlic clove
1 tablespoon minced gingerroot
2 teaspoons pickling salt
1 teaspoon ground cinnamon
1 cup dark raisins

Peel and seed the cucumbers. Peel the green tomatoes. Seed and dice the yellow, sweet banana peppers. Cook all ingredients, except the raisins. Near the end, add the raisins.

JSP/RWB10(4OZ)15(8OZ)20(16OZ)A or JS**R.** Age chutney 2 to 6 months. DOB = 9/15/1994.

* May substitute tomatillas

Variation: Spanish Flag Chutney—Use colors of the Spanish flag: yellow tomatoes instead of red or green tomatoes, red peppers instead of yellow banana peppers, and light brown sugar instead of dark brown sugar for a slightly sweeter chutney to complement fish.

The next simple chutney or sauce is called **Shirley Sauce** and is a sweeter-tasting sauce. Many chefs who put sugar in pasta sauce approximate a less-sweet version of this sauce. Bernard Cretier, the chef and owner of Le Vichyssois Restaurant in Lakemoor, Illinois, once said he makes a similar sauce with yellow or orange tomatoes. In fact, years ago Chef Cretier purchased many organic yellow or orange tomatoes from Jamlady for French sauces and soups. **This recipe is the bare bones of chutney with fruits, onions, hot peppers, sugar, vinegar, and salt. This recipe looks so simple one might be tempted to ignore it as average, but it is above average.**

This simple chutney, Seedless Shirley or Hot Seedless Shirley, is made from tomato meats with no tomato seeds or skins. The original recipe calls for whole chopped tomatoes and seeded green peppers with white distilled vinegar. Jamlady has found a good red or white wine vinegar improves the recipe. Whole or seeded hot peppers may be substituted equally with seeded, not-hot peppers or use a 50 to 50 ratio. **Any pepper variety, *habaneros* to *poblanos*, may be used to transform this mellow ketchup-type sauce into a sudorific agent.** Although the base recipe is the same, each change of pepper will impart perceivable differences in this sauce.

This recipe illustrates how and why a chef may have a recipe but cannot make an identical product. In this recipe, plum tomatoes will taste different from "slicers." We used to deliver tomatoes to local Mexican restaurants. The owners never wanted plum tomatoes, and not because they are less juicy, but because they taste different and have a firmer texture.

Jamlady has changed the tomato variety used in Shirley Sauce by using ½ orange or yellow tomatoes and ½ red tomatoes or by using all yellow tomatoes. With so many varieties of tomatoes, there are equal numbers of modified Shirley Sauces that may be made from the same basic recipe. Shirley Sauce needs no aging. It can be used as a salsa, taco, or chili sauce and is wonderful on fish, rice, grilled meat, meatloaf, hamburgers, and brats. Shirley Sauce is good in pasta dishes (**Shirley Pasta Salad—Chilled Shirley** or **Fettuccini/Angel Hair with Shirley—Hot Shirley**). Just add the pasta and sautéed seafood or chicken to the Shirley Sauce.

Hot Orange Seedless Shirley Sauce

- 12 large Lemon Boy/orange tomatoes
- 2 large diced onions
- 12 large jalapeño/Serrano peppers
- 2 cups sugar
- 2 cups red wine vinegar
- 2 tablespoons pickling salt

Plunge the tomatoes in boiling water and then in cold. Remove all skins and seeds; retain the meats (plunge method). Cook all ingredients until thick. JSP/RWB10(4OZ)15(8OZ)20(16OZ)A or JS**R.**

Variation: Old-Fashioned Shirley Sauce—Use little, old-fashioned pear tomatoes.

Typical Indian apple chutney contains apples, raisins, onions, garlic, peppers, some kind of sugar, and lots of spices. *The Ball Blue Book* (1977, 31) shows a recipe for apple chutney with no vinegar, which is really sweet apple chutney or apple conserve with spices. As far as Ja0mlady is concerned, many apple chutney recipes have entirely too much sugar. Few market customers desire an overly sweet chutney with no vinegar.

Look closely at these sweet apple chutney recipes. Notice they are basically apple preserves with peppers, onions, raisins, and spices. The cook who formulated the sweet apple chutney recipe uses sugar to address the preservation and pH issues, because the recipe contains low-acid vegetables (peppers and onions).

Calculations of water activity also come into play in many of these recipes. Most customers would rather have some vinegar and not so much sugar. **If we toss out "sweet apple chutney" from Jamlady's chutney category, when it probably is not chutney anyway, then we have a definition of chutney as a "sweet-and-sour" with a kicker. This pleases Jamlady very much.**

This next recipe, **Spicy Hot Pear Chutney,** is wonderful with grilled chicken, roast turkey, or warmed Brie cheese and crackers. All sorts of pears may be used, but try to select a pear cultivar without a "sandy" texture.

Spicy Hot Pear Chutney

16 cups cubed pears
1 cup diced red/white onions
8 sliced garlic cloves
6 red hot finger peppers*
5 cups cider vinegar
3 cups brown sugar
1 tablespoon pickling salt
1 cup raisins**

Peel and cut the pears, onions, and garlic. Mince the hot peppers. Cook all ingredients, except the raisins, until nearly thick. Add the raisins; stir well, and complete the cooking. JSP/RWB10(4OZ) 15(8OZ)20(16OZ)A or JS**R.**

* Hot peppers are optional or use not-hot peppers for Not-Hot Pear Chutney.

** May substitute currants

Jamlady Tip: Quarter the recipe for speed and improved taste or use multiple pans.

Variation: Spicy Hot Apple Chutney, Spicy Hot Pear-Apple Chutney, Spicy Hot Asian Pear Chutney, Hot Spicy Asian Bartlett Chutney, Spicy Hot 3-Pome Chutney—Use apples, Asian pears, or a combination of pears, apples, and Asian pears.

Hot Indian Apple Chutney

16 tart apples*
½ cup minced gingerroot
2 ¾ cups light brown/white sugar
1-2 tablespoons pickling salt
4 ½ cups red wine vinegar
1 cup fresh apple juice**
½ cup diced chili peppers
1/3 cup crushed mustard seed
½ cup diced onions
10 minced garlic cloves
¾ cup light or dark raisins
¾ cup currants

Juice the apples. Peel and mince the gingerroot. Layer the apples and sugar. Add 1 tablespoon salt, vinegar, and apple juice. Wait ½ hour. Heat; slowly add the sugar and then the ginger, chilies, onions, mustard seed, and minced garlic. Cook; add the raisins and currants near the end. Add the rest of the salt (optional). Stir well. JSP/RWB10(4OZ)15(8OZ)20(16OZ)A. Age 6 to 12 months.

* Use peeled, unevenly cubed or sliced apples.

** Juice the apple peels or downed apples (Champion juicing machine recommended).

The **idea of infusions** to make jam, jelly, chutney, sauce, tea, and rice is not new, but sometimes we need to rethink and expand an idea. This next chutney was an attempt to use a rose-hips infusion in a chutney.

Jamlady hopes others will try more herbal infusions in their canned products. **With newly identified adaptogens or adaptogenic herbs (see *The Jamlady Cookbook,* 56, 199), it should be possible to incorporate more of these herbs, tropical fruits, and exotic vegetables into our crafted foods with interesting results and concomitant medicinal benefits.** These new foods are known as **functional foods.**

Jamlady believes some of the infusions need to be stronger than used here, but still, this chutney was well received. Actually, some fermented sauces or infusions like soy sauce or balsamic vinegar are already being used in creative pickling. Tea infusions, medicinal jellies, and exotic fruits could be used in more recipes. This area of research is underdeveloped. Jamlady and I believe artists and homemakers, not just scientists, need to participate in this scientific inquiry. **People need different and meaningful activities to balance their lives—to keep themselves whole and stabilized.**

From Jamlady's research notes on October 25, 1994:

This chutney is called Christmas Chutney because it is made on Oct. 25th to be eaten on Dec. 25th. This chutney is symbolic of God's love, as rose hips are from rose bushes. Gifting this chutney is a gift of your love and mother Earth's love, beauty, and grace. The infusion of rose hips symbolizes the infusion of God or Mother Earth into our lives. The apple is biblically symbolic, even though many experts say Eve ate a tomato and not an apple!

Christmas Chutney

- 8 ounces dried rose hips*
- 5 cups white wine vinegar
- 20 peeled, sliced apples
- 2¼ cups sugar
- 2 large diced onions
- 2 chopped bell peppers
- 2 tablespoons mustard seed
- 1-3 dried, crushed chili peppers
- 1 teaspoon pickling salt
- 12 ounces dark raisins

Boil the dried rose hips in vinegar for 2 minutes; steep 2 to 3 hours. Strain the infusion and discard the rose hips. Measure the reserved vinegar again, adding more vinegar to make 5 cups. Cook all ingredients, except the raisins; add them last. Stir well. JSP/RWB10(4OZ)15(8OZ)20(16OZ)A. Age 3 months. DOB: 10/25/1994.

* May use 12 to 16 ounces rose hips.

"The birth of new knowledge is always worthy of recognition." —Jamlady

Pearcot Chutney

- 16 ounces Old English Candied Fruit and Peel Mix
- 1 cup water
- 10 cups peeled, cut pears
- 6 peeled, cut apples
- ½ cup dried, cut apricots
- 2 cups sugar
- 2 minced chilies
- 2 cups vinegar
- 3 tablespoons minced gingerroot
- 1 teaspoon ground allspice
- 1 cup macadamia nuts

Cook the Old English Candied Fruit and Peel Mix with 1 cup water until soft. Add the rest of the ingredients, except the nuts, and cook until thick. Add the nuts. JSP/RWB10(4OZ)15(8OZ)20(16OZ)A or JS**R.**

English Lamb Chutney

3½ pounds cut Granny Smith apples
3 quarts cider vinegar
5 cups mint leaves
9 cups diced onions
50 large, skinned, seeded plum tomatoes (8 cups)
6 cups sugar
½ cup mustard seed
½ cup minced gingerroot
3 tablespoons pickling salt
2 pounds dark raisins
10 ounces currants

Peel and cube or slice the apples. Heat the vinegar, pour it over the mint, and steep for ½ hour. Strain; use the mint-infused liquid. Cook all ingredients together, except the raisins and currants, until nearly thick. Add the raisins and currants. JSP/RWB10(4OZ)15(8OZ)20(16OZ)A or JS**R.** pH = 4.10 or lower. Half or quarter this recipe for a home-size batch, cook in multiple pans, or use a large, jacketed steam cooker.

Bev's Fruity Tomato Chutney is excellent on potato cakes, meatloaf, hamburgers, and in sour cream dips. Seal in 4-ounce jars for single servings or to take on picnics.

Bev's Fruity Tomato Chutney

12 cups tomato meats*
14 peeled, sliced apples
6 cups red wine vinegar**
3 diced medium onions
5 chopped red bell peppers
3 cups sugar
12 ounces sliced prunes
1 tablespoon minced ginger
4 minced garlic cloves
4 chopped chilies
1 tablespoon ground allspice
½ teaspoon pickling salt
½ teaspoon pepper
1 cup raisins

Cook all ingredients together, except the raisins. Add the raisins when nearly thick. JSP/RWB10(4OZ)15(8OZ)20(16OZ)A or JS**R.**

* May quarter or half the recipe
** May substitute white or white wine vinegar

Mrs. Ruby Bartlett Chutney

12 large pears (8 cups)
20 cups red tomato meats*
12 cups brown sugar
12 cups white vinegar
1 cup fresh pear/apple juice (optional)
8 cups sliced green onions
5 cups diced green bell peppers
1 cup minced fresh gingerroot
24 chopped jalapeño peppers
10 sliced garlic cloves
10 cinnamon sticks
1 tablespoon pickling salt
4 cups raisins

Peel and cube/slice the pears. Cook all ingredients, except the raisins, until almost thick. Add the raisins and JSP/RWB10(4OZ)15(8OZ)20(16OZ)A. Age 3 to 6 months.

* **May cut the recipe by a half, quarter, or tenth.**

Many types of chutney may be used with cream cheese as a sandwich filling. Try this next chutney on toasted bread with cream cheese and a leaf of ruby-leaf lettuce, or serve it as a nice accompaniment to meats, rice, and fried vegetables. The following recipe is a market favorite!

Bev's Fruity Tomato Chutney with sour cream and shrimp chips.

Pear and Walnut Chutney with cream cheese sandwich.

Pear and Walnut Sandwich Chutney

8 cups sliced pears
4 sliced apples
$2\frac{3}{4}$ cups sugar
2-3 sliced chili peppers
$1\frac{1}{2}$ cups cider vinegar
$\frac{1}{8}$ teaspoon ground allspice
3 tablespoons minced gingerroot
1 teaspoon crushed coriander seeds
1 cup dates or raisins
1 cup walnuts

Peel the pears and apples; slice. Cook all of the ingredients together, except the raisins and walnuts. When nearly thick, add the raisin and walnuts. JSP/RWB10(4OZ)15(8OZ)20(16OZ)A or JS**R.**

Caution: Canning chutney can be safe if you follow the recipe. Test the pH of any altered recipe.

CREATING SAFE CHUTNEY RECIPES

Pumpkin chutney has been around for a long time and often contains tomatoes and/or apples. The vinegar and sugar in a pumpkin-chutney recipe should sufficiently reduce the overall pH to under 4.0. Pumpkins are low acid and have a pH around 4.80 to 5.50. Adding apples with a pH range of 2.90 to 4.00 and ripe tomatoes with a pH range of 4.42 to 4.65 potentially improves the pH situation, depending on the measures of each. However, red tomatoes are not always below the 4.6 safety line, and the most acidic tomato is not comfortably under the safety line. For this reason, pumpkin chutney formulations with tomatoes and apples need to be carefully adjusted with an acidifier to lower the completed pH.

There are also recipes for zucchini or marrow chutney. The pH of squash is 5.00 to 6.20, which is higher than pumpkin. Likewise, squash chutney may be made with apples or tomatoes and apples and would also need pH adjustment. In these next recipes, the tomatoes may be green or red, with green tomatoes being more tart and firm. Likewise, eggplant chutney or jam needs a lot of vinegar or another acid to bring them into range for safe canning.

In the marrow recipes I have analyzed, there are usually about 8 pounds marrow, apples, and onions in a ratio of 4:2:2 to about 6 to 7 cups vinegar, 2 cups sugar, and 1 to 2 tablespoons salt, and less than 3 tablespoons ginger or hot peppers. The rest is spice. Another recipe in measured pounds had a ratio of 2:2:2 (pumpkins to tomatoes to apples) with 2 cups sugar and $3\frac{1}{2}$ cups vinegar. Yet a third recipe used a total of $6\frac{1}{2}$ pounds of low-acid vegetables: $2\frac{1}{2}$ pounds pumpkin to 2 pounds tomatoes to 2 pounds onions with 4 cups vinegar and 2 cups sugar. So, one might predictably say that similar formulations should be safe.

Anyone in this fashion is able to figure out a recipe before making it, and it will probably test out within range. How it will taste is another story. However, one must remember to **always check new formulations with a pH meter; for the one time something gets miscalculated, may be the time you have failed to check the pH, or some newly added ingredients may have an unexpected impact on the pH.** Failing this, refrigerate new creations, and do not assume they are shelf-stable.

Jamlady has devised a limited variable-design problem whereby cooks may be creative even if they have no pH meter. **What you should not do with this recipe is decide that you want less vinegar and more pumpkin.** Measure accurately, and follow the directions. Use leftover, end-of-the-season pumpkins to experiment, or grow some lovely marrow this year.

Basic Pumpkin or Marrow Chutney

Create your own!

- 2½ pounds pumpkin or marrow cut into chunks
- 4 cups white or red wine vinegar (5% acidity) or 1-2 tablespoons balsamic vinegar with 4 cups red wine vinegar or 3½ cups vinegar and ½ cup malt vinegar
- 6 tomatoes or 3 apples and 3 tomatoes or 6 apples or 2 red tomatoes, 2 green tomatoes (peeled), and 2 apples
- 2 medium onions
- 1 cup raisins or currants
- 2 cups brown or white sugar
- 1 tablespoon pickling salt
- 4 minced garlic cloves
- 1 teaspoon clove or 1 tablespoon allspice (both optional)
- 1 teaspoon freshly ground pepper or 12 black peppercorns (optional)
- 2 tablespoons ginger (optional)

Alternate spices: rosemary, tarragon, sage, paprika, cardamom, cinnamon, or crushed juniper berries. Sample a new spice in a small amount of basic chutney before committing it to the whole batch. Now, with this basic formula, manipulate a few controlled variables to gain understanding of what constitutes a safe formulation.

Caution: Test your chutney; the pH needs to be safely under 4.6 pH or JSR.

Mr. Pumpkin Chutney: 2½ pounds peeled, cut pumpkin (Musquee de Provence preferred), 4 cups red wine vinegar, 2 red tomatoes (meats), 2 peeled, cut green tomatoes, 2 peeled, cut tart apples, 2 diced medium onions, 1 cup raisins, 2 cups brown sugar; 1 tablespoon pickling salt, 4 sliced garlic cloves; 1 teaspoon clove; 1 teaspoon ground black pepper; and 1 sprig fresh rosemary.

Variation: Gingered Pumpkin Chutney—No clove or rosemary, but use ginger and allspice to taste instead.

Jamlady wants to substitute pineapple for tomato in marrow chutney, as it is good in marrow jam and pineapple chutney. Jamlady says, "You stir Grand Marnier into everything else, so why not into chutney?" Try Grand Marnier in marrow, apple, and pineapple chutney. And, pumpkin chutney with pistachio nuts and grated lemon peel is another super combination. See how that pH meter can come in handy?

MORE CHUTNEY RECIPES

Eggplant, *Solanum melongena,* native to Asia and Africa, is grown in lots of gardens. There are many exciting recipes to make with these beautiful purple, orange, or white fruits. Below are two eggplant recipes; one for **eggplant chutney** and the second for **eggplant caviar,** a relish. Arguably, it is also chutney. Normally eggplant caviar is not canned, but this recipe, born August 18, 1998, has a pH reading of 3.92 to 3.98.

Originally, this first chutney was called **eggplant chutney,** but because eggplants are in the nightshade family, it is also called **nightshade chutney.** Patrons tend to show more interest in **"nightshade chutney"** than eggplant chutney, finding it ghoulish-sounding and appropriate for Halloween curries and rice, grilled pork chops, or pita chips with sour cream.

Nightshade Chutney

2 pounds eggplant
1 pound sliced tart apples
1-2 teaspoons cut gingerroot or ground ginger
3 medium diced onions
1 teaspoon mustard seed
1-3 minced hot peppers (optional)
1-2 teaspoons lemon juice or balsamic vinegar
¼ teaspoon turmeric or cinnamon
Pickling salt (to taste)
1¾ cups red wine vinegar or malt vinegar
1¼ cups light brown sugar

Peel and cut the eggplant and apples into ½-inch x 1-inch pieces. Cook the eggplant, apples, ginger, onions, and spices in the vinegar. When tender, add the sugar. Cook until thick enough. Check the pH. JSP/RWB10(4OZ)15(8OZ)20(16OZ) or JS**R.** Fresh eggplant's pH = 4.75 to 5.50.

The next recipe for eggplant caviar uses wonderful clover-ginseng honey, good red wine vinegar, and jalapeño peppers. Our taste consultant, George Vicory, says, "This stuff is great even on Ritz® crackers!" We also recommend sesame crackers or ***lahvosh*** (Armenian cracker bread).Warm fried bread "tangos" with this caviar spread. Use caviar on fried green tomatoes, with lamb and rice, or as a side condiment for onion *frittatas.*

Hot Eggplant Caviar

2 chopped, large tomato meats
3¾ cups chopped onions
3-4 finely minced garlic cloves
2 cups chopped jalapeño peppers
2½ cups red wine vinegar
1 cup raw beekeeper's honey
7 cups coarsely chopped eggplant
½ cup fresh lemon juice
¼ cup salt
2 teaspoons dried parsley
½ teaspoon ground clove (optional)

Plunge the tomatoes in boiling water, then cold; peel and retain only the meats. Set them aside. Cook the onions, garlic, and peppers with red wine vinegar; add the honey. In a separate dish, cover the eggplant with water and ¼ cup lemon juice and parboil 2 to 3 minutes in the microwave. Drain the eggplant; add it to the onion mixture. Add the salt, spices, and remaining ¼ cup lemon juice; cook. When the caviar is half-cooked, add the reserved tomatoes meats. Optional: Add balsamic vinegar to taste or to adjust the pH. Test the caviar for a pH in the range of 3.92 to 3.98. Add any needed lemon juice to achieve a 3.98 reading. Cook until somewhat thick, JSP/RWB10(4OZ)15(8OZ)20(16OZ)A or JS**R.**

Caution: For canning Hot Eggplant Caviar, do not cut the salt, honey, lemon juice, or vinegar in this recipe and do not increase the vegetables.

Variation: Regular Eggplant Caviar—Exchange sweet peppers for hot peppers.

The **ground cherry,** *Physalis alkekengi,* isn't commonly grown for commercial markets, but it grows well in home gardens. Ground cherries are an edible member of the Chinese Lantern/Nightshade Family. **Ground cherry recipes taste best when the cherry flavor predominates, as too many other flavors hide the true and subtle taste of the ground cherry. The pH of the raw ground cherries sampled in our test kitchen tested around 4.23 to 4.25. The completed chutney's pH tested around 3.78 before the apples were added and around 3.6 after the apples were added.** Another way to look at this recipe is: the onion is the only vegetable or fruit in the recipe above the 4.6 safety line. A 50:50 measure of vinegar and onions in a *jardinière* recipe is sufficient for a shelf-stable product. So, this recipe made with 5-percent-acidity vinegar should be all right, but the pH will be higher. If you'd like it lower, decrease the onions or increase the vinegar. Use this nutty and "pineappley tasting" chutney with grilled or roasted chicken, quail, squab, or other fowl.

Ground Cherry Chutney

4¾ pounds ripe ground cherries*
4 cups white wine vinegar (6-percent)**
4 cups sugar
3 cups chopped apples
3½ cups chopped onions

Husk and wash the ripe ground cherries*; measure out 4¾ pounds of ground cherries. Cook all of the ingredients on low heat until thick (about 1 hour). JSP/RWB10(4OZ)15(8OZ)20(16OZ)A.
* **Caution: Unripe ground cherries are toxic.**
** Completed pH = 3.6 with recommended 6-percent vinegar (Dell'Alpe Brand). If using 5-percent vinegar, decrease the onions or increase the vinegar accordingly.

The sugar beet or **garden beet,** *Beta vulgaris,* is native to southern Europe. The plant is normally a biennial, producing a bulbous root one year and a seed stalk the following year. **While many people like to see greens on their beets, it is really best to remove the tops from the beets so the moisture is not pulled from the beet by the leaves.** Don't wash the beets, separate the tops from the bulb, and refrigerate both.

Many cultivars of beets are available: some white, orange, red, candy-striped, or purple. The white beets from farmer Nick Nichols of Marengo, Illinois, are called **"Bassanos."** Swallowtail Garden Seeds offer a white **Albina Verduna;** an Italian heirloom called the **Chioggia,** which is a candy-striped cultivar; **Forona,** which is the purple Danish beet; **Golden,** which is a sweet-and-mild yellow beet; and **Red Ace,** which is the "best all-around red beet." Ohio State's horticultural fact sheet recommends the **Detroit Dark Red** for canning and pickling. Mayo Underwood, www.UnderwoodGardens.com, recommends **Bull's Blood** and **Ruby Queen** beets. The juice from the Bull's Blood, says Underwood, **"is used to make the only red-food coloring allowed by Swedish law"—so imagine how well this beet will dye pink pickled eggs!** Select a beet variety suitable for your climate and needs.

Beetroot chutney is classically made with red beets, apples, onions, gingerroot, and cider vinegar. Jamlady's original white beet version is made with pears, ginger, onions, white wine vinegar, brown sugar, ground coriander, hot peppers, and the surprise—dried cranberries! White beets actually predate red beets. White beets taste the same as red beets, but they do not stain or bleed as red beets do.

White Bassano Chutney

1 pound white beets
1 tablespoon minced gingerroot
3 minced chili peppers
½ cup diced onions
1 cup white wine or cider vinegar
¾ pounds peeled, cubed pears
½ teaspoon salt
½ teaspoon coriander
1 cup light brown sugar
¼ cup dried cranberries (optional)*

Partially cook the beets; peel. Then cut the beets into ½-inch x ½-inch cubes. If fully cooking the beets to slip the skin, the beets will become too soft for this recipe. With the lid on, cook the beets, ginger, peppers, onions, and vinegar for 10 minutes. Add the ¾-inch x ¾-inch peeled pears, salt, coriander, and sugar; cook in an open pan until thick. Add the cranberries near the end. JSP/RWB15(8OZ)20(16OZ)A. pH = 4.03. DOB = 11/3/1999. If you prefer a pH under 4.0, then add an additional ¼ cup vinegar and ¼ cup sugar. To add more hot pepper, decrease the onions in equal measure.

* Add ¼ cup sugar and ¼ cup vinegar with the cranberries.

Variation: If you prefer **Red Beetroot Chutney**, use these measures and follow the same directions: 6 pounds beets, 3 pounds apples (or pears), 4½ cups cider vinegar, 3¼ cup white or brown sugar, 2½ cups diced onions (about 4), 5 tablespoons minced ginger, 1½ teaspoons salt, and ½ cup raisins (optional). If adding a ½ cup raisins, add an additional ½ cup sugar and ½ cup vinegar. Alternate spices: instead of ginger, use crushed allspice berries, mustard seed, coriander, or pepper.

Many diabetics do not want to use added sugar or artificial sweetener. Many say if a product tastes too sweet, even if it is not sweetened with real sugar, then they crave sweet things. **This Cantaloupe and Peach Chutney has no added sugar or artificial sweetener.** On October 3, 1995, this recipe was created of necessity when the melon man got "rained-out" and gifted Jamlady three cases of melons.

Cantaloupe and Peach Chutney

- 10 peeled, diced peaches
- 3 pounds diced onions
- 1 tablespoon whole clove
- 1 tablespoon ginger peels
- 2 large muskmelons or cantaloupes
- 3 cups white or cider vinegar
- 2½ cups dark raisins
- 2 cups apple juice
- 2 cups diced, dried apricots
- 1 cup golden raisins
- 4 tablespoons minced ginger
- 3 tablespoons ground ginger
- 8 chopped garlic cloves
- 1 tablespoon ground nutmeg
- 2 teaspoons ground allspice

Peel and dice the peaches and onions. Put the clove and ginger peels in a spice bag. Peel and chunk the muskmelons. Cook all ingredients together, except the raisins. Stir well, adding the raisins when nearly thick. Chutney may be completed in a microwave, but do not superheat and wait for cooling between warm ups (on-off method). JSP/RWB15(8OZ)20(16OZ). pH = 4.0 or add ¼ cup to ½ cup more vinegar for a lower pH.

Cantaloupes or muskmelons, *Cucumis melo,* native to western Africa, are usually a vining plant, but compact varieties do exist. **True cantaloupes, *Cucumis melo cantalupensis,* do not usually grow in the United States. American cantaloupes or muskmelons, *Cucumis melo reticulates,* do grow in the United States.** This orange-fleshed muskmelon is round or oval and visually appears to have netting atop its green-grey skin. While often eaten raw, this melon may also be utilized by the canner.

Muskmelon and Pineapple Chutney

10 cups cubed muskmelon
6 cups fresh or canned pineapple in 100% juice
6 cups cider vinegar*
6 cups light brown sugar*
9 ounces grated gingerroot
20 minced garlic cloves
18 minced Serrano peppers
3 pounds dark raisins
1-2 cups macadamia nuts*

Cook all ingredients, except raisins and nuts, until thick. Add the raisins and nuts. JSP/RWB10(4OZ)15(8OZ)20(16OZ)A or JSP/**R** or JS**R** (see note below). DOB: 10/13/1995.

* **Note: pH = 4.22. For 2 cups macadamia or other nuts, add ½ cup more vinegar and ½ cup more sugar.** Test the pH before canning or add an additional ½ to 1 cup vinegar and ½ to 1 cup sugar.

Mango Chutney

12 large mangoes
4½ cups white wine vinegar*
4 cups sugar
4 large sliced apples
½ cup minced gingerroot
¼ cup lemon juice
12 minced red Serrano peppers**
12 clove
2 tablespoons mustard seed
30 ounces dark raisins

Prepare the mangoes into 1-inch x 2-inch pieces or use 16 large peeled peaches (cut into chunks) or equivalent measure of other fruits. Cook all ingredients, except the raisins, which are added near the end. JSP/RWB10(8OZ)15(16OZ). Age 2 to 6 months. pH = 3.84. Serve with meats, fried vegetables, cheese, rice, or curries.

* May substitute red wine or cider vinegar
** May substitute red finger peppers

Variation: Peach Chutney, Nectarine Chutney, or **Apricot Chutney**—Instead of mangoes, use peaches, nectarines, or apricots (or a mixture) to make this world-famous chutney.

Green Mango Chutney

6 cups sliced green mangoes
3¼ cups sugar
1¼ cups white wine vinegar
¼ cup grated gingerroot
3-4 minced chili peppers
1-2 minced garlic cloves
¼ cup diced onions
½ teaspoon pickling salt
1½ cups currants or raisins

Cook all ingredients, except the raisins, which are added near the end. If unsure of the chutney's thickness, refrigerate it prior to canning. JSP/RWB15(8OZ)20(16OZ)A.

Trio of tamarillos.

The **tamarillo, tree-tomato,** or ***tomate de Árbol,*** *Solanum betaceum,* is a semi-tropical, South-American fruit that is grown in New Zealand as a cash crop. This old fruit crop takes about eighteen months to produce fruits and cannot tolerate frost. **The tree tomato or tamarillo was originally named *Solanum betaceum* in 1799, by Cavanilles. In 1845, it was moved to the genus *Cyphomandra* where it stayed until 1995. That year Bohs, using molecular studies and genetics, returned it to *Solanum.* Several wild species of the tree tomato in Bolivia may prove to be the progenitors of today's tamarillo (Heiser and Anderson 1999, 379-384; http://www.hort.purdue.edu/newcrop/proceedings1999/v4-379.html). In recent years, the tree tomato has been given the made-up name of tamarillo.**

An officer from the New Zealand Tamarillo Growers Association, Inc. sent Jamlady a copy of Jan Bilton's book *Tamarillo Cook Book* (1986) and several recipe leaflets produced by the association. Jamlady thanks the Tamarillo Growers Association, Inc. for their permission to reprint these recipes.

Fresh Tamarillo Chutney

- 1 cup caster sugar (superfine sugar)
- 1 tablespoon water
- 4 tablespoons cider vinegar
- 1 teaspoon green peppercorns
- 1 teaspoon pink peppercorns* (optional)
- 2 pounds peeled, diced tamarillos

Place the sugar in a heavy pan with water and melt over low heat. Cook until the mixture becomes golden (i.e. it caramelizes). Add the vinegar, peppercorns, and tamarillos. Bring to a boil; let it stand.

This chutney keeps for up to two weeks in the refrigerator or JSP/RWB10(8OZ)A. **The fresh and ripe tamarillos we tested for this photo shoot measured 4.06 pH.**

***Caution: Pink peppercorns may cause allergic reactions. The recommended substitution is white peppercorns.**

Tamarillo Guacamole: 1 large avocado, juice ½ lemon, salt and pepper, ½ to 1 teaspoon chili seasoning, 1 tablespoon mayonnaise, and 2 tamarillos. Mash the avocado flesh with the lemon juice, seasonings, and mayonnaise; add the peeled, diced tamarillos and serve. **Tamarillo Mayonnaise:** Mix mashed tamarillos with mayonnaise.

The sweet-tart, egg-shaped tamarillo fruit grows on a 12-foot-tall tree and is usually shipped to the United States from May to September. **The red tamarillo has a golden flesh and red seeds, and the golden-skinned variety is golden throughout.** Both the seeds and the flesh are edible, but the skin is not eaten as it is astringent tasting. Tamarillos are reasonably high in fiber, vitamins (C, A, E, and B), phosphorus, potassium, and may be used in cold fruit soup. Some sources show the pH of the tamarillo to be 4.21 to 4.30, but our tamarillos tested out around 4.06 to 4.07. Tamarillos may be substituted for tomatoes in most tomato recipes.

Red Tamarillo Chutney

3 tart, green apples
1 seeded bell pepper
3 jalapeño peppers
2-3 red tamarillos
2 ripe plum tomatoes
1½ cup red wine vinegar
1 cup brown sugar
1 peeled, cubed pear*
1 diced medium onion
1 tablespoon minced gingerroot
1 minced garlic clove
1 teaspoon cinnamon
⅓ teaspoon salt
½ cup raisins
½ cup dried currants

To make this original Jamlady recipe, peel and slice the apples; dice the peppers. Halve the tamarillos and scoop out the flesh; discard the skins. Obtain the tomato meats (plunge method). Cook all ingredients, except the raisins and currants. When thick, add the raisins and currants. JSP/RWB15(8OZ) 20(16OZ)A.

* May substitute 1 to 2 tamarillos

Crab apple products are in high demand, but making chutney from peeled, cored crab apples is labor intensive. However, for the discerning epicure, the hard work may be worth it.

Jamlady's Cadillac Chutney

4 pounds crab apple pieces
2 cups crab apple juice*
2-3 handfuls of aromatic mint
4 tablespoons fresh-cut mint
3 cups brown sugar
3 cups cider vinegar
3 peeled, sliced pears
Pinch ascorbic acid crystals
2 cups diced onions
1 cup chopped dates
1 tablespoon grated gingerroot
1 cup chopped dates
1 cup golden raisins
½ cup dried currants

Use a pinch of ascorbic acid crystal in the wash water to reduced oxidation. Wash and grade 4 pounds crab apples and additional crab apples to yield 2 cups of crab apple juice. Peel the larger crab apples, cut them into pieces, and measure out 4 pounds. Juice the crab apples with a very small pinch of ascorbic acid crystal. Simmer the handfuls of mint in the apple juice for 10 minutes; infuse for 20 minutes. Strain, reserving the infusion, discard the mint. Cook all remaining ingredients, except the dried fruit (dates, raisins, and currants). When thick, add the fruit. The dried fruit are best added at the end, because they absorb some liquid and maintain their shape. JSP/RWB10(4OZ)15(8OZ)A.

* When it clogs, clean the Champion juicing machine. Jamlady and I always worry we will break the machine, but in twelve years, it has not happened.

Crab Apple Chutney

2 pounds crab apples
1 pound sliced tart green apples
4 medium limes
2 ounces peeled, minced gingerroot
½ pound tallow (rendered suet)
2 cups sugar
10 ounces dried currants

Peel and core the crab apples and tart green apples. Peel the limes; remove/discard the pith (white portion) and seeds. Juice the lime pulp in a Champion juicing machine or similar machine. **Reserve the juice and the extruded dry material, or juice and chop the pulp.** Cut the peel with scissors to 1/16-inch x 1/16-inch or ⅛-inch x ⅛-inch. Cook 2 ounces ginger and bagged ginger peels (left from peeling the ginger) in ½ cup water for 5 minutes. Reserve the juice and chopped ginger; discard the bagged peels. Grate the hard tallow in a food processor. **To make tallow from scratch:** save fat from beef cuts or purchase fatty beef scraps. Cook the fat scraps slowly to obtain the rendered fat; strain the fat and chill until hard. Grate ¼ pound tallow and brown slightly. Add the rest of the ingredients; cook 20 to 25 minutes or until thick. JSP/RWB10(4OZ)15(8OZ)A**R. Label "Keep Refrigerated."** In the old days, properly acidified tallow recipes were considered to be shelf-stable; today they are not. Although labor-intensive, this chutney is worth the effort. Use it with grilled chicken or sharp cheese.

This next recipe, a variation on Crab Apple Chutney, demonstrates the ease with which key limes can be macerated in a Champion juicing machine. The pulp and juice are extruded separately, but both may be used.

Key Lime Chutney

1 pound key limes
2 cups fresh apple juice
½ pound chopped tallow (rendered suet)
12 peeled, sliced tart apples
2 cups golden raisins
4 cups sugar
½ cup peeled, minced gingerroot
¼ cup sliced, skinless almonds

Slice the limes, remove the seeds, and run the limes through a professional Champion juicing machine or use a grinding machine. Reserve the juice, pulp, and rind. To obtain the apple juice: juice tart, misshapen, and small apples. Brown the suet; add the limes, lime juice, and rest of the ingredients (except the almonds). Cook until thick. Add the almonds. JSP/RWB10(4OZ)15(8OZ)20(16OZ)**R.**

Chokoloskee Island Chutney is a fruity chutney for use with fish and seafood but is also perfectly delightful with fowl. Utilize both the watermelon flesh and its rind. Make **Chokoloskee Island Chutney** (or watermelon molasses or watermelon jam) from the flesh and Pickled Watermelon Rinds or Watermelon Rind Preserves (*The Jamlady Cookbook*, 193) from the rind. This chutney is just the chutney for a shore dinner out on one of the Ten Thousand Islands in Florida and was made to go with broiled or fried flopping-fresh fish, boiled crab, or grilled fowl. Because Chokoloskee is Jamlady's favorite fishing and vacation spot, she named this chutney for this beautiful, unspoiled island.

Chokoloskee Island Chutney

- 8 cups watermelon cubes
- 3 cups sugar
- 2 cups diced fresh pineapple
- 1½ cups dark raisins*
- 1½ cups red wine vinegar
- 1 cup chopped white onions
- 1 peeled, seeded lemon
- 1 peeled, seeded orange
- 4 ounces candied lemon peel
- ¼ cup lemon juice
- 2 ounces peeled, minced gingerroot
- 5 true cinnamon sticks
- 30 whole clove (spice bag)
- 30 coriander seed (spice bag)

True cinnamon sticks are recommended. Seed and cube (½ inch) the watermelon. Use no citrus pith (bitter white part). Cook all ingredients until thick. Remember, the chutney will be thicker when cool. JSP/RWB10(8OZ)A. pH = 3.90.

* May substitute golden raisins or dried currants

Sunshine Chutney is gingered and made with papaya, nectarines, and blood oranges. Fresh papaya is low in pectin. The citrus peels provide the necessary pectin to thicken this chutney. Papaya aids digestion, which is an extra benefit for a tasty condiment.

True cinnamon, Cinnamomum zeylanicum *Nees. is tan in color, and* Cinnamomum cassia *Blume, Cassia, or Chinese Cinnamon is brown and somewhat bitter. Cassia buds, a spice used in pickling, are from* C. cassia.

Sunshine Chutney

8 cups 1-inch papaya cubes
4 blood oranges
9-10 ounces grated ginger
3 cups water
4 cups white/red wine vinegar
4 cups light brown sugar
2 cups white sugar
4 cups sliced nectarines*
8 ounces candied lemon peel
¼ teaspoon ascorbic acid crystals**
Per spice bag:
25 whole clove
5 cinnamon sticks
15 coriander seeds
1 crushed whole nutmeg

Buy a 4-pound papaya. Prepare slivered orange rinds and sliced orange flesh; discard all citrus pith. Microwave the orange rind (rind only) and grated ginger in 3 cups water for 10 to 15 minutes. Cook the orange rind/ginger mixture (including liquid) with vinegar and spice bag for 5 minutes; add both sugars. Boil for 5 minutes; add the fruit (papaya, nectarines, and orange slices), candied lemon peel, and simmer slowly until acceptably thick. JSP/RWB10(4OZ)15(8OZ)A. Completed pH = 3.96 to 4.04. DOB: 6/24/1996.

* With skins juiced and juice used

** Use with peeled fruits to prevent browning.

If you love chutney, try this seedless version of elderberry chutney made with a top-quality red wine vinegar, stoned raisins, ginger, clove, cayenne, and mace. Other versions of elderberry chutney contain mustard seed.

Elderberry Chutney

1½ pounds elderberries
2 cups red wine vinegar
3 ounces raisins
6 whole clove
1 pound chopped onions
2-3 ounces light brown sugar
¼ ounce ground ginger
1 teaspoon salt
Dust of cayenne
Mace (to taste)

Juice the elderberries with a Champion juicing machine to obtain all the pulp; discard the seeds. Elderberry chutney may be made from juiced salvage after the juice has been heat extracted for jelly, but the best chutney is made from fresh berries. Run the elderberries through the juicing machine many times until the seeds begin to feel warm. "Blenderize" the vinegar, raisins, and clove; add the pulp and other ingredients and simmer for 10 minutes. JSP/RWB15(4OZ)15(8OZ)A. **Note: For more intense flavor, heat-extracted elderberry juice may be cooked down and added into this chutney with sugar to taste. The pH of fresh elderberries is 3.6 to 3.8.**

Caution: Don't eat too many raw elderberries. They do have some cyanide, which usually is destroyed by heat. Please see other references to cyanide in this book.

On September 14, 2000, because we had many peaches, Jamlady helped me invent **Nellie Melba Chutney.** We had just made peach chutney and mango chutney using the same recipe and several batches of Jamlady's Original Peach Melba Jam (see *The Jamlady Cookbook,* 104). With two cups of raspberry puree left over from Nellie Melba Jam and lots of peaches, we decided to try a Nellie Melba Chutney. **Since raspberries are expensive,**

this recipe is a good way to obtain the raspberry flavor without the raspberry cost. Jamlady and I believe most creative endeavors come from scarcity, plenty, deliberate focus, or limitation. Next time you hear yourself saying, "I can't make this or that, because I don't have the exact ingredients," think of what you can make. Seize the opportunity. Listen to your inner Jamlady.

When canning creatively, especially with low-acid fruits or vegetables, always check the final pH. The pH must be comfortably under 4.6. Aim for 4.0 or under. If the pH is too high, acidify with vinegar or some other high-acid juice, fruit, or rind. Study the pH scale. **Low numbers are high-acid, and high numbers (4.6 and up) are low-acid. Botulism can grow in a sealed canning jar when conditions for growth include: room temperature, low-acid, low-salt, and low-sugar. Do not can low-acid vegetables or fruits without understanding pH.**

If you buy a pH meter, make sure to get a temperature probe and an electrode that is the non-clogging type (made for jam making, as well as pickle making). **If you're reasonably intelligent and diligent, do not be intimidated by a pH meter or experts—who might imply a careful homemaker can't really use a pH meter appropriately.** Meters usually come with instructions (read them thoroughly) and a technical service phone number. Some newer pH meters are all metal. If you can't afford to buy a pH meter, see if your library, local extension office, or local rental-all place will allow you to borrow or rent one.

Nellie Melba Chutney

2 cups raspberry pulp*
12 large peaches**
4½ cups red wine vinegar
4 cups sugar
6 peeled, cubed apples
½ cup minced gingerroot
¼ cup fresh lemon juice
10 Serrano peppers
2 tablespoons mustard seed
12 clove
20 ounces raisins

* Juice whole raspberries 15 times until the seeds run hot and dry. Measure out 2 cups of raspberry pulp. Peel and slice the peaches. Cook all ingredients together, except the raisins. When almost thick, add the raisins. Stir well. JSP/RWB10(4OZ)15(8OZ)A.

** May substitute mangoes, nectarines, or apricots.

Variation: Charlotte Church Chutney—Make this chutney with mangoes. Name the apricot variation for your favorite vocalist (Apricot-Raspberry Chutney).

Rhubarb chutney is an old-time rhubarb-lover's delight. Serve it with pork, ham, venison, lamb, chicken, and curries. **Rhubarb, *Rheum rhaponticum,*** is often made into chutney with clove and cinnamon, but this recipe is flavored with ground mustard, fresh gingerroot, and garlic.

Rhubarb Chutney

8 cups sliced rhubarb
2 pounds brown sugar
1 cup diced onions
1 cup cider vinegar
2½ ounces peeled, minced ginger
½ tablespoon pickling salt
3 minced garlic cloves
1 teaspoon ground mustard
⅛ teaspoon pepper
1 pound dark raisins

Wash and trim 2 pounds rhubarb; processor slice. Cook all the ingredients, except the raisins, until thick. Add the raisins; cook 3 minutes. JSP/RWB10(4OZ)15(8OZ)A. For a small batch, half or quarter the recipe.

Caution: Discard all rhubarb leaves; they are toxic!

Variation: Add raspberry puree to rhubarb chutney for **Raspberry Rhubarb Chutney.** Raspberries have a pH of 2.8 to 3.6. Add 1 cup raspberry puree, ¼ cup more vinegar, and ¼ cup more sugar.

Note: There isn't very much vinegar needed in this recipe, because rhubarb has a 3.1 to 3.2 pH, so other low-acid ingredients like onions (in smaller measure) do not impact the overall pH that much. Ginger has a pH of 5.6 to 5.9 and raisins, 3.8 to 4.1.

Rhubarb and Date Chutney may be made with 4 pounds rhubarb, ¾ pound dates (low-acid), 1 medium onion (low-acid), 3 cups light brown sugar, 4 cups red wine vinegar, 1 tablespoon grated fresh ginger (low-acid), and other spices such as pepper, coriander, allspice, and 1 hot pepper.

Rhubarb and figs go well together, but Jamlady and I have not yet made that combination in chutney, only in a preserve. To compute it out, combine the ingredients from ½ of a rhubarb chutney recipe plus ½ of a fig chutney or fig preserves recipe (see *The Jamlady Cookbook,* 68). If using a half-fig preserves recipe, add in a tad more vinegar or to taste. Figs have a pH of almost 6.0, so any chutney made must be acidified sufficiently to 4.2 or under. If you need a recipe tested and can't find local help, e-mail Jamlady@Jamlady.com for assistance.

A WORD ABOUT PH

The pH of vinegar and lemon juice, two ingredients often used to regulate pH, are approximately in the same range. I tested 5-percent acidity **cider vinegar, red wine vinegar,** and distilled **white vinegar;** the readings were **2.40, 2.36, and 2.34,** respectively. Many canners incorrectly believe they may add equal amounts of an ingredient with a pH of 2.2 to another ingredient with a pH of 6 and get a pH of 4.1. Such is not always the case. The reason has to do with buffering capacities, as well as other factors. **One big problem some home canners have is they do not know what they do not know.** Canners, like many of us, make some assumptions based on a little, no, or wrong information. **What seems logical, just might be wrong. While Jamlady recommends zero reliance on a mathematical calculation that assumes 1 cup of pH 3.0 mixed with 1 cup of pH 5.0 equals a product with the pH of 4.0, this method of computation might be useful in guesstimating formulations for canned food products that will ultimately be tested. These products should then be made, tested, and canned only if the pH is safely under 4.6. For those who do not understand why one cannot rely on such a mathematical calculation, even one weighted for the number of cups of a substance, Jamlady and I can only say you need to read up on buffering capacity, molarity, and pH. Keep in mind, a buffer is a substance that tends to keep a chemical system balanced by causing resistance to changes in pH. If you have never taken chemistry, or are rusty on the basic concepts of molarity, it might be useful to talk with a chemistry expert who can explain the topic well.** Remember always to test newly created product before hermetically sealing it in a jar. Always be mindful of the dangers of adding high pH (low-acid) ingredients to chutney recipes without adequately compensating by adding low-pH (high-acid) ingredients to the same mixture. Then always double-check the safety of the recipe by measuring the final ground-up product. Even with pickles, grind the pickle juice with the pickles to measure the pH, or measure the juice, the solids, and the juice with the ground-up solids. **Please consult the pH chart, located in the back of this book, for approximate pH values for each ingredient used in any given recipe. If you cannot locate the pH for any fruit or vegetable, test it yourself or send Jamlady an e-mail for help.**

Dates from the date palm, *Phoenix dactylifera,* with a 6.20 to 6.40 pH need to be acidified for canned chutney. Date chutney pairs well with apples and cheese. **Heaven is a toasted muffin with Brie cheese, date chutney, and fresh, juicy pear slices on the side.**

Date Chutney

5½ cups chopped dates
3 cups brown sugar
2½ cups red wine or malt vinegar
1 pound diced red onions or shallots
½ cup allspice berries (in spice bag)
6 tablespoons pickling salt
1 teaspoon ground ginger

Chop about 2 pounds pitted dates and measure out 5½ cups. Cook all ingredients until thick. Either refrigerate, labeling **"Refrigerate Only,"** or check the pH, adjusting it with more vinegar if necessary. For chutney under 4.2, JSP/RWB15(4OZ)15(8OZ)20(16OZ)A or JS**R.**

Note: The pH of dates may vary. Dromedary dates (so they say) have a maximal pH of around 4.88, but other brands of dates could be 6.4 or higher. A 4.88 pH date provides a wider margin of safety in a canned product.

Rubus Pome Chutney

15 cups apples
1 cup peeled, minced gingerroot
8 cups white wine vinegar
1 cup distilled water
4 cups raspberries*
4 cups sugar
1 cup diced onions
1 cup dried currants
Juice of 4 lemons
4 tablespoons mustard seed
2 minced garlic cloves
1 pound golden raisins
2 cups pecan pieces

To make this raspberry-apple chutney, peel and slice the apples. Cook the ginger for ½ hour with 1 cup vinegar and 1 cup distilled water. Add the rest of the ingredients, except the raisins and the pecans, and cook until nearly thick. Add the raisins and cook until thick. Add the pecans and JSP/RWB15(8OZ)20(16OZ)A.

* May substitute seedless raspberry puree (see previous instructions in Nellie Melba Chutney)

Variation: Blackberry-Apple Chutney—Use blackberries instead of raspberries.

Use blueberry chutney on fried potato cakes with sour cream, crackers and cream cheese, cream-cheese stuffed celery, and meats. Who said to put that blueberry chutney on your French fries and Tater Tots®?

Blueberry Chutney

1-2 minced hot pepper pods
4½ cups fresh blueberries*
1 medium diced onions
1¾ cups wine vinegar
⅝ cup light brown sugar
2½ teaspoons mustard seed
2 tablespoons grated gingerroot
¼ teaspoon ground ginger
1/16 teaspoon ground nutmeg
½ cup raisins or currants

Seed the hot peppers. Wash and stem the blueberries. Cook all ingredients, except the raisins/currants, until thick. Add the raisins. JSP/RWB15(8OZ)20(16OZ)A.

Variation: Huckleberry Chutney—Use *huckleberries.

In the Midwest, the term **huckleberry** describes two low-growing berry species, *Vaccinium canadensis* and *V. pennsylvanicum.* The **New England huckleberry** is *Gaylussacia,* spp. The **whortleberry** or **bilberry** is *V. myrtillus* and *V. corymbosum* Linn. The **High bush blueberry** is *V. corymbosum.* **The Midwest huckleberries are called blueberries in New England.**

Gooseberries, *Ribes* spp., are shrubby plants of various species. ***Ribes hirtellum* is the edible American gooseberry.** *Ribes speciosum* is a fuchsia-flowered gooseberry. Gooseberries, cousins to currants, are low in pH (2.8 - 3.1). They may be distinguished from currants by their thorns. Gooseberries have a stem end and a bloom end. Both ends need to be removed prior to cooking. The head-and-tailing takes considerable time, but the tasty gooseberry chutney is worth the extra effort.

Red Gooseberry Chutney

7-8 cups red gooseberries
3¼ cups red wine vinegar
3¼ cups sugar
2 cups diced red onions or shallots
1 tablespoon pickling salt
½ teaspoon mustard seed
½ teaspoon pepper
1 cup dried currants

Prepare 3½ pounds gooseberries (see above). Cook all ingredients, except the currants, until nearly thick. Add the currants. JSP/RWB15(8OZ)20(16OZ)A.

The next recipe, Worcestershire Sauce, is actually ground-up chutney that is cooked and strained to produce the sauce.

Worcestershire Sauce

3 pounds diced apples
3 chopped onions
2 pounds sugar
2 tablespoons ground ginger
4 tablespoons pickling salt
1 chopped, seeded orange
1 gallon vinegar
½ teaspoon cayenne pepper
2 tablespoons whole clove

Peel the apples and onions. Cook all of the ingredients for 3 hours; strain. JSP/RWB10-15*(8OZ)A or JS**R.**

* For a thicker product

Spicy Old-Fashioned Chili Sauce

8 quarts diced tomato meats
2 cups diced bell peppers
5 cups red wine vinegar
4 cups diced onions
3 cups sugar
12 minced hot-pepper pods
3 tablespoons dried parsley or celery tops
2 tablespoons celery seed
2 tablespoons pickling salt
2 tablespoons minced gingerroot
1 tablespoon minced garlic
1 tablespoon ground clove
1 tablespoon ground cinnamon
1 tablespoon ground allspice

Boiling-water plunge the red tomatoes to obtain the meats. To make a hotter sauce, substitute some sweet peppers for hot. Slowly cook all ingredients down for 4 hours. Reduce the liquid, using the on-off method. JSP/RWB15(8OZ)15(16OZ)A.

Medium-Hot Chili Sauce

6½ cups diced bell peppers
4 cups diced onions
7½ quarts tomato meats
2 cups sugar
1–1½ cups diced Serrano peppers
6¼ cups vinegar
2 tablespoons pickling salt

Per spice bag:
4 tablespoons celery seed
2 tablespoons mustard seed
2 bay leaves
2 teaspoons whole clove
2 teaspoons ground ginger
2 teaspoons ground nutmeg
4 cinnamon sticks

Seed the bell peppers, peel the onions, and dice both. In boiling water, plunge the tomatoes to obtain the meats. Cook all ingredients until thick. Stir well; discard the spice bag. JSP/RWB15(16OZ)A. pH = 4.0.

Hot Lemon-Boy Chili Sauce

16 cups yellow tomato meats
3 cups cider or white wine vinegar
2 cups diced onions
1 cup sugar
1 cup diced red bell peppers
1 cup diced yellow bell peppers
1 cup diced green/red bell peppers
1 cup diced Serrano peppers
1 tablespoon pickling salt

Per spice bag:
2 tablespoons celery seed
1 tablespoon mustard seed
6 bay leaves
1 teaspoon whole clove
6 cinnamon sticks
1 teaspoon ground nutmeg
1 teaspoon ground ginger

Boiling-water plunge the tomatoes to obtain the meats. Cook all ingredients together until thick. JSP/RWB15(16OZ)A. Serve on fish, omelets, *frittatas*, or brats.

Spicy Damson Plum Chutney

3 pounds sectioned plums
Plum pits (spice bag)
1 pound sliced tart apples
1 large diced Spanish onion
3 minced garlic cloves
2 cups brown sugar
2 cups red wine vinegar
1 tablespoon pickling salt
2 tablespoons minced gingerroot
2 tablespoons ground clove
5 minced Serrano peppers

Pit the plums and cut into large pieces. Cook all ingredients until thick. JSP/RWB15(8OZ) 20(16OZ)A.

This recipe makes a sweeter chutney than most and is made with honey. A similar, spicier version (whole plums with vinegar and sugar syrup) was noted in a recipe for spiced plums (Lemcke 1899, 27). Use this simple chutney (relish) with meats, curries, cottage cheese, and rice. And to the lady who asked, "Do all chutneys have raisins?" The answer is—no!

Simple Plum Chutney

1 large orange
$8\frac{1}{2}$ cups chopped plums
$\frac{5}{8}$ cup red wine vinegar
Dash of nutmeg*
$2\frac{1}{4}$ cups raw clover or orange blossom honey
1 cup nuts (optional)

Seed the orange; chop. Use firm and coarsely chopped plums. A good, light honey from a local beekeeper is recommended. Cook the plums, oranges, vinegar, and nutmeg until thick, stirring well. Add the honey and nuts at the end. JSP/RWB15(8OZ). Makes eight 8-ounce jars.

* Or use spice bag (clove, cinnamon, allspice, or mace).

Make Banana Chutney from "on sale" bananas. Regular bananas range in pH from 5.00 to 5.29. Red bananas usually have a lower pH (4.50 - 4.75).

Banana Chutney

3 tablespoons pickling spice
$\frac{1}{2}$ pound minced gingerroot
$7\frac{1}{2}$ cups cider vinegar*
20 peeled, cut bananas
$2\frac{1}{2}$ pounds diced onions
4 cups brown sugar
2 pounds sectioned dates
1 tablespoon pickling salt
$1\frac{1}{2}$ pounds raisins

Put the pickling spice in a spice bag. Microwave the ginger in 2 cups of vinegar for 3 minutes. Pour the ginger/vinegar mixture into a cooking pan along with the rest of the ingredients (except the raisins). Cook the chutney on low until nearly thick. Add the raisins. Stir well. Discard the spice bag. JSP/RWB15(8OZ)20(16OZ)A. pH = under 4.0.

* May substitute some malt vinegar for cider vinegar

The tropical tree **guava,** *Psidium guajava,* is not a particularly attractive tree, but its fruit has been eaten for years. Chutney may be made from both guavas and tamarinds (Dooley, E. 1950. *Puerto Rican Cook Book*) if you have a source for the fruits. This basic guava chutney is not very different from basic tomato chutney, except it is made with fresh guavas.

Guava Chutney

5 pounds prepared guava
2 pounds brown sugar
2 quarts vinegar
2 pounds seedless raisins
1 minced garlic clove
1 tablespoon minced gingerroot or ground ginger
½ tablespoon mustard
3 tablespoons salt
Turmeric (optional, to taste/color)
2-3 diced hot peppers

To 5 pounds seedless, skinless guava pulp, add the brown sugar and vinegar. Simmer until tender. Stir well. Add chopped, seedless raisins and garlic; cook a bit more. Add the ginger, mustard, salt, a little turmeric, and peppers. Refrigerate overnight. Heat again. JSP/RWB15(8OZ)A.

Cranberry Chutney

Rind of 1 orange or 2 lemons
1 pound fresh cranberries
2 cups sugar
2 cups red/white wine vinegar
Juice of 1 orange or 2 lemons
½ teaspoon ground coriander
1/16 teaspoons ground clove

Grate the rind of 1 orange or 2 lemons, using no white pith. Cook all ingredients until thick. JSP/RWB15(8OZ)A.

While many recipes in this chapter are for canned chutney, this next recipe, **Cranberry, Ginger, and Lemon Chutney or Joe Watson's Cranberry Chutney may be frozen or canned.** Other chutney recipes may be frozen as well. Just freeze a small amount to see how it turns out when defrosted.

Joe Watson's Cranberry Chutney was given to Jamlady and me by a loyal market patron, Mr. Thomas J. Watson, who received it from his grandmother. We decided to test the pH of Joe's recipe. The pH of cranberries is 2.7. The highest pH of peppers is around 5.45. The pH of gingerroot is 5.6 to 5.9. The pH of lemon is around 2.2. The highest pH of onions and garlic is around 5.85. Doing the "guesstimates," the recipe should be able to be canned; the pH should be well under 4.0. In fact, it is under 4.0 without any vinegar in the recipe.

One day Joe Watson delivered two newly made batches of his cranberry chutney to us. **A pH test revealed numbers of 3.25 and 3.47 for the two different batches. Both batches were well under 4.0; therefore this recipe may be canned safely.** Of course, Joe's chutney may be frozen; freezing is faster. Then again, if your freezer is full or you want the chutney for hostess gifts, can it. **This chutney exemplifies a product that may be canned and is also vinegar free.** This chutney may be canned because of all the high-acid ingredients. Thinking back, we also have made a lime-and-crab-apple chutney with no added vinegar, and it too had a low pH.

Joe says he buys his crystallized ginger at a Japanese market in Arlington Heights, Illinois, because the price is reasonable. Shop around for large quantities of crystallized ginger, because candied ginger is cost prohibitive in some stores. To make your own, see the recipe in Chapter 1. The lovely, large pieces of candied ginger (pictured on page 37) were purchased at Emmanuel's Marketplace in Stone Ridge, New York.

This recipe is special and unique; unlike most chutney recipes, there are no apples, raisins, or vinegar. There are many unimpressive chutney recipes, but the Joe Watson Family recipe is not one of them. It's spectacular! Make it, freeze it, or can it, and definitely gift it to your friends.

Ingredients for Joe Watson's Cranberry Chutney: cranberries, sugar, grated lemon rind, sliced lemons, freshly grated gingerroots, chopped onions, candied ginger pieces, sliced garlic cloves, a cinnamon stick, dry mustard, salt, and minced, seedless jalapeño peppers.

Place all ingredients in the pan, except the sugar.

Add the sugar to the ingredients in the pan. Stir the sugar into the other ingredients in the pan; start cooking.

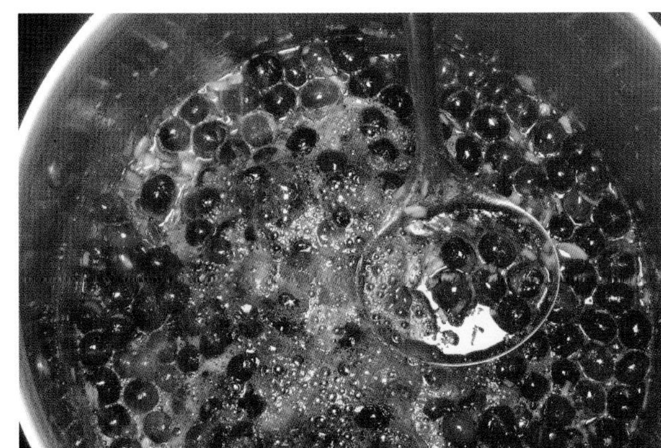

As the chutney begins to cook, the sugar will start to melt and the cranberries will begin to pop open.

Fill the jars with the thick chutney. Don't overcook, as the chutney will thicken when cool. Attach the lid and tighten the ring.

Process the jars in a rolling-water bath. Remove the jars from bath, and set them on a towel.

Joe Watson's Cranberry Chutney on Camembert cheese with water crackers.

Joe Watson's Cranberry Chutney. Eat it. Refrigerate it. Can it. Freeze it.

Joe Watson's Cranberry Chutney

1 minced jalapeño pepper
½ cup crystallized ginger
1 medium lemon
12 ounces fresh cranberries
2 cups sugar
⅓ cup minced onion
1 minced garlic clove
1 true cinnamon stick*
½ teaspoon dry mustard
½ teaspoon salt

Seed the hot pepper. Cut the crystallized ginger into midsize or large pieces. Grate or cut in slivers the outer lemon rind. Discard all pith and seeds. Dice the lemon; retain the pulp and lemon juice. In a stainless-steel pot, boil all the ingredients until thick and the cranberries pop open. Alternately, set aside half of the ginger to add at the very end. JS**R**, JS**F**(freeze), or JSP/RWB15(8OZ)A.

* ***Cinnamomum zeylanicum*** **Nees.** is tan in color, not brown. Remember to leave 6-percent headspace to allow for expansion in both canning jars and freezer containers. Allow the chutney to cool before freezing. Purchase good-quality crystallized ginger and true cinnamon sticks.

Cranberries are very versatile. **Fine chutney may be made with cranberries, sugar, whole oranges, onions, raisins, shelled pistachios, dried figs, ginger, salt, cinnamon, cayenne pepper, and dry mustard** (see Chef2Chef's **Cranberry-Fig Chutney with Cinnamon and Pistachios** or J. Sahni's recipe in the November 1988 issue of *Bon Appétit* magazine). Cranberries go well with many other fruits and berries so all sorts of chutney combinations may be made. There is no reason fresh figs may not be used instead of dried figs (*Bon Appétit* recipe), except that fresh figs do not retain their shape, and an extended cooking time would be needed to evaporate the extra moisture.

Caution: Just remember to use a pH meter when experimenting with canning recipes.

Once fall arrives, everyone looks for mincemeat for that special holiday dinner. This mincemeat, better known as **"mock mincemeat,"** has no real meat. It satisfies both vegetarians and meat eaters. However, do not assume the taste is anything less than great! This low-fat recipe adds no butter, margarine, or suet.

Green Tomato-Apple Mincemeat

32 tart apples
¼ teaspoon ascorbic acid crystals
32 green tomatoes
1 minced outer rind of an orange
12 cups sugar
4 pounds washed raisins (dark and/or golden)
3 cups candied lemon or mixed peel
1⅓ cups cider vinegar
1 cup dried currants
2⅔ tablespoons pickling salt
2 tablespoons ground cinnamon
1 teaspoon ground clove
1 teaspoon ground nutmeg
1 teaspoon ground allspice

Peel and quarter the apples. Float them in water containing ¼ teaspoon ascorbic acid crystals. Drain and slice. Wash and slice the green tomatoes; peeling them is optional. Cut the orange peel from the orange, discard the orange pith, and use only the outer rind. Cook all ingredients together about 1 to 1¼ hours or until thick. Makes 11 quarts; halve the recipe for smaller batch. The color darkens to brown when almost done. JSP/RWB25(32OZ)A.

Variation: Frozen Mincemeat Pies—Make complete pies and freeze, or freeze the pie fillings in smaller pie pans; reset them later into crusts for baking. Double bag the pies to avoid "freezer tastes."

We have always been leery of meat or tallow recipes stored in warmer temperatures with brandy on top. If you keep this mincemeat and suet recipe refrigerated, and bake it before eating, it should be fine. Make a few days before the holidays but don't cold store too long.

Mincemeat with Brandy

1 pound tart apples
8 ounces suet
12 ounces seedless raisins (2½ cups)
8 ounces sultanas (1½ cups)
8 ounces dried currants (1½ cups)
8 ounces mixed, chopped peel (1 cup)
12 ounces soft brown sugar (2 cups)
Juice and grated rind of 1 lemon
Juice and grated rind of 1 orange
½ teaspoon ground mixed spice
¼ teaspoon ground nutmeg
¼ pint brandy (⅝ cup)

Peel, core, and chop the apples finely. Shred the suet. Wash and dry the raisins, sultanas, and currants. Mix the prepared ingredients in a large bowl with the chopped peel, brown sugar, grated citrus rinds, citrus juices, and the spices. Stir well. Add half of the brandy; stir well. According to the recipe maker, "Pack the mincemeat loosely into sterile jars, and spoon the remaining spirits over the top; seal" (in maker's terminology, **I believe seal means to close the jar only**—no processing. JS**R.**). According to one recipe tester, this mincemeat will keep up to 9 months with brandy. Jamlady and I recommend this mincemeat be used within a week and that it not be tasted until baked. Make sure the brandy completely covers the top. Keep the jar upright and Refrigerated at all times.

Variation: Freeze the filling directly in the completed pie, or can meatless mincemeat and add in the canned meat when you bake the pie. Use commercially canned meat as the Amish do. If you do not have a source for the canned beef, contact Miller Orchards in Nappanee, Indiana, or stop by its store and orchards. If you wish to can any product containing meat, a pressure-cooker is required, as the product must be processed at temperatures higher than is possible in a RWB.

Jamlady has an Amish friend who used to make an excellent mincemeat with canned meat. The beef used had been previously canned, and she mixed this beef with the meatless mincemeat recipe. Then she canned the mixture in a rolling-water bath. While she has successfully made and sold this meat version of mincemeat for over ten years, she is no longer allowed to make it this way due to the potential for botulinus growth, even in previously cooked and canned meat. Please see the previous variation.

A NOTE ON PRESSURE-COOKERS

If you have never used a pressure-cooker, be careful. Should the seal of a pressure cooker be old or worn, there is the potential for a blast of hot liquids and an incredible mess. I have cleaned ceilings twice and sworn off pressure-cookers. Jamlady wasn't much help—she kept saying—"I told you so."

Caution: Even when properly maintained, a pressure-cooker has the potential for dangerous accidents. You just would not believe what happens when you fall asleep and forget to turn off the pressure-cooker. Set an alarm if you are tired and canning into the wee hours of the morning. A pressure-cooker is not needed for any recipes in this cookbook. However, if you wish to can real mincemeat filling safely, you will need to can it in a pressure-cooker especially made for canning.

SOLO FRUITS AND TOMATO JUICE

Solo fruits may be canned in season and enjoyed throughout the year. If you have a pear or apple tree in your backyard, you might want to try your hand at canning plain, minted, or otherwise flavored pears in a simple syrup, making frozen or fresh pear pies with nutmeg, cinnamon or peppermint extract, or canning fruit juice. In season, Jamlady and I often make pear, apple, sour cherry, raspberry, blackberry, or strawberry rhubarb pies. We do not bake them directly; instead, we seal them twice and freeze. These pies are tasty during the off-season and come in handy when a quick dessert is needed. Sometimes we just take the frozen pie to a friend's house and bake it there. Pie fillings may be canned as well, but usually it is just as easy to can the solo fruit or freeze the pies or pie fillings. Reference pages forty-six thru forty-nine of *The Jamlady Cookbook.*

Tomato juice, tomato puree, and V-8 type juices may all be canned with a RWB if they are acidified with citric acid to well under 4.6 pH. Jamlady and I have formulated and tested this recipe for Snappy Tomato Juice. Acidify this recipe and measure everything accurately. Plain tomato juice should also be acidified with citric acid (sour salt). **Use ¼ teaspoon citric acid per pint of tomato juice or**

Snappy Tom drink with dilly bean, pickled garlic, pickled carrot stick, and pickled onion.

tomato puree. One 5-ounce container of citric acid will process approximately 50 quarts of tomatoes. Formulating mixed vegetable juices is more difficult than it appears; for if you add too much citric acid to bring the pH below 4.6, it may make the juice too tart to the taste. **This Snappy Tomato Juice is good as a non-alcoholic drink or with vodka for a super Bloody Mary!** Break out the Stoli® and dress up your Bloody Mary with a pickle (dilly bean, hot pickled carrot stick, pickled Brussels sprouts, pickled celery sprig, or pickled asparagus stalk).

Snappy Tomato Juice

Juice the tomatoes in a Champion juicing machine or other juicer. Measure out 7 quarts tomato juice. Add 2 large, sliced jalapeño peppers, 4 teaspoons citric acid, 3 to 4 thinly sliced garlic cloves, 2 teaspoons celery seed, 1 teaspoon dried parsley leaves, ½ teaspoon ground black pepper, and ½ teaspoon salt. Simmer for 1 hour. Run the entire contents through the juicing machine again, JSP/RWB35(16OZ)A. pH reading = 4.04. Makes 12 pints.

Note: I have noticed at least one canning expert lists 15-minute processing times for pints of ketchup and chili sauce but 35 minutes for pints of acidified tomato juice, and 40 minutes for quarts. I do not see the logic of that, as the given pH of my tomato juice or Snappy Tomato Juice is always around 4.04, and I don't see where heat penetration should be a problem. However, I have not run tests, and the USDA presumably has (sometime in the 1970s). Ruth Hertzberg's *Putting Food By* (1976, 132) recommends 15 minutes for pints and quarts that have been acidified with ½ teaspoon citric acid per quart. I agree with her, but I can't prove it with my own tests. Therefore, I took the time to consult experts on this matter. They too are in conflict about this. Until somebody does further studies, I will not make a recommendation about the times for processing tomato juice. Process as you see fit, after informing yourself on the matter. Jamlady does not recommend cold packing tomatoes or tomato juice.

Note: If you care whether your tomato juice "separates" in the jar, you will have to cook your tomatoes prior to juicing them. Most of us just shake up the juice if it separates. Think about the extra work and mess, and perhaps you will just juice the tomatoes, cook them a little, acidify them, and can them like most of us do. And no, the vodka won't take care of separating tomato juice, but maybe after one drink, you won't care about it anyway.

Caution: Do not fail to add the citric acid. It is critical. Do not add more jalapeño peppers without increasing the citric acid and testing the pH. Actually, the addition of more citric acid may make the juice too tart.

Caution: Do not can stewed tomatoes or tomato juice without some citric acid. Refer to the pH chart in this book. Most tomato varieties have a pH under 4.6, but a few do not. Hermetically sealing a tomato product, 4.6 pH or higher, potentially can manufacture *botulismotoxin* (botulinus toxin). If you open a canned jar and the toxin is present, you may never know it—especially if you cook the product before eating it. However, if you drink the cold tomato juice and it contains the toxin, it could be deadly. Boiling temperatures kill the deadly toxin but not the spores that grow the toxin. So, heed Jamlady's warning, and use citric acid to can tomatoes. Of course, acidification may be accomplished with vinegar, lemon juice, or some other acid, but these acidifiers may impart a taste that is less desirable.

Appendix A

Approximate pH of Foods

For more information on this topic, see *The Jamlady Cookbook,* by Bev Alfeld.
Please note: Single numbers indicate single test.

Apples 2.90-4.00
Apricots 3.30-4.80
Artichokes 5.60
Asparagus 5.00-6.70
Avocados 6.27-6.58
Bananas, red 4.50-4.75
Bananas, yellow 5.00-5.29
Beans 5.60-6.50
Beers 4.00-5.00
Beets 4.90-6.60
Bilberries 2.80-3.70
Blackberries 3.20-4.50
Blood, human 7.35-7.45
Blueberries, Maine 3.12-3.33
Boysenberries 3.00-3.30
Bread, white 5.00-6.00
Broccoli, cooked 6.30-6.52
Brussels sprouts 6.00-6.30
Butter, melted 5.70-6.80
Cabbage 5.20-6.80
Cactus, pear cactus (tuna or *Opuntia tuna*) . 5.30-7.10
Cantaloupe 6.13-6.58
Carrots 4.90-5.30
Cauliflower 5.60-6.00
Celery 5.70-6.00
Chayote (*christophene,* French) (*Sechium edule*) 6.00-6.30
Cheese 4.10-7.44
Cherries 3.20-4.20
Cherries, maraschino 3.47-3.52
Cherries, 'Royal Ann' 3.80-3.83
Chicory 5.90-6.05
Chives 5.20-6.35
Cider 2.90-3.30
Coconut, fresh 5.52-6.18
Corn 5.90-7.30
Corn syrup, Karo Light . . . . . 4.6 maximum
Corn syrup, Karo Dark . . . . . 5.0 maximum
Cranberries 2.30-2.70
Cream of coconut, canned 5.51-5.87
Cucumbers 5.12-5.78
Cucumbers, dilled pickles 3.20-3.60
Cucumbers, sour pickles 3.00-3.40
Currants, red 2.90
Dates, canned 6.20-6.40
Dates, 'Deglet Noor' (Sun Fresh) 5.50-6.00
Eggplant 4.75-5.50
Eggs, newly laid . . . . . 6.58 (as CO_2 in egg decreases with time the albumen pH rises)
Eggs, white 7.96
Eggs, yolk 6.80
Elderberries 3.60-3.80
Fennel, Anise 5.48-5.88
Fiddleheads, defrosted . . . . . 6.00-6.80 (tentative, needs to be retested)
Figs, 'Calimyrna' 5.05-5.98
Flour, wheat 7.60-8.00
Garlic cloves 5.30-6.30
Gelatin dessert 2.60
Gelatin, plain jell 6.08
Gingerroot 5.60-5.90
Gooseberries 2.80-3.30
Grapefruit 3.00-3.75
Grapes, 'Concord' 2.80-3.00
Grapes, 'Niagara' 2.80-3.27
Grapes, seedless or seeded 2.90-4.50
Grapes, wild . . . . . 3.14 (single test, Illinois)
Ground cherries 4.25-4.35
Guava 4.60
Guava, canned 3.70-4.00
Honey 3.70-4.20
Horseradish, freshly ground 5.35
Jams 3.50-4.50
Jellies, fruit 2.80-3.40
Ketchup 3.89-3.92
Kiwano fruit 4.40
Kiwi fruit 3.10-3.50
Kumquat, Florida 3.64-4.25
Leeks 5.52-6.17
Lemons 2.20-3.20
Lettuce 5.80-6.15

Limes 1.80-2.35
Loganberries 2.70-3.50
Mangoes, Florida 3.40-4.63
Maple syrup 6.50-7.00
Melba toast 5.08-5.30
Melons, casaba 5.78-6.00
Melons, honeydew 6.00-6.67
Melons, Persians 5.90-6.38
Milk, acidophilus 4.90-4.25
Milk, condensed 6.33
Milk, cow 6.30-6.80
Milk, evaporated 5.90-6.30
Milk, goat 6.48
Milk, human 6.60-7.60
Molasses 4.90-5.40
Mushrooms 6.00-6.70
Nectarines 3.92-4.18
Okra pods 5.50-6.60
Olives, green fermented 3.50-4.60
Olives, ripe 6.00-8.00
Onions, red 5.30-5.80
Onions, white 5.40-5.80
Onions, yellow 5.32-5.60
Oranges 3.00-4.35
Oysters 6.10-6.60
Papaya . . . . . 5.10-5.72 (fourth month papaya = 6.66)
Parsley 5.70-6.03
Parsnips 5.30-5.70
Peaches 3.30-4.05
Peanut Butter 6.28
Pears, 'Bartlett' 3.50-4.60
Peas, chick (*garbanzo*) 6.48-6.80
Peas, cooked 6.22-6.88
Peas, dried (split green), cooked 6.45-6.80
Peas, dried (split yellow), cooked 6.43-6.62
Peppers 4.65-5.93
Peppers, green 5.20-5.93
Persimmons 4.42-4.70
Pickles, dill 3.20-3.60
Pickles, sour 3.00-3.40
Pimentos 4.40-4.90
Pineapples 3.20-4.10
Plums 2.80-4.00
Plums, blue 2.80-3.40
Plums, 'Damson' 2.90-3.10
Plums, 'Green Gage' 3.60-4.30
Plums, red 3.60-4.30
Plums, yellow 3.90-4.45
Pomegranates 2.93-3.10
Potatoes 5.40-5.90
Potatoes, sweet 5.30-5.60
Prunes, dried, stewed 3.63-3.92
Prune, pureed 3.30-4.30
Pumpkins 4.80-5.50
Quince, freshly cooked 3.12-3.40
Radishes, red 5.85-6.05
Radishes, white 5.52-5.69
Raisins, seedless 3.80-4.10
Raspberries 2.80-3.60
Red pepper relish 3.10-3.62
Rhubarb stalks 3.10-3.40
Rice, white, cooked 6.00-6.68
Romaine lettuce 5.78-6.06
Rose hips 3.70
Rowanberry (mountain ash) 3.70
Salmon 6.10-6.35
Sauerkraut 3.30-3.60
Shallots 5.30-5.70
Shrimp 6.80-7.00
Sorrel leaves 2.90-3.70
Soursop, fruit (*guanábana*) 5.00
Soursop, pulp . . . . 3.70 (some pulps are acidified prior to shipping)
Soy sauce 4.40-5.40
Spinach 5.10-6.80
Squash 5.00-6.20
Strawberries 3.00-4.30
Swiss chard, cooked 6.17-6.78
Tamarillos (tree tomatoes) . . . . 4.06 (single test)
Tangerines 3.32-4.48
Tomatoes, green 4.20
Tomatoes, vine ripened . . . . 4.42-4.65 (safety level = 4.6)
Tomato puree 4.30-4.47
Tuna fish 5.90-6.10
Turnips 5.29-5.90
Vinegar 2.30-3.40
Vinegar, cider 3.10
Walnuts, English 5.42
Water Chestnuts 6.20
Watercress 5.88-6.18
Watermelon 5.18-5.60
Water, tap 6.50-8.00
Wines 2.80-3.80
Worcestershire sauce 3.63-3.67
Yams, cooked 5.79-6.81
Yeast 5.65
Zucchini, cooked 5.69-6.10
Zwiebach 4.84-4.94

Note: Please alert Jamlady regarding any discrepancies in this chart or to suggest future additions to this pH section.

Appendix B

Information Guide

Bronson Laboratories
350 S 400 W, Suite 102
Lindon, UT 84042
800/235-3200
Pure ascorbic acid crystals and other supplements. Use crystals on your fresh fruit as well as in recipes.

Cole-Parmer Instrument Co.
625 E. Bunker Court
Vernon Hills, IL 60061
800/323-4340 or 847/549-7600
Sells pH meters, standard buffer solutions, probes, and large stainless steel-trays.

Chop-Rite Two, Inc.
531 Old Skippack Road
Harleysville, PA 19438
800/683-5858
#16T cherry stoner

Cook, Seal, and Process
Box 874
Crystal Lake, IL 60014
815/459-9518
or
Jamlady.com
3202 Northwest Highway, J
Cary, IL 60013
www.jamlady.com
Homemade jellies, jams, preserves, chutneys, relishes, pickles, and other condiments. Small batch products have the recipe attached to the jar. Canning equipment, canning supplies, group and individual instruction, and books. To arrange a Jamlady workshop, please e-mail Jamlady at Jamlady@Jamlady.com.

Cumberland General Store
P.O. 4468
Alpharetta, GA 30023
800/334-4640
Food mills, food grinders, cherry pitters, hand-thrown crocks (2-, 3-, 5-, and 10-gallon size) and canning tools.

CutleryAndMore.com
951 Nicholas Boulevard
Elk Grove, IL 60007
847/545-1722 or 800/650-9866
www.cutleryandmore.com
Jamlady recommends All-Clad's 8 quart, 10¼" x 5 5/16", stainless stock pot with lid and heavy bottom for making jam, and a tall stainless stock pot, 13" x 13", with core bottom and ¾" high rack for the bottom for processing jars. Commercial stock pot, canning pots, racks, knives, strainers, stainless ladles, etc. Ask for Michael; tell him Jamlady sent you!

E.C. Kraus Home Wine Making Supplies
733 South Northern Boulevard
Independence, MO 64053
816 254-7448
Sells pH papers and other wine making supplies.

Eurofresh Market
130 Northwest Highway
Palatine, IL 60074
847/202-0333
Bulk spices, unusual vegetables, and inexpensive wine vinegar in gallon containers.

Healthnut Alternatives
7 Dunham Drive
New Fairfield, CT 06812
800/728-1238
www.ezjuicers.com

Sells Harsch fermentation crocks, juicing machines, steam juicers, and other culinary gadgetry. Jamlady recommends the Champion juicing machine (commercial model). Ask for Brian; tell him Jamlady sent you.

Joseph's Marketplace
29 Crystal Lake Plaza
Crystal Lake, IL 60014
815/444-9866
Imported foods and global selection of fruits and vegetables.

Lorann Oils, Inc.
4518 Aurelius Road
Lansing, MI 48910
888/456-7266 or 517/882-0215
Wholesale oils and flavorings. Available retail where many cake decorating supplies are sold and at some pharmacies.

Micro-Essential Laboratory, Inc.
4224 Avenue H
Brooklyn, NY 11210
718/338-3618
Sells buffer solutions and pH test papers.

Miller Orchards
501 W. Randolph Street
Nappanee, IN 46550
574/773-3923
Fresh apples, canned meats, apple butter, and other homemade products. Ask about homemade cider vinegar.

Polstein's Hardware
7615 13th Avenue
Brooklyn, NY 11228
718/232-5055
Canning equipment and books.

Precision Foods, Inc.
11457 Olde Cabin Road
St. Louis, MO 63141
800/647-8170
Pickling lime, pickling salt, citric acid, and Home Jell and Home Jell Lite (LM) pectins.

Rare Fruit Growers, Inc.
www.crfg.org/descr/descr.html
A six-page list of exotic fruit trees, complete with Latin names. Review of books on topics related to gardening, fruits, canning, endangered species, etc. Members receive *Fruit Gardener* magazine.

The Council for Responsible Genetics
5 Upland Road, Suite 3
Cambridge, MA 02140
617/868-0870
www.gene-watch.org
Publishes a catalog of all growers and seed companies that have signed "The Safe Seed Pledge." Those listed pledge not to sell genetically engineered seeds or plants.

The Fisher Chicago Hometown Nut Store
906 S. Northwest Highway
Barrington, IL 60010
847/382-4202
Bulk spices, teas, nuts, dried fruits, and other gourmet products.

The Spice House
1512 North Wells Street
Chicago, IL 60610
312/274-0378
www.thespicehouse.com
A great selection of world-wide spices. True cinnamon is available in both ground and stick form.

Underwood Gardens
1250 Galloway Drive
Woodstock, IL 60098
815/338-6279
www.underwoodgardens.com
Sells organic heirloom seeds.

United Pickle Products
4366 Park Avenue
Bronx, NY 10457
718/933-6060
www.gusspickles.com/
The oldest continually operating pickle manufacturer in New York City, selling nationwide.

Walton Feed
135 North 10th
P.O. 307
Montpelier, ID 83254
800/847-0465
www.waltonfeed.com
CLEARJEL®, grains, and bulk food for co-ops.

Appendix C

Annual Pickle Festivals or Events

Atkins Picklefest
May Festival (third weekend in May)
Atkins, AR
479/641-1993
The 2008 Picklefest will mark the seventeenth year of this annual pickle festival, which draws over 8,000 attendees. This fest includes pickle eating and pickle juice drinking contests, arts, crafts, food vendors, tractor pull, rodeo, petting zoo, pony rides, beauty contest, and a parade.

California Rare Fruit Growers, Inc.
www.crfg.org/descr/descr.html
A six-page list of exotic fruit trees, complete with Latin names. Review of books on topics related to gardening, fruits, canning, endangered species, etc. Members receive *Fruit Gardener* magazine.

Dillsburg Picklefest
May Festival (third Saturday in May)
Dillsburg Area Business Association
Box 359 (Dill Tavern on Baltimore Street in Dillsburg to the Maple Shade Barn at the corners of Greenbrier Lane and Harrisburg Pike.)
Dillsburg, PA 17019
www.dillsburgbusiness.org
info@dillsburgbusiness.org
This fest draws about 1,000 people annually for a pickle-eating contest, 5k run, 1k-fun run, craft and business fair, car show, and a living history event, which includes civil-war-era encampments, exhibits, and demonstrations. Refreshments are available; make sure to have a bowl of their famous pickle soup. On New Year's Eve, Dillsburg has a second pickle event, which includes music, dancing, bingo, a magician, fireworks, food, and Mr. Pickle dropping into the "Pickel Barrel" at midnight. According to town sources, the fest began as a play on the town's name; there is no pickle factory in town.

Greenlawn—Centerport Historical Society Pickle Festival
September Festival (last weekend in September)
The John Gardiner Farm
900 Park Ave. (Corner of Little Plains Road and Park Avenue)
Greenlawn, NY 11740
631/754-1180
GCHA-Info@usa.net
The 2008 festival will mark the twenty-ninth year of this pickle festival that celebrates the turn-of-the century pickle industry in Greenlawn. This festival is a fundraiser for the Greenlawn-Centerport Historical Association. About 1,500 attendees enjoy the one-day event each year. Partake of the fun trying a hayride or a walking through a corn maze. Pickles, produce, and food offerings like homemade chowder and hot dogs are for sale.

Lake County International Pickle Festival
October Festival (third or fourth Friday in October)
Lake County Historical Museum
317 W. Main St.
Tavares, FL 32778
352/343-9600
dkamp@co.lake.fl.us
This pickle festival's first year was in 2007, but director Dr. Diane Kamp expects the festival to draw 500 to 1,000 attendees in year 2008 and to double annually thereafter. Dozens of pickle-related contests and demonstrations are scheduled for this festival. Decorate a four-foot pickle, throw a pickle, taste a pickle, write some pickle poetry, can a pickle, answer some pickle trivia questions, or recite a pickle tongue twister. There's a perfect contest for everyone; and don't forget to guess the number of pickles in the pickle jar.

Linwood National Pickle Festival
August Festival (third weekend in August)

Linwood Park Board
Linwood Bicentennial Park
565 Center Street
Linwood, MI 48634
989/686-0002
Year 2008 will mark the thirty-second year of this annual event. This festival may be the longest continually held pickle festival in America. Come and enjoy their weekend ball tournaments for men and women, music on Friday and Saturday night, karaoke on Sunday, canning contest, pickle contest, two parades, and pickle mania contest. The festival's free pickles are provided by Heinz, Sechler, and Vlasic.

North Carolina Pickle Festival
April Festival (fourth weekend in April)
Mt. Olive, NC
919/658-3113
www.ncpicklefest.org
moacc@bellsouth.net
April 2008 will mark the twenty-second year for this festival. The estimated 20,000 attendees enjoy vendors, rides, book sale, entertainment, free pickles, and a host of other activities. The town of Mt. Olive also has an annual event on December 31 where their three-foot, lighted pickle drops into a "perfectly preserved redwood pickle tank at the stroke of seven o'clock." The event is held at the corner of Cucumber and Vine at 7:00 P.M.; it's over by 7:05 P.M. so folks can be sleeping by midnight.

NY Food Museum
NYC International Pickle Day
September/October Festival
Orchard Street, Manhattan's Lower East Side
212/966-0191
www.nyfoodmuseum.org
nyfoodmuse@aol.com
Ten thousand or more people attend this free all-day event. Featuring free samples of pickles from around the world and exhibitions on home canning, pickle history, pickling science, ethnic traditions, and historical Lower East Side picklers.

Polanki Annual Polish Soup Festival
Norway House
7507 West Oklahoma Avenue
Milwaukee, WI 53201
http://www.polanki.org/soupfestival.html
polanki@polanki.org
This annual festival, while not exclusively a pickle festival, serves *Chlodnik* (Chilled Cucumber Soup), *Czarnina* (Duck Blood Soup), *Grzybowa* (Mushroom Soup), *Kapusniak* (Cabbage Soup), *Zupa Fasolowa* (Bean Soup with Ham), *Zupa Ogórkowa* (Dill Pickle Soup), and *Zupa Pomidorowa z Ryzem* (Tomato Soup with Rice). Soup offerings may vary from year to year. Reservations are required. PACIM (Polish American Cultural Institute of Minnesota) also has a similar annual Polish Soup Festival in October. They offer *Kapusniak z Kiszonej Kapusty* (Sauerkraut Soup) and other soups made with pickles. For more information, contact PACIM.org.

Rosendale International Pickle Festival
November Festival
Community Center
Route 32
Rosendale, NY 12472
845/658-9649
www.picklefest.com
info@picklefest.com
This wonderful pickle festival is held in the quaint town of Rosendale, which is located about ninety miles from New York City. Each year about 7,000 people flock to this festival to eat pickles, enjoy international entertainment, and to see who wins the best pickle competition. The judges for the pickle competition are: Eri Yamaguchi (author of *The Well-Flavored Vegetable Cookbook,* a Japanese pickling cookbook, and restaurateur), Chef Patrick Wilson (James Beard winner), and Bev Alfeld (award-winning author and journalist). Be greeted by Mr. Pickle and see all the wonderful food, vendors, and performances. The festival is always the Sunday before Thanksgiving.

Smiths Falls Lions Club Pickle Fest
September Festival (first or second Saturday in September)
The Smiths Falls Lions Club
P.O. Box 123
Centennial Park
Smiths Falls, Ontario K7A4S9
Activities and events at this annual festival include pickle demonstrations, sampling, and judging. There are also pickles for sale, a farmers' market, wine tasting, and entertainment. A chicken BBQ is held each year, and there is a sidewalk sale. Year 2007 was the second year of the festival. About 1,500-2,000 people are expected at the 2008 event. For more information, contact Mr. Wilf Toop, Smith Falls Lions Club.

St. Joe Pickle Fest
August Festival (second full weekend in August)
Riverdale School
State Road 1
St. Joe, Indiana 46785
260/337-5470
www.gourmetpickles.com/pickle/fest.html
The 2008 festival will mark the twelfth year of this festival. Their pickle cook-off contest has produced winners like pickle ice cream and a Lemon Pickle Pop Cake with Pineapple Coconut Topping. The festival features thirty-nine varieties of pickles from nearby Sechler's gourmet pickle factory.

Winchester Pickle Festival
September Festival (fourth Saturday in September)
Main Street (Route 10)
Winchester, NH
603/239-4202
www.winchester-nh.gov
The 2008 festival will mark the eleventh year of this festival. Come and taste some fried pickles or pickle ice cream. There is a pickle-eating contest, a judged homemade-pickle contest, an international pickle-anything contest, and a toss the pickle contest. Enjoy the entertainment and pickle parade; shop around the various crafters' booths.

WORLD-WIDE CUCUMBER OR PICKLE FESTIVALS

There also appears to be quite a few cucumber/pickle festivals in other countries. There is one in Kédainiai, Lithuania, in June. It is called the *Agurku Sventé* or Cucumber Festival and is held in Kédainiai's Central Park. One source, www.baltictimes.com/news/articles/18156, states a cucumber-flavored alcoholic liqueur, *agurku trautine,* is available at this festival, which also includes presentations on growing cucumbers and over one hundred culinary dishes made of cucumbers.

There also appears to be an International Cucumber Festival in Suzdal, Russia, which has been held for at least seven years.

If you know of any festivals not listed here, please email Jamlady@Jamlady.com or mail the information to Bev Alfeld, c/o Pelican Publishing Company, 1000 Burmaster Street, Gretna, LA 70053. We will endeavor to include any unlisted pickle or cucumber festival in subsequent printings of *Pickles to Relish.*

Index